# Specialty Competencies in Forensic Psychology

# Series in Specialty Competencies in Professional Psychology

SERIES EDITORS

Arthur M. Nezu, PhD, ABPP and Christine Maguth Nezu, PhD, ABPP

SERIES ADVISORY BOARD

David Barlow, PhD, ABPP

Jon Carlson, PsyD, EdD, ABPP

Kirk Heilbrun, PhD, ABPP

Nadine J. Kaslow, PhD, ABPP

Robert Klepac, PhD

William Parham, PhD, ABPP

Michael G. Perri, PhD, ABPP

Norma P. Simon, EdD, ABPP

TITLES IN THE SERIES

*Specialty Competencies in School Psychology*
Rosemary Flanagan and Jeffrey A. Miller

*Specialty Competencies in Organizational and Business Consulting Psychology*
Jay C. Thomas

*Specialty Competencies in Geropsychology*
Victor Molinari (Ed.)

*Specialty Competencies in Forensic Psychology*
Ira K. Packer and Thomas Grisso

*Specialty Competencies in Couple and Family Psychology*
Mark Stanton and Robert K. Welsh

IRA K. PACKER
THOMAS GRISSO

# Specialty Competencies
# in Forensic Psychology

OXFORD
UNIVERSITY PRESS

Oxford University Press, Inc., publishes works that further
Oxford University's objective of excellence
in research, scholarship, and education.

Oxford New York

Auckland   Cape Town   Dar es Salaam   Hong Kong   Karachi
Kuala Lumpur   Madrid   Melbourne   Mexico City   Nairobi
New Delhi   Shanghai   Taipei   Toronto

With offices in
Argentina   Austria   Brazil   Chile   Czech Republic   France   Greece
Guatemala   Hungary   Italy   Japan   Poland   Portugal   Singapore
South Korea   Switzerland   Thailand   Turkey   Ukraine   Vietnam

Copyright © 2011 by Oxford University Press, Inc.

Published by Oxford University Press, Inc.
198 Madison Avenue, New York, New York 10016
www.oup.com

Oxford is a registered trademark of Oxford University Press

**Library of Congress Cataloging-in-Publication Data**
Packer, Ira K.
Specialty competencies in forensic psychology / Ira Packer, Thomas Grisso.
   p. ; cm. — (Series in specialty competencies in professional psychology)
Includes bibliographical references and index.
ISBN 978-0-19-539083-4 (pbk. : alk. paper)
1. Forensic psychiatry.  2. Core competencies.   I. Grisso, Thomas.  II. Title.
III. Series: Series in specialty competencies in professional psychology.
[DNLM: 1. Forensic Psychiatry.  2. Professional Competence—standards. W 740]
RA1151.P3325 2011
614'.1—dc22                                                      2011003691

ISBN 978-0-19-539083-4 (Paper)

9 8 7 6 5 4 3 2 1

Printed in the United States of America
on acid-free paper

# ABOUT THE SERIES IN SPECIALTY COMPETENCIES IN PROFESSIONAL PSYCHOLOGY

This series is intended to describe state-of-the-art functional and foundational competencies in professional psychology across extant and emerging specialty areas. Each book in this series provides a guide to best practices across both core and specialty competencies as defined by a given professional psychology specialty.

The impetus for this series was created by various growing movements in professional psychology during the past 15 years. First, as an applied discipline, psychology is increasingly recognizing the unique and distinct nature among a variety of orientations, modalities, and approaches with regard to professional practice. These specialty areas represent distinct ways of practicing one's profession across various domains of activities that are based on distinct bodies of literature and often address differing populations or problems. For example, the American Psychological Association (APA) in 1995 established the Commission on the Recognition of Specialties and Proficiencies in Professional Psychology (CRSPPP) to define criteria by which a given specialty could be recognized. The Council of Credentialing Organizations in Professional Psychology (CCOPP), an inter-organizational entity, was formed in reaction to the need to establish criteria and principles regarding the types of training programs related to the education, training, and professional development of individuals seeking such specialization. In addition, the Council on Specialties in Professional Psychology (COS) was formed in 1997, independent of the APA, to foster communication among the established specialties to offer a unified position to the pubic regarding specialty education and training, credentialing, and practice standards across specialty areas.

Simultaneously, efforts to actually define professional competence regarding psychological practice have also been growing significantly. For example, the APA-sponsored Task Force on Assessment of Competence in Professional Psychology put forth a series of guiding principles for the assessment of competence within professional psychology, based, in part, on a review of competency assessment models developed both within (e.g., Assessment of Competence Workgroup from Competencies Conference—Roberts et al., 2005) and outside (e.g., Accreditation Council for Graduate Medical Education and American Board of Medical Specialties, 2000) the profession of psychology (Kaslow et al., 2007).

Moreover, additional professional organizations in psychology have provided valuable input into this discussion, including various associations primarily interested in the credentialing of professional psychologists, such as the American Board of Professional Psychology (ABPP), the Association of State and Provincial Psychology Boards (ASPBB), and the National Register of Health Service Providers in Psychology. This widespread interest and importance of the issue of competency in professional psychology can be especially appreciated given the attention and collaboration afforded to this effort by international groups, including the Canadian Psychological Association and the International Congress on Licensure, Certification, and Credentialing in Professional Psychology.

Each volume in the series is devoted to a specific specialty and provides a definition, description, and development timeline of that specialty, including its essential and characteristic pattern of activities, as well as its distinctive and unique features. Each set of authors, long-term experts, and veterans of a given specialty were asked to describe that specialty along the lines of both functional and foundational competencies. *Functional competencies* are those common practice activities provided at the specialty level of practice that include, for example, the application of its science base, assessment, intervention, consultation, and where relevant, supervision, management, and teaching. *Foundational competencies* represent core knowledge areas that are integrated and cut across all functional competencies to varying degrees, and dependent on the specialty, in various ways. These include ethical and legal issues, individual and cultural diversity considerations, interpersonal interactions, and professional identification.

Whereas we realize that each specialty is likely to undergo changes in the future, we wanted to establish a baseline of basic knowledge and principles that comprise a specialty highlighting both its commonalities with other areas of professional psychology as well as its distinctiveness. We look forward to seeing the dynamics of such changes, as well as the emergence of new specialties in the future.

Although forensic psychology was formally recognized as a specialty by the ABPP in 1985 and by the CRSPPP in 2001, its origins can be traced back to early applications of psychology to law during the time psychology was being differentiated from the more general field of philosophy.

As it is currently applied, the specialty took organizational shape from the 1960's to the 1990's, and today forensic psychology is one of the most popular areas of specialization among emerging psychologists. The demand for forensic training, continuing education, and research is palpable in many graduate level professional programs and at events sponsored by the American Psychology-Law Division 41 of the APA or the American Academy of Forensic Psychology. Therefore, the demand for a comprehensive text focused on the competencies required in the specialty has never been greater. Drs. Packer and Grisso provide a guide to understanding legal systems, evaluations, and consultations encountered in day-to-day forensic practice that is simultaneously sophisticated, scholarly, and user-friendly. It should be required reading for all those interested in pursuing the forensic specialty practice.

Arthur M. Nezu<br>
Christine Maguth Nezu

## References

Kaslow et al. (2007). Guiding principles and recommendations for the assessment of competence. *Professional Psychology: Research and Practice, 38*, 441–451.

Roberts et al. (2005). Fostering a culture shift: Assessment of competence in the education and careers of professional psychologists. *Professional Psychology: Research and Practice, 36*, 355–361.

# CONTENTS

# AUTHOR ACKNOWLEDGMENTS

Much of our thinking about standards and competencies in forensic psychology has been influenced by our association with the American Board of Forensic Psychology and the American Academy of Forensic Psychology. We acknowledge their efforts for the past three decades to shape the field of forensic psychology and to forge many of the standards that this volume describes. We offer special thanks to Kirk Heilbrun for his insightful comments on an early draft of the manuscript.

Ira K. Packer
Thomas Grisso

# PART I

# Introduction to
# Forensic Psychology

# ONE

# Definition of Forensic Psychology

For more than a century, psychology has been applied to analyses of law, performing evaluations of individuals to inform legal decisions, studying the legal process and legal decision making, and assisting attorneys and judges in matters that can be informed by psychological knowledge of human behavior. Across time, many of these activities have come to be identified as "forensic psychology," and some persons who engage in them have come to be called "forensic psychologists."

Textbooks contain a variety of definitions of forensic psychology. They all refer to psychology's application to law, but they differ somewhat in their breadth and inclusiveness. These differences often are related to the purposes for which the definitions were developed.

This volume is in a series that focuses on applied specialties in psychology for purposes of credentialing or certification through the American Board of Professional Psychology. The definition of forensic psychology that is most relevant for that context is the one that is used for recognition of forensic psychology as *an applied specialty* by the American Psychological Association (APA). The definition of the specialty as contained in the most recent (2007) petition for recognition is:

> "the professional practice by psychologists within the areas of clinical psychology, counseling psychology, school psychology, or another specialty recognized by the American Psychological Association, when they are engaged as experts and represent themselves as such, in an activity primarily intended to provide professional psychological expertise to the judicial system" (http://cospp.org/specialties/forensic-psychology)

As we will describe later, an analysis of this definition indicates that it defines a professional specialty for purposes of identifying certain psychologists with a primary area of practice, associated with specialized training, background, and experience in providing services to legal institutions and proceedings. It defines those who are recognized as being *specialized* to practice forensic psychology.

Other definitions of forensic psychology, with equal authority, are quite different from this definition of a professional specialty. For example, the draft revision of the American Psychology-Law Society's (AP-LS) *Specialty Guidelines for Forensic Psychology* (2008) is intended to provide guidance for *all psychologists* when they engage in professional activities that provide psychological expertise in any judicial, administrative, or other quasi-legal situation. As such, the *Guidelines* offers a broad definition of forensic psychology that is applicable to many psychologists who would never consider themselves "forensic psychologists." Large numbers of psychologists, for example, regularly testify in civil commitment hearings in the course of their ordinary clinical duties, yet they have no special training in the application of psychology to law or legal proceedings. Nor do they define themselves as "forensic psychologists" and would not meet APA's criterion as specialized in forensic psychology. The AP-LS *Guidelines* offers them guidance when they apply their psychological knowledge in legal proceedings. But it does not define them as specialists in forensic psychology—that is, as professionals who are especially trained to engage in the application of psychology to legal institutions or proceedings.

The term *specialty* in the AP-LS *Guidelines'* title defines guidelines for a *special application* of psychology, but it does not intend to define *forensic psychology* as a *professional's area of specialized practice*. The latter—defining forensic psychology as a specialized area of practice—is the purpose of the definition used for APA recognition. We employ that definition in this volume, because that is the focus of the series of volumes of which this one is a part.

This chapter begins by deconstructing the definition used for APA recognition of the specialty. It discusses the ways that the specialty of forensic psychology is different from, and similar to, other related professional fields, activities, and identities. This is followed by a brief history of the development of forensic psychology, from its roots in the late nineteenth century to its recognition by APA as a specialty in the early twenty-first century. Finally, we sketch the boundaries of forensic psychology in three ways: We examine its unique knowledge base and skill sets, the problems that it addresses, and the populations that it serves.

## I. Distinguishing Forensic Psychology as a Specialty

A careful examination of the definition of forensic psychology suggests the difficulties that its framers encountered in its development. Why the "judicial system" and not the "legal system?" Why "the professional practice of forensic psychology" rather than "scientific studies related to law?" Defining a specialty involves distinguishing it from other specialties and more general fields of psychological endeavor, and these carefully chosen phrases reflect that effort. The following discussion shows how they shape the intended meaning of forensic psychology as a specialty.

### A. "PROFESSIONAL" PRACTICE

Throughout the definition, it is clear that a key feature of forensic psychology is its application of psychology to law and legal questions. Yet psychologists apply psychology to law at many levels. The field of Law and Psychology, described later, includes many experimental and social psychologists who study judicial and jury decision making, the law's presumptions about human behavior, the reliability of witness evidence, and a host of other questions about the law that psychology is uniquely prepared to address. Moreover, sometimes those psychologists who research these areas provide "professional psychological expertise" when they enter the courtroom to describe their research or consulting to lawyers and policy-makers about how to apply it.

The definition of forensic psychology, however, uses words and phrases that do not include all psychologists who are primarily engaged in applying psychology to law and legal systems, even when they sometimes testify in court. Two distinctions are made in this regard.

First, the definition focuses on the "practice" of providing "professional" expert services. The use of these terms seeks to describe psychologists who are *engaged primarily in the practice of taking psychology into the legal forum, on a day-to-day basis,* and offering it to fact-finders as assistance in their legal decision-making process. This distinguishes them from other psychologists involved primarily in research that promotes the application of psychology to law or from clinical psychologists who occasionally find themselves in circumstances in which they are asked to provide clinical information to courts.

A similar distinction is found in the field of law itself. Legal scholars as well as attorneys who represent clients in legal cases are both "lawyers." Both may involve application; legal scholars, for example, may seek to change legal systems or influence the direction of law by offering the legal system their theories and case analyses. But these two types of lawyers are distinguished by the degree to which they "practice" law. It might be said that legal scholars study and analyze law to promote a better legal system and better legal outcomes. But practicing attorneys are devoted to using the law in the daily course of cases that they represent. Similarly, many psychologists may do research, consult, and occasionally testify in ways that apply psychology to law. But forensic psychologists, under the specialty definition, are devoted to using psychology in the daily course of services that they provide to persons involved in legal cases. Some authorities now use the term *legal psychology* to refer to a field of applied psychological research on legal issues, reserving *forensic psychology* for the professional practice of applying psychology to legal forums (Douglas, Otto, & Borum, 2003).

The second feature of the definition that distinguishes *forensic psychology* from *legal psychology* is its reference to "clinical psychology, counseling psychology, school psychology, or another specialty recognized by the American Psychological Association." Many psychologists who seek applications of psychology to law work in a range of nonclinical subareas in psychology, such as experimental, social, personality, and developmental psychology. When they apply their science to law, rarely do they inform the law about clinical characteristics of people about whom the court is making a decision. In contrast, forensic psychologists' expert opinions are almost always focused on clinical issues.

Note that this emphasis on professional practice as a touchstone for forensic psychology will not always make for easy identification regarding who, among those in the field of "Law and Psychology," are or are not included in the specialty. For example, some legal psychologists who are primarily researchers may, at some point in their careers, begin offering frequent testimony based on their research, such that it becomes their primary activity as a psychologist. Moreover, depending on the nature of their research, much of their testimony might offer evidence that could be construed as "clinical." In such cases, the erstwhile legal psychologist might be identified appropriately as practicing the specialty of forensic psychology.

### B. "SPECIALIZED" PRACTICE

If forensic psychology is "clinical" and involves "professional practice," then how does it differ from practice by the other "clinical" specialties in psychology—especially clinical psychology and clinical neuropsychology, whose theories and methods often are the basis for the expertise of forensic psychologists? And does it encompass all clinical practice within legal contexts?

The most obvious difference between the other clinical specialties and forensic psychology is found in the definition's reference to providing "professional psychological expertise to the judicial system." Later in this chapter, we describe more specifically what this phrase means. In general, however, the definition acknowledges that a practice devoted to applying clinical psychological knowledge to legal questions requires additional knowledge and skills that are not essentially clinical: for example, *(1)* knowing how clinical constructs are relevant for legal questions; *(2)* having special knowledge and expertise in the use of methods and analytic processes that meet legal requirements for addressing those questions; and *(3)* being able to communicate one's information in a way that is appropriate within the context of the law, the judicial process, and the framework within which legal professionals operate.

The definition in no way suggests that psychologists in other clinical specialties cannot provide psychological information in legal proceedings. Many psychologists engaged in clinical practice find themselves testifying about a patient from time to time. From a legal perspective, an "expert," for purposes of courtroom testimony, is any professional who is qualified, by training and experience, to form an opinion about a specific question before the court in a specific case. Thus, there is no need to qualify for specialization in forensic psychology to offer expert opinions in legal contexts.

The relevant distinction in this regard is the acceptance of referrals *with the prior knowledge* that they will be asked to form and communicate an expert opinion in the case. Put another way, in the practice of forensic psychology, the reason for one's referrals is not a request for the provision of clinical services but, rather, is entirely for the purpose of *producing evidence* for use in legal proceedings. This distinguishes the practice of forensic psychology from circumstances in which any clinician, having been referred a patient for diagnosis or treatment in the course of their clinical practice, might *later* be asked to provide a court information that was not originally acquired for purposes of addressing the law's concerns. Thus, the specialty of forensic psychology limits who may offer services to legal clients as a forensic psychologist but in no way limits who may provide expert psychological testimony.

Finally, given that the definition of forensic psychology is "clinical," does it encompass the activities of all clinical psychologists who primarily practice in legal settings? For example, many psychologists devote their careers to providing therapeutic services to persons with mental illnesses while they are in jails and prisons. Are they practicing the specialty of forensic psychology?

The definition of the specialty uses phrases that suggest that they are not. It refers to expertise in the *judicial* system. It does not refer to forensic psychology's domain as the *legal* system, a broad concept that includes courts and law enforcement (which encompasses the work of police departments, jails, and correction agencies). In contrast, the term *judicial system* refers more narrowly to "the system of law courts that administer justice" (www. dictionary.com).

This distinction between service to the courts and service to law enforcement and corrections has several implications. Before the specialty of forensic psychology was acknowledged by the APA, Law and Psychology had developed a loose tradition—but not necessarily a consensual one—of referring to the former as "forensic psychology" and the latter as "correctional psychology." But it is important not to construe this difference as a mere statement about "where one works" or that a psychologist must be one or the other. Many psychologists who provide clinical treatment in correctional facilities might also engage in evaluations designed for use in courts, such that they need the qualifications associated with the specialty in forensic psychology. Therefore, the definition narrows the specialty of forensic psychology, such that engaging in clinical therapeutic practice with persons in jails and corrections does not, *by itself*, constitute the practice of forensic psychology.

## II. A Brief History of Forensic Psychology

Forensic psychology's roots are found in early interests in applying psychology to law even as psychology itself was being differentiated from the more general field of philosophy. Organizational development of forensic psychology began in the 1960s and took its present form by 1990. The modern substantive foundations of the specialty began to take shape in the 1970s, and the APA's formal recognition of forensic psychology as a specialty arrived about 30 years later, in 2001. These aspects of forensic psychology's development are described in this brief history; more detailed information can be found in Bartol and Bartol (2005) and Brigham and Grisso (2003).

### A. EARLY APPLICATIONS OF PSYCHOLOGY TO LAW

Students of the earliest psychology laboratories in the late 1800s—especially that of Wilhelm Wundt—began applying scientific methods to legal questions. Among them was Von Schrenk-Notzing, often acknowledged as the first forensic psychologist (although his activities would not have met the current definition of the specialty). He performed research on the effects of pretrial publicity in murder cases and sometimes offered testimony based on his findings.

Munsterberg, another of Wundt's students, wrote a book (*On the Witness Stand*) in 1908 that described wide-ranging potential applications of psychology to law, including judging the accuracy of witness recall, crime detection, false confessions, and crime prevention. His ideas aroused widespread attention in the United States, but his treatise offered little empirical evidence to support his views (indeed, it included no citations) and was written in an arrogant style that did not sit well with legal scholars.

William Marston, a student of Munsterberg, specialized in studies of jury selection and research that led to the development of the modern polygraph. His work frequently brought him into the courtroom, most notably in the case of *Frye v. U.S.* (1923), which produced the legal decision that, in many states, still defines the requirements for the admissibility of evidence through expert testimony. Marston also consulted regularly to police and attorneys on identifying deceptive reports by witnesses and suspects (Bartol & Bartol, 2005).

The work of early psychological test developers, such as Binet, Simon, and Terman, played a significant role in psychology's services to law and the courts. Their development of intelligence tests early in the twentieth century led to applications in the selection of law enforcement officers. These new psychological tests of intellectual abilities also became one of the empirical foundations for evaluations of delinquent youth in juvenile courts. The first juvenile court, created in Cook County (Chicago) in 1899, soon had a clinic (1909) devoted entirely to providing the courts with evaluations of youth to assist judges in deciding how to respond to delinquency, child welfare, and dependency cases. Indeed, the claim might be made that the first psychologist to meet all parts of the current definition of the specialty of forensic psychology was Grace Fernald, who, with William Healey (a neurologist), developed Cook County's "Juvenile Psychopathic Institute." This clinic was devoted entirely to providing "individual studies" of youth for the juvenile court (Grisso, 2006; Healey, 1923; Jones, 1999).

For the most part, however, the activities that we most readily identify with the current definition of forensic psychology as a professional specialty were not greatly apparent until the 1950s. This is not surprising when one considers that clinical psychology itself did not develop as a recognized subfield in psychology until the 1930s and 1940s. Psychologists' involvement in diagnosis and treatment of disorders was encouraged during World War II when the large number mental casualties of war exceeded the need that could be covered by psychiatrists. The evolution of the community mental health movement of the 1950s provided further avenues for the involvement of psychologists in clinical evaluation and treatment. By the 1960s, many psychologists were providing clinical services in correctional programs, bringing them closer to everyday practice within the legal system (Brodsky, 1973).

Through all of these avenues, an increasing number of psychologists began to enter the courtroom to testify on issues of mental illness and disability in criminal cases. Their practice was limited, however, by the fact that the laws of most states designated psychiatrists as the proper experts for such cases (Greenberg, 1956). Various events of the 1960s removed some of these barriers, especially a 1962 U.S. Supreme Court case, *Jenkins v. United States*. An earlier U.S. Supreme Court case (*People v. Hawthorne*, 1940) had established that professionals should be qualified as experts based on their knowledge of the specialized matters relevant to a case rather than on the basis of their degree. Similarly, in *Jenkins*, the Court ruled that psychologists, despite their lack of a medical degree, could offer opinions as expert witnesses concerning the nature and existence of mental disorders, as long as they could demonstrate that they had training, knowledge, and experience about those matters.

## B. THE EARLY ORGANIZATION OF THE PROFESSION

The earliest organization for psychologists who practiced clinically in service to the legal system was the American Association of Correctional Psychologists (1954). Its focus, however, was more on applications in correctional institutions than in courts. It was the founding of the AP-LS in 1969 that provided the foundation for the growth of forensic psychology as a professional specialty serving the judicial system. (For a detailed history of the first 20 years of the AP-LS, *see* Grisso, 1991.)

Thirteen psychologists attended the inaugural meeting of the AP-LS at the 1969 American Psychological Association convention. They had acquired more than 100 charter members within a few months. Yet only about one-half of the members would have been identified as forensic psychologists engaged primarily in professional practice of the type identified by the current definition. The other half were academicians involved primarily in research that applied psychological theories and methods to better understand the legal system, the legal process, the quality of legal evidence, and the rationality of its decisions.

Nevertheless, the organization's two founders, Jay Ziskin and Erik Dreikurs, were both motivated by the application of clinical psychological practice in the courts. Dreikurs was interested primarily in promoting the practices of forensic psychologists, whereas Ziskin, the first AP-LS president, bridged the interests of the two main types of members—he sought research to improve forensic practice. His vision of an empirical base for forensic practice was laudable and eventually became one of forensic psychology's most pressing objectives. But his strategies did not sit well with his colleagues. Ziskin almost immediately fell out of favor with the organization when he published a book for lawyers, *Coping with Psychiatric and Psychological Testimony* (1970), showing them how to challenge almost all clinical psychological evidence based on then-current practices. His book opened with the assertion, "Psychiatric and psychological evidence ... frequently does not meet reasonable criteria of admissibility and should not be admitted in a court of law" (Ziskin, 1970, p. 1).

During the 1970s, the AP-LS developed its strength primarily as an organization to drive psychological research aimed at legal and social change. Its leadership reflected the growth of Psychology and Law as a scientific organization but less so as a professional practice involving the clinical application of psychology to judicial decision making. Many psychologists in the AP-LS who had the latter interests began to identify the need for an organization that would provide standards for forensic psychology as a practice. Thus was born the American Board of Forensic Psychology (ABFP; Kaslow, 1989).

In 1978, Florence Kaslow and several other forensic psychologists proposed to the AP-LS that it was important to establish a process for credentialing of forensic psychologists, much as forensic psychiatry had done a year earlier. The executive board of the AP-LS suggested that Kaslow set up a committee to study the matter. This soon led to the AP-LS' decision to provide the committee $1,000 to assist them in developing an entirely independent corporation called the ABFP. The ABFP developed a process of review regarding candidates' training and experience, including written and oral examinations for attaining the diplomate in forensic psychology. The new Board also developed the American Academy of Forensic Psychology (AAFP), an organization for all psychologists who had achieved diplomate status. The AAFP became the mechanism for providing continuing education toward improvement in the quality of forensic psychological services and preparation for ABFP certification.

A few years later, both the AP-LS and the ABFP/AAFP found their way into the organizational mainstream of psychology. In 1980, the APA formed a new Division 41 for Psychology and Law, and the AP-LS then merged with Division 41 in 1983. The ABFP became a specialty of the American

Board of Professional Psychology in 1985, and the AAFP continued to be the "faculty" of forensic psychology diplomates. By 1991, the AP-LS and the AAFP had collaborated to produce the first formal guide for forensic psychological practice, the *Specialty Guidelines for Forensic Psychologists* (Committee on Ethical Guidelines for Forensic Psychologists, 1991).

The 1970s and 1980s also saw the development of the first specialized training opportunities for forensic psychologists and psychiatrists. By 1980, a significant proportion of psychology graduate fellowship programs with APA accreditation were offering courses in Psychology and Law, many of them focusing on forensic applications (Grisso, Sales, & Bayless, 1982). However, until the late 1980s, there was not even a small collection of post-doctoral programs to prepare forensic psychologists for practice (Bersoff et al., 1997; Otto, Heilbrun, & Grisso, 1990). Currently there are more than 20 such programs.

## C. THE MODERN SUBSTANTIVE FOUNDATIONS OF FORENSIC PSYCHOLOGY

The modern principles, methods, and practices that form the foundation of forensic psychology are very new. One must realize that at the time that the AP-LS and the ABFP were taking shape, there were literally no general textbooks in forensic psychology or forensic assessment and no journals devoted to psychology and law or forensic mental health practice. The forensic psychologists of the 1970s had almost no literature to represent their "field."

As the 1970s progressed, however, many psychologists began developing a conceptual and research base on which the future of forensic psychological practice would be built. The period between 1970 and 1990 witnessed three kinds of contributions.

First, some of the most significant works of this era documented and described the weaknesses in forensic psychological assessments and typical expert witness practices at that time. Mental health professionals' roles and performance in the courtroom sustained serious criticism, in light of limits in their methods and inappropriate use of clinical information as though it were dispositive of the legal question. Research on clinicians' judgments about individuals' future risk of violence revealed a greater likelihood for clinicians to be wrong than right when concluding that a person was likely to be violent in the future (as reviewed in Monahan, 1981). Others performed research describing marked inadequacies in the practices of judges, attorneys, and clinicians in cases in which questions of competence to stand trial were raised (McGarry et al., 1968; Roesch & Golding, 1980). Discourse on the proper roles of mental health professionals in corrections and the courts identified difficult issues that needed to be addressed before psychology and psychiatry could assist the courts with integrity (Brodsky, 1973; Monahan, 1980).

As the 1980s progressed, it became clear that an empirically based practice of forensic psychology, as summarized by Grisso (1987), was not yet secured and would require considerable research to provide the profession with a firm claim to an empirical foundation. But the work of the 1970s had at least established that objective. The field would need to set aside the days in which expert opinions by mental health professionals were based simply on extrapolations from clinical practice and were accepted by courts on the basis of deference to the expert's profession. Forensic psychology needed to be grounded in its own set of principles, concepts, methods, and science-based knowledge.

Second, several works began providing the conceptual building blocks for a systematic approach to forensic mental health assessment (FMHA) in certain specific areas of forensic assessment. For example, Monahan (1981) identified a set of factors that would have to be studied, measures that would have to be created, and interpretive logic that would be required to develop effective assessments of risk of violence. Grisso (1986) offered an analysis of the essential components common to all legal competencies and then used these components as a template to apply to the development of new instruments for assessing competence to stand trial, competence of parents in guardianship cases, and other legal competencies. Lidz et al. (1984; *see also* Appelbaum & Roth, 1982; Tepper & Elwork, 1984) produced a conceptual analysis of legal criteria for competence to consent to treatment, thus providing a set of psycholegal concepts that eventually would be used to guide the development of structured methods to assess patients' capacities in this civil area of competency. In what would become a classic in the field, Melton et al.'s (1987) *Psychological Evaluations for the Courts* offered conceptual clarity regarding these matters pertaining to a broad range of forensic assessments.

Third, an important development in the new field of FMHA during the1970s and 1980s was the first appearance of *forensic assessment instruments* (Grisso, 1986). These were tools that used new psycholegal concepts as the structure for relatively standardized procedures designed to obtain psychological data relevant for a specific legal question. Clinical instruments for assessing diagnostic conditions, personality traits, and cognitive capacities would still be important in forensic assessments. But the new forensic assessment instruments provided an interpretive bridge between general psychological capacities and abilities or predispositions related to specific legal questions.

The first major instruments of this type that were developed with a systematic program of research were the *Competency Assessment Instrument* and the *Competency Screening Test*, both products of a National Institutes of Mental Health research grant (by psychiatrist Louis McGarry and psychologist Paul Lipsitt; cited as Laboratory of Community Psychiatry, 1973). They were followed in the 1980s by other tools designed to assess competency to stand trial (e.g., *Interdisciplinary Fitness Interview*: Golding & Roesch, 1983; *Georgia Court Competency Test*: Wildman et al., 1979), as well as tools that could guide assessments for criminal responsibility (*Rogers Criminal Responsibility Assessment Scales*: Rogers, 1984), capacity to waive *Miranda* rights (Grisso, 1981), and competence to consent to treatment (e.g., Roth et al., 1982).

As specialized principles and methods for forensic psychology grew, so did the literature that began to represent the field. The first volume of *Perspectives in Law and Psychology*, a book series developed by the AP-LS, appeared in the 1970s (Sales, 1977). For 30 years, the series has continued to be an important source of guidance for forensic psychology. The first general textbooks in forensic psychology appeared in the 1980s, many of them continuing as revised editions today (Monahan & Walker, 1985, 2006; Rosner, Harmon, & Ronnie, 1989—later Rosner, 2003; Saks & Baron, 1980; Shapiro, 1984—later Shapiro, 1991; Shuman, 1986, 2005; Weiner & Hess, 1987, 2005; Wrightsman, 1987, 2006; as the period closed, Brodsky, 1991, 1999). Many of these new textbooks included chapters pertaining to forensic mental health assessment. However, two general textbooks appeared in the 1980s that were devoted solely to forensic mental health assessments and have continued in revised versions to the present: Grisso's *Evaluating Competencies—Forensic Assessments and Instruments* (1986, now 2003), and Melton et al.'s *Psychological Evaluations for the Courts* (1987, now 2007).

The first books on specific areas of forensic assessment appeared in the 1980s as well; for example, Roesch and Golding (1980) and Grisso (1988) on competency to stand trial, and Rogers' books on insanity evaluations (1986) and assessment of malingering and deception (1988). The appearance of forensic assessment texts began to provide an identity for forensic psychology, helping to establish the first clear notions of a consensus (and issues that needed to be resolved) regarding the nature of the field.

The appearance of the first journals in law and psychology provided a forum for research on populations and methods of importance for forensic psychology. Table 1.1 shows (in the first list) the first mainline journals for the field that developed in the 1970s. The second list shows journals (including those developed within forensic psychiatry) that continue to

TABLE 1.1 **Journals Pertaining to Law and Psychology/Psychiatry and Forensic Psychology/Psychiatry**

**Earliest Journals**

*Behavioral Sciences and the Law*
*Criminal Justice and Behavior*
*International Journal of Law and Psychiatry*
*Bulletin (now Journal) of the Academy of Psychiatry and the Law*
*Law and Human Behavior*
*Law and Psychology Review*

**Subsequent Journals**

*Aggression and Violent Behavior*
*American Journal of Forensic Psychiatry*
*American Journal of Forensic Psychology*
*British Journal of Forensic Practice*
*Child Abuse and Neglect*
*Criminal Behavior and Mental Health*
*Family Court Review*
*Forensic Reports (no longer published)*
*International Journal of Forensic Mental Health*
*International Journal of Forensic Psychology*
*International Journal of Offender Therapy and Comparative Criminology*
*Journal of the Canadian Society of Forensic Sciences*
*Journal of Clinical Forensic Medicine*
*Journal of Forensic Medicine*
*Journal of Forensic Psychiatry*
*Journal of Forensic Psychiatry and Psychology*
*Journal of Forensic Psychology Practice*
*Journal of Forensic Sciences*
*Journal of Interpersonal Violence*
*Legal and Criminological Psychology*
*Psychiatry, Psychology and Law*
*Psychology, Crime and Law*
*Psychology, Public Policy and Law*

provide an ever-expanding forum for forensic psychology research and practice.

D. THE AMERICAN PSYCHOLOGICAL ASSOCIATION'S RECOGNITION
OF FORENSIC PSYCHOLOGY AS A SPECIALTY

Although forensic psychology was recognized as a specialty by the ABPP in 1985, it was not until 2001 that it obtained formal recognition as a specialty by the APA. This delay was not specific to forensic psychology but, rather, was a function of internal debates within the APA about the nature of psychological practice and the tension between those who considered psychologists to be generalists (e.g., Matarazzo, 1987, *American Psychologist*, pp. 893–903: "There is only one psychology, no specialties, but many applications") versus those who advocated for recognizing specialties within the broad and general framework of psychology as a discipline. It was not until 1995 that the latter group prevailed, and the APA developed the Commission for Recognition of Specialties and Proficiencies in Professional Psychology (CRSPPP), with the mandate to review petitions for recognition of specialties, with the ultimate decision being made by the APA Council of Representatives. This represented the first time that the APA had implemented a *de jure* process for recognizing specialties. In this context, in 2001, the AP-LS of the APA and the ABFP submitted a petition to CRSPPP. In 2001, the APA accepted this petition and formally recognized forensic psychology as a specialty.

Specialty recognition by the APA is for a 7-year period, at the end of which the specialty must submit a renewal petition, documenting that it is still a distinctive area of practice, with empirical support, a system for education and training, and established guidelines for practice. By 2007, the petition was submitted by the Forensic Specialty Council, which is an organization comprised of representation from the AP-LS, the ABFP, and the AAFP, and the APA granted re-recognition in 2008. A significant advance from the initial petition was that by 2007, the Forensic Specialty Council had developed Education and Training Guidelines for Forensic Psychology (http://cospp.org/specialties/forensic-psychology), which will be described in more detail below.

**Education and Training Guidelines**   In 2007, with input from Forensic Psychology Postdoctoral training directors, the AP-LS, the ABFP, and the AAFP, the Forensic Specialty Council developed Education and Training Guidelines (E&T). These are designed to provide guidance to Postdoctoral Fellowship Programs (also known as Residency Programs) and to establish standards for training forensic psychologists. These guidelines were endorsed by the Council of Specialties in Professional Psychology and thus were accepted by the APA's Commission on Accreditation. The significance of this development is that as of 2008, Forensic Psychology Postdoctoral programs can now apply for formal accreditation.

The E&T guidelines were based on several basic principles:

1. the necessity for broad and general education and training in the science and practice of psychology;
2. recognition that forensic psychology is a postdoctoral specialty, meaning that additional training is required beyond the graduate level;

3. fellowship training should cover a broad range of topics within forensic psychology, with the goal of attaining competency in at least two different areas of forensic practice;
4. fellowship training should prepare fellows to meet criteria for becoming board-certified specialists in forensic psychology by the ABPP.

## IV. Characteristics that Define the Specialty

As defined earlier in this chapter, that which defines forensic psychology as a specialty is its relation to law, legal process, and legal decision makers. To explore how this relation leads to defining characteristics of the specialty, it is important first to consider more specifically who it is that forensic psychologists serve and what it is they are asked to do. Then we will offer an analysis of the types of special expertise that is required to offer those services "to the judicial system."

### A. WHOM FORENSIC PSYCHOLOGISTS SERVE

Descriptions of most other specialties in professional psychology are likely to define their clients as individuals or families. Forensic psychologists, however, have long recognized that their clients often are better defined not as individuals but as the entities that forensic psychologists serve, such as courts or legal agencies (Monahan, 1980). In doing so, of course, they evaluate individuals who come before the courts or who are in the custody of various legal agencies. Often those individuals may benefit from the services that the forensic psychologist provides. But the forensic psychologist would not be seeing them if they were not the object of a legal proceeding. Thus the people who forensic psychologists evaluate would rarely be called the forensic psychologist's "patients."

Forensic psychologists do have "clients," yet only in rare circumstances are those clients the individuals about whom legal decisions are being made. Forensic psychologists' clients typically are attorneys, courts, other judicial entities, probation and law enforcement officers, and correctional programs, for whom they perform evaluations that will provide relevant psychological information to assist in reaching legal decisions. In this context, forensic psychologists are primarily obligated to legal system professionals who require their services—not to the individuals whom they evaluate. This does not mean that they have no ethical or clinical obligations to the individuals whom they evaluate, only that their overarching obligation is to provide the legal system with relevant and valid information for use in making a legal decision.

The legal institutions and professionals whom forensic psychologists serve are quite extensive. They include the criminal, civil, juvenile, and family courts in federal, state, and tribal jurisdictions. They include judges, prosecuting attorneys, and attorneys representing defendants, appellants, respondents, or wards about whom those courts are making decisions. They include correctional and probation programs that need to make decisions about placement and treatment of persons who are in legal custody for criminal or civil reasons.

The individuals forensic psychologists are asked to evaluate are extremely varied with regard to demographic and clinical conditions. They include adults and adolescents accused of crimes or delinquencies, as well as those who have been found guilty and for whom questions are raised about sentencing and placement. Many of them have serious mental disorders, substance abuse disorders, and intellectual disabilities. They include men and women of all ethnic and cultural backgrounds, although minority ethnic groups are represented in greater proportion than in the general population. They include persons with various disabilities being seen in civil court proceedings involving their potential involuntary commitment to restricted treatment facilities or their need for guardianship. Forensic psychologists are also asked to evaluate children, parents, or whole families in cases involving child welfare or divorce-related custody questions. In brief, forensic psychologists evaluate an extraordinary range of people, as one would expect, given the many ways in which the law becomes involved in the lives of citizens in every community in the nation.

### B. WHAT FORENSIC PSYCHOLOGISTS DO

Table 1.2 (from Heilbrun, Grisso, & Goldstein, 2009) offers a list—divided into three groups—of the most common types of evaluations that forensic psychologists are asked to perform for legal proceedings. Detailed descriptions of these evaluations are provided in the Oxford University Press series of 20 volumes, *Best Practices in Forensic Mental Health Assessment* (Grisso, Heilbrun, & Goldstein, editors). Published separately (between 2009 and 2012), each volume is devoted to one of these evaluations.

Evaluations in the first group arise as a result of charges against persons claiming that they have committed illegal behaviors. They arise in the criminal justice system if the defendant is an adult (or an adolescent charged as an adult) and in delinquency courts if the defendant is charged as a juvenile. Each of the evaluations listed here is, in effect, a "referral question" asked by the court or attorney who requests the evaluation. Some

TABLE 1.2 **Systems-Based Classification of Forensic Mental Health Assessments (FMHAs)**

**Criminal Justice and Juvenile Justice Delinquency Subsystem**
- Capacity to waive Miranda rights (and validity of confessions)
- Competencies
  - Competence to stand trial
  - Competence to plead
  - Competence to waive counsel
  - Competence to testify
  - Competence to be sentenced
  - Competence to be executed
- Jurisdiction (Transfer to/from juvenile court to/from criminal court)
- Criminal responsibility (mental state at time of the offense)
- Sentencing (in juvenile justice, Disposition)
- Risk of future offending (aggression; sex offending; recidivism)
  - For pretrial secure placement
  - For placement after adjudication
  - For post-corrections release or placement

**Civil Justice and Juvenile Justice Child Welfare/Domestic Affairs Subsystem**
- Civil commitment
  - Mental illness and dangerousness
  - Risk of sex offense recidivism after completion of criminal sentence
- Competence to consent to treatment/research
- Guardianship and conservatorship
- Personal injury under workers' compensation and tort laws
- Employment discrimination/harrassment
- Testamentary capacity
- Fitness for duty
- Termination of parental rights
- Child custody

**Criminal Justice, Civil Justice, and Juvenile Justice**
- Jury selection
- Eyewitness identification
- Abuse and neglect

are "pre-trial questions." For example, a person's capacity to have waived *Miranda* rights is relevant when a court is deciding whether the state will be allowed to use information obtained during police questioning as evidence in a future trial. Other pretrial competencies address whether a defendant's present disabilities have an impact on the defendant's capacity to participate in the trial process. Other evaluations pertain to special questions that arise after a defendant is found guilty, focusing on treatment needs, risk of re-offending, or mitigating factors that are relevant for sentencing decisions. Criminal responsibility evaluations are the only forensic evaluations that are relevant for the stage at which guilt is argued.

In the second group, forensic evaluations are requested in a wide variety of civil and child welfare legal cases. Some of these pertain to legal decisions about a person's need for protection as a result of their disabilities: whether they need involuntary commitment to hospitals or protection from their incapacities to make important decisions that will have an impact on their own welfare. Other evaluations in this category focus on individuals who make claims of entitlement regarding their disabilities or injuries, with the evaluation focusing on the fit between the law's definition of conditions that afford such entitlement and the person's actual disabilities (what they are, how they arose, and what consequences they are likely to have).

Finally, a large subset of these civil forensic evaluations pertains to the welfare of children under the custody of their caretakers. They involve, in part, the evaluation of the specific needs of a child and the capacities of current or future caretakers to meet those needs. Outcomes can result in completely terminating the relationship between a child and parents or, in divorce custody cases, will often conclude by limiting the nature and extent of the parent's relationship with the child.

Finally, a few types of forensic evaluations occur across the criminal, civil, and juvenile justice systems. Evaluations related to child, elderly, or other domestic abuse and neglect cases, for example, can be requested for use in criminal courts when a defendant is facing criminal charges for abuse, in civil courts when a person is being sued by the alleged abused party, or in juvenile and family courts when parents are being investigated to determine whether it is safe to leave the child in their continued care. Other evaluations listed here are "jury selection" and "eyewitness identification." These are forensic psychological practices that do not involve evaluations of individuals but, rather, the application of psychological science in consultation to professionals seeking assistance in trials. As noted earlier in the definition of the specialty of forensic psychology, the mere fact that one is engaged in these consultations does not mean that one is practicing forensic psychology. But these consultations are among the activities of some forensic psychologists who regularly provide professional psychological expertise to the judicial system.

The evaluations and consultations in Table 1.2 do not describe all of the things that forensic psychologists do. Some forensic psychologists work in settings in which individuals involved in the legal system receive treatment—for example, special mental hospital units for patients who are in the correctional system, or "forensic units" where persons with serious mental illnesses are hospitalized while they are being treated to restore their competence to stand trial. If their practice focuses primarily on providing clinical treatment to those populations, their practice does not fall under the specialty definition, which focuses on providing consultation "to the judicial system" and "in legal proceedings." But some clinicians who provide treatment in legal settings are also required to offer opinions and consultations to courts regarding the individuals they are treating. In such circumstances, their treatment activities can be said to be a part of their practice of the specialty of forensic psychology.

In summary, the range of populations and evaluations included in the specialty of forensic psychology are extremely varied. Does this mean that professional qualification for the specialty of forensic psychology requires the necessary expertise to offer this range of services? It does not, of course, any more than the specialty of clinical psychology requires qualifications to assess, diagnose, and treat adults and children with the full range of mental, behavioral, developmental, and substance disorders. A forensic psychologist who is highly qualified to perform evaluations related to criminal judicial questions might not be qualified to address issues in civil and juvenile cases. Therefore, we have described the domain of populations and activities within forensic psychology rather than the domain of individual forensic psychologists' practices.

## C. UNIQUE REQUIREMENTS OF THE SPECIALTY

Although the domain of services that forensic psychologists provide is extensive, there are certain types of knowledge and ability that *(1)* are required for practices across this domain and *(2)* are relatively unique among the professional specialties as a consequence of the focus of forensic practice on service to the judicial system. What do psychologists who practice forensic psychology as a specialty need to know and be able to do that is different from the practice of clinical psychologists in general? What makes forensic psychology a "specialty?"

One might imagine that "knowledge of law" would be one of those factors. Yet all psychologists must know the laws that pertain to their practice of psychology. In this sense, "knowledge of law" is not a unique feature of forensic psychology as a specialty. However, the need for the forensic psychologist to know about laws that often have little to do with general clinical practice is unique. They need to know not only how the law defines their practice but also how it defines the legal system's manner of reaching legal decisions. Put another way, they must understand the client that defines their specialty and for whom they are providing a service. Most of the specific, unique requirements that follow are related to the fact that forensic psychologists work in a system that is neither psychological nor clinical and that has different functions and purposes than the profession for which many psychologists are trained.

## Legal Analysis

*The practice of forensic psychology requires the ability to find, read and analyze law.*

This ability is not required by any other professional psychology specialty as a fundamental matter of competent practice.

Each of the types of evaluations or consultations that forensic psychologists are asked to perform are defined by laws that describe the meaning of the referral questions (in Table 1.2). Some of these laws are in federal or state statutes, but many are in a complex labyrinth of previous legal cases decided by courts in the jurisdiction in which the referral is being made. Taken together, these past legal cases refine—and sometimes completely change—whatever guidance the statutes provide in defining the legal question the forensic psychologist's evaluation is supposed to address. In many areas of law, legal definitions are not static; they change somewhat from year to year. Moreover, the definitions are often different from one jurisdiction (e.g., state) to another. The situation is similar to the chaotic world in which a clinician would be practicing if different hospital systems had somewhat different definitions and diagnostic criteria for the same mental disorder, with definitions changing continuously on the basis of clinical experience, and with the clinician being required to employ the current definition relevant for the hospital system in which the clinician is working. Such diversity and instability would seem almost unmanageable. Yet under similar definitional circumstances, the forensic psychologist is expected, at any moment and for any case, to offer a clear and reasonably accurate definition of the laws that pertain to the evaluation performed for that case.

Even the comparison to an ever-changing diagnostic system does not do justice to the complexity of this demand on forensic psychologists, because it is not only the definition of one's referral question that is involved. Laws also have an impact on what data the forensic psychologist can and cannot collect, as well as the methods that can and cannot be used, when performing the forensic evaluation.

One cannot expect textbooks to describe these legal definitions in a way that is specific to one's own forensic practice in one's own jurisdiction. The pace of textbooks cannot keep up with continuous changes in law, and the jurisdictional variations are too great to be handled by most general texts.

Therefore, the practice of forensic psychology is more effective when the professional has the ability to find, read, and analyze law. Forensic practice is enhanced when one knows how to find statutes and search for new legal cases that may provide relevant definitions for one's practice, although the law's archival system is nothing like the retrieval of scientific information in psychology. Practice is enhanced when one is able to read what one finds, although the format and terms in legal documents are not taught in the typical psychology graduate school curriculum. Having found and read the relevant law, one must interpret it. This requires analytic methods that presuppose a knowledge of the structure of law and its application, much of which does not follow the empirically based, result-driven logic with which psychologists are trained. These specialized abilities to find, read, and analyze law are not essential to provide competent forensic psychological assistance to the courts. But the ability to do so, when required by their role, characterizes individuals for whom forensic psychology is their specialty as defined by the APA.

## Translating from Law to Psychology

> *The practice of forensic psychology requires the knowledge and ability to translate what the law wants to know into theories, constructs, and behaviors that the psychologist can observe and that will be relevant for addressing the legal question.*

The law defines what it wants to know about human behavior when it asks for a forensic psychologist's evaluation and opinion. But it defines what it wants to know in ways that are entirely inadequate for purposes of developing one's evaluation. It usually does not use psychology's terms and concepts for human abilities or disabilities when defining legal constructs like "competence to stand trial," "risk of harm to others," or "parenting to meet the child's needs." The first of these legal constructs has no comparable counterpart in clinical psychology. The second is a construct that almost all clinical psychologists must be able to define and measure, but it has many different meanings in law—depending on the specific criminal or civil question for which it is raised—that most clinical psychologists would not be expected to be able to identify. The third concept will be well-known as a clinical question by some psychologists (those trained in child and family practice) but not necessarily as a legal construct that may have to address different abilities and circumstances than would be common in general clinical child practice.

Therefore, forensic psychologists must know the law's meanings of certain constructs about human behavior in a way that allows them to translate what the law wants to know into things that can be observed and measured. They must also be able to recognize when the law wants to know something that *cannot* be deduced from observations and measures that are available to psychology to recognize the limits of our scientific expertise in addressing legal questions about human behavior. Forensic psychology has produced a substantial body of theoretical and empirically based literature to assist clinicians in this process of translating legal constructs into terms and concepts that are amenable to psychological evaluation.

### Comprehending Legal Systems

*The practice of forensic psychology requires understanding the legal systems in which one provides forensic psychological services.*

Clinical psychologists recognize that their knowledge of human behavior and human disabilities, and their knowledge of assessment and treatment methods, is not all that is required to engage in effective and competent practice. They must also be familiar with the ways in which hospitals and clinics operate to implement their methods effectively within the demands of that context. They must also be familiar with the people in health provider settings to communicate with them in ways that promote best practices for patients.

Similarly, forensic psychologists must be thoroughly knowledgeable regarding the legal settings in which they practice, be they jails, courts, forensic hospitals, or prisons. Some of this knowledge relates to the formal rules and procedures within which the forensic psychologist must provide a service. But often a grasp of the "culture" and unwritten social assumptions within such settings are of equal importance to anything one might learn from formal instruction. If psychologists approach legal settings with expectations based on their knowledge of clinical settings, they will fail to conduct their evaluations, or to communicate their results, in ways that will allow them to be used by their clients.

### Competence in Principles and Methods of Forensic Mental Health Assessment

*The practice of forensic psychology requires knowledge of special principles and assessment methods specifically developed for forensic evaluations.*

During the past 40 years, the field of forensic psychology has developed principles for applying psychology to assessment questions raised in legal proceedings. The field has also developed a large number of structured assessment tools that have been designed specifically to obtain data relevant for various types of forensic evaluations outlined in Table 1.2. These principles and assessment methods are described in a growing literature that represents consensus regarding their value and importance, represented by such texts as Heilbrun's (2001) *Principles of Forensic Mental Health Assessment,* Melton et al.'s (2007) *Psychological Evaluations for the Courts,* Grisso's (2003) *Evaluating Competencies,* and the aforementioned Oxford series (Grisso, Heilbrun, & Goldstein, 2009) on *Best Practices in Forensic Mental Health Assessment.* These specialized principles and methods for forensic assessments typically are not part of the curriculum of general clinical psychological training. They are essential, however, for performance of forensic evaluations and therefore are a unique characteristic of forensic psychology as a specialty.

This is not to say that all of the principles and methods employed in forensic psychological evaluations are distinct from general clinical assessment theories and methods. To the contrary, forensic psychology uses virtually all of the methods and strategies developed in the field of clinical psychological assessment. The newer, distinctly forensic methods have been developed to augment clinical psychology's rich array of methods and instruments, primarily by measuring concepts and employing content that comes closer to the meanings of the legal constructs that forensic psychologists are asked to address.

## Specialized Clinical Knowledge for Legal Populations

*The practice of forensic psychology requires clinical knowledge of the special characteristics of populations for whom the legal system requests forensic evaluations.*

Persons who are facing criminal, civil, and juvenile legal proceedings often manifest clinical and personality characteristics that distinguish them from the general diagnostic classes to which they belong. In the criminal and juvenile delinquency systems, many persons with mental disorders have more extensive histories of illegal and violent behavior than their diagnostic counterparts outside the legal system. Knowledge of factors that are related to violent behavior, therefore, is of significantly greater importance for forensic work than for general clinical work. This also creates a need to understand the special contexts (e.g., adult prisons, juvenile correctional programs) in which future aggression might occur, because these environments possess characteristics that are unlike those encountered in general clinical practice. Some of the relevant research literature is in the annals of psychology and psychiatry, but much of it is in other disciplines, most notably criminology.

### Understanding Data as Legal Evidence

*The practice of forensic psychology requires a translation of psychological data into legal evidence, including the limits that the law places on the manner in which such evidence can be introduced and used in judicial settings.*

This special demand for forensic examiners is, in a sense, the opposite of the one noted earlier regarding "translation from law to psychology." Having conducted the evaluation, the forensic examiner must know how to "back-translate," such that the clinical information one has acquired is put in a form that is relevant as legal evidence. One's evaluation may have caused one to acquire various types of clinical information that would be improper, according to rules of legal evidence, if it were included in one's report to the court. For example, if a report on competence to stand trial included information that would explain why an examinee committed a particular offense, most jurisdictions' rules of evidence would render the evaluation and the report inadmissible in the legal proceeding. Most forensic questions restrict the reporting of clinical information in one way or another. Forensic examiners must know those restrictions generally and in their own specific jurisdictions.

### Ethics in the Context of Legal Systems

*The practice of forensic psychology requires knowledge of the ways in which general professional ethical obligations create special demands in forensic contexts.*

The general ethics codes for psychology apply to forensic psychologists in their work in service to legal systems. But they raise issues and require specialized applications that differ from general clinical practice. Perhaps the most basic foundation for these differences is in the role of the forensic examiner to the examinee. Forensic examiners are not ultimately responsible for the welfare of the examinee. The forensic examiner's primary duty is to provide unbiased, truthful, and accurate information for a legal decision maker. In most instances, there is no "doctor–patient" relationship between forensic psychologists as their examinees.

Forensic evaluations are always done, of course, in a context that seeks to minimize avoidable harm to the examinee and honors every legal right of the examinee. But it is inevitable that forensic examiners' findings will sometimes create conditions that are not desirable from the examinee's perspective and may even be potentially damaging. For example, a court may increase an examinee's conditions of confinement partly in response to clinical information about the examinee's likelihood of future violence, and the confinement itself might be in conditions that could exacerbate the examinee's distress.

Managing these conditions, while abiding by the principles of psychology's ethical codes, is an important part of the special expertise of a forensic psychologist. They are aided in this effort by a number of "specialty guidelines" for psychologists involved in various types of forensic evaluations (e.g., APA, 2009: Guidelines for Child Custody Evaluations in Family Law Proceedings). Often these have been promulgated by subspecialty organizations associated with such forensic evaluation as adult defendants, delinquency defendants, parents in child custody cases, and children in abuse and neglect cases.

# TWO

# Conceptual Foundations of Forensic Psychology
*The Legal Basis*

As discussed in Chapter 1, forensic psychology involves the application of psychological knowledge and expertise to the legal system. Although forensic psychologists are not expected to be legal scholars, competent practice requires that they be knowledgeable about the legal system and the "legal doctrines that give relevance" (Melton et al., 2007, p. 87) to the mental health evaluations that they perform. Without such knowledge, psychologists are not likely to be aware of the psychological attributes that are most relevant for addressing the forensic referral question, the functional capacities that need to be addressed, and the relevance of their clinical data to the legal issue at hand. For example, concepts of legal causality often differ from psychological approaches to understanding causality, in both criminal and civil context. In addition, laws typically focus on narrow conceptualizations of functional abilities relevant to specific areas of competency. The same clinical status may have different implications for different legal competencies, such as competency to stand trial, criminal responsibility, competency to make treatment decisions, or competency to manage one's affairs.

This chapter will briefly summarize the legal knowledge domains that are relevant to forensic psychologists. It will begin with an overview of the legal system and then discuss legal concepts relevant to substantive areas of forensic practice, based on case law and statutes. The next chapter in this section (Chapter 3) will focus on areas of psychological research that are uniquely, or predominantly, relevant to areas of forensic practice. The final chapter in this section (Chapter 4) will discuss assessment strategies and instruments specifically developed for forensic practice.

## I. Understanding the Legal System

Laws that govern issues addressed by forensic psychologists may be determined either by statute (i.e., laws passed by a State legislature or, in Federal
cases, by the Congress of the United States) or by case law. Case law refers
to precedents established by the courts that are relevant to the particular
jurisdiction. Forensic psychologists should have a basic understanding of
the structure of the court system and the scope of authority of particular
courts.

### A. FEDERAL COURT SYSTEM

The trial court in the federal system is called the district court. This court
has jurisdiction in criminal cases involving federal offenses (such as kid-
napping across state lines), claims of entitlement under federal law (e.g.,
social security, Americans with Disability Act), rules of evidence in Federal
court (e.g., *Frye v. United States,1923; Daubert v. Merrell Dow,1993*, discussed below), and claims that a state or federal statute is unconstitutional
(such as commitment of sex offenders following completion of their criminal sentences). Appeals of decisions made at the district court level are
heard by judges in a circuit court of appeals. The country is divided into
12 circuits, each having jurisdiction over a number of states. It is important to keep in mind that a decision made by a circuit court of appeals is
binding only within that circuit. Therefore, federal law could be interpreted
differently in different states. Such differences often form the basis for an
appeal to the U.S. Supreme Court. In addition, any decision made by a
circuit court can serve as the basis for a petition to the Supreme Court,
although that court has discretion as to whether to agree to decide the case
(known as granting, or denying, *certiorari*).

Although the U.S. Supreme Court is the highest legal authority in the
nation, there are important distinctions regarding the scope of that authority. When the Supreme Court rules on issues related to federal law or federal
courts (such as the issue of setting standards regarding when new methodologies can be accepted into evidence, as in *Daubert v. Merrell Dow* [1993],
discussed below), these rulings pertain only to federal courts and are not
binding on state courts, which are free to establish their own standards.
However, when the Supreme Court rules that a practice or law is unconstitutional, such as its ruling in *Atkins v. Virginia* (2002) that execution of
mentally retarded defendants is unconstitutional (as discussed below), this
is binding on all jurisdictions, State and Federal. In these latter cases, the
Court's ruling establishes the minimal standards that must be adhered to.

However, this allows an individual state to provide *additional* safeguards (e.g., although the Supreme Court ruled in *In re Gault* [1967] that juveniles do not have a constitutional right to a jury trial, this does not prevent a state from enacting laws that do provide this extra protection by providing juveniles with such a right).

## B. STATE COURT SYSTEM

State courts are organized differently than the federal court system. Most states have separate courts for different types of cases. For example, minor crimes and civil claims for small sums of money are often heard in a lower court (sometimes called a "district court," although the terminology is not uniform across states), whereas more serious crimes and claims for larger sums of money are heard in a higher court (sometimes called "superior courts"). There are other special-jurisdiction courts, such as courts for children and juveniles, probate courts, and more recently developed "drug courts" and mental health courts. Most states have an appeals court system similar to the federal system—court of appeals and a state supreme court, although some have only a supreme court. The state supreme court has final jurisdiction over matters of interpretation of state law, unless it is in conflict with the Constitution or a federal law. Although the structure of state courts is similar across jurisdictions, the names used for these courts differ. Thus, although in most states the highest court is the state supreme court, in New York the courts that adjudicate felonies are called supreme courts, and the highest court is called the Court of Appeals.

## C. CRIMINAL PROCEEDINGS

Criminal proceedings involve charges that an individual (a defendant) has violated a state or federal law. Because violation of a criminal statute can involve serious loss of liberty (imprisonment) or even death (capital punishment), the state or federal government has the burden of proof (i.e., the defendant is considered innocent until proven guilty) and must prove guilt by a very high standard—that is, "beyond a reasonable doubt." Defendants are entitled to be represented by an attorney, and the state or federal government is required to provide an attorney if the defendant is indigent and cannot afford one.

Children and adolescents are treated differently in the criminal system. Juvenile courts were first established in 1899 (*see* Chapter 1), with the idea that the focus was more on rehabilitation than punishment. However, as society became more concerned with violence by juveniles (in the 1990s), the balance between rehabilitation and punishment shifted more toward the latter for juveniles. States enacted laws to change the standards under which juveniles could be charged as adults (known as "waiver hearings," as jurisdiction was waived from juvenile court to adult court) as well as enhanced punishment. Relevant case law will be discussed below in the section on Juvenile Assessments.

## D. CIVIL WRONGS

Civil wrongs, referred to legally as torts, involve disputes between two parties. The party seeking compensation is called the plaintiff, and the party being sued is called the defendant. As the consequences of civil proceedings do not involve loss of liberty, the burden and standard of proof are different than in criminal matters. The plaintiff has the burden of proof and must meet this burden by the lower standard of "preponderance of the evidence." This simply means that the plaintiff has to demonstrate that his or her claim is more likely than the defendant's to be true. Of relevance to forensic psychologists, civil suits often involve depositions prior to trial. In a deposition, attorneys have the opportunity to question a witness (including expert witnesses) under oath, without the presence of a judge or jury. This provides an opportunity for the opposing attorney to discover what the witness intends to testify about, and any statements made in the deposition can be used at the trial.

## E. DIVORCE AND CHILD CUSTODY

Divorce proceedings are heard in family or probate courts, and within this context, the most likely case to involve a forensic psychologist will be those in which there is an issue of child custody. As discussed below, most states determine custody arrangement based on the best interest of the child (rather than simply based on the rights of each of the parents, as would be the case in tort law). Furthermore, in addition to attorneys for each of the parents, courts may appoint a *guardian ad litem* for the children involved; the term simply means that this person is appointed for the purpose of the lawsuit only (*ad litem*) to represent the interests of the children, separate from the interests of either parent.

## F. CIVIL COMMITMENT AND GUARDIANSHIP

Another type of civil case involves attempts to either limit the rights of certain individuals to make decisions on their own behalf, because of disability (by appointing a guardian to make those decisions) or to deprive the individual of liberty by civilly committing him to an institution (such as a psychiatric hospital). Although these cases are civil in nature and do not involve punishment as in criminal cases, they differ from other civil cases in that they involve loss of liberty and rights for the individuals involved. In civil commitment cases, in which an individual can be locked up involuntarily, the burden of proof is placed on the petitioner (i.e., the party seeking to commit the respondent), and the U.S. Supreme Court (*Addington v. Texas*, 1979) has ruled that the standard is *clear and convincing evidence*. This is an intermediate standard between *preponderance of evidence* used in civil cases and the most stringent *beyond a reasonable doubt* used in criminal cases. The Supreme Court's rationale is that the Fourteenth Amendment, which includes the provision that no state can "deprive any person of life, liberty, or property, without due process of law," establishes that individuals have significant liberty interests that necessitate a higher standard of review before they can be committed involuntarily.

## II. Criminal Adjudications

### A. COMPETENCE TO STAND TRIAL

Evaluations of a defendant's competence to stand trial are the most common form of evaluation in the criminal justice system. This concept is also referred to as adjudicative competence (e.g., Poythress, Bonnie, Monahan, Otto, & Hoge, 2002) to reflect the reality that many defendants do not actually proceed to a trial but resolve their cases through plea bargaining. It is a concept that stems from the legal system's interests in ensuring both that defendants obtain a fair trial and that the dignity of the court proceedings be upheld. If a trial proceeds while the defendant is not able to comprehend what is transpiring, and/or cannot provide relevant information to the defense attorney, then justice cannot be served. In the case of *Dusky v. United States* (1960), the U.S. Supreme Court established the minimal standard for competence to stand trial to be whether the defendant "had sufficient present ability to consult with his lawyer with a reasonable degree of rational understanding and whether he had a rational as well as factual understanding of the proceedings against him" (p. 402). All states have adopted a comparable standard, although the exact wording may vary across jurisdictions.

The most common clinical conditions that impair competence to stand trial are severe mental illnesses (e.g., psychotic disorder, bipolar disorders) and mental retardation. Some jurisdictions specify in their statutes that incompetency must be tied to a mental disorder, although others are silent on this point, which leaves open the option of other factors impairing competency (such as cultural issues, or immaturity—as in the case of juveniles). In all jurisdictions, the standard is a functional one, meaning that the presence of a mental disorder, even one that incapacitates the individual in other spheres of life, is not sufficient for determining that a defendant is impaired in those domains that are clearly related to the defendant's ability to understand and assist.

Legal Burden and Standard of Proof   Although competence to stand trial is relevant to criminal cases, the standard of proof is different than that required to prove guilt (which is beyond a reasonable doubt). In 1992, Teofilo Medina was found competent to stand trial in a California court after a protracted and contested hearing. His case was appealed, eventually to the U.S. Supreme Court, on the grounds that California law had placed the burden of proof on him, by a preponderance of the evidence (meaning more likely than not), to demonstrate that he was incompetent. He argued that this violated his due process rights of the Fourteenth Amendment. The Supreme Court (*Medina v. California*, 1992) rejected this argument and ruled that states could place the burden on the defendant. However, in the case of *Cooper v. Oklahoma* (1996), the Supreme Court ruled that it was unconstitutional for a state to require the defendant to demonstrate incompetency by the stricter standard of clear and convincing evidence. Such a requirement could lead to situations in which a defendant would be forced to stand trial when he had shown by a preponderance of the evidence that he was incompetent but could not prove so to a higher degree. The Supreme Court ruled that such an outcome would undermine the basic fairness of the trial process and stated that: "difficulty in ascertaining whether a defendant is incompetent or malingering may make it appropriate to place the burden of proof on him, but it does not justify the additional onus of an especially high standard of proof" (p. 366).

Elements of Competence to Stand Trial   As noted, most cases do not end up going to trial, as the matter is resolved during plea bargaining. In those circumstances, defendants plead guilty or no contest in return for a lighter sentence. As such, the demands on the defendant are different; although there is no need to sit through a potentially lengthy trial and understand all the testimony and its implications, the defendant gives up significant rights by such a plea (e.g., the right against self-incrimination, the right to a trial by jury, and the right to have the prosecution prove guilt beyond a reasonable doubt). Thus, when a defendant pleads guilty (whether as part of a plea bargain or without any such deal), it may be argued that there are heightened demands on decision-making ability. Courts have struggled with the concept of whether the decision to plead guilty requires a higher standard of competency. Although previous decisions had suggested a higher standard, in the case of *Godinez v. Moran* (1993), the U.S. Supreme Court ruled that the standard for competency was a uniform one, regardless of whether the defendant pled not guilty and went through a trial with the assistance of an attorney or decided to represent himself and plead guilty. In arriving at this decision, the Court emphasized that decision making is an important element of all types of criminal proceedings—not limited to cases in which the defendant chooses to plead guilty.

A related issue addressed by the Supreme Court in *Indiana v. Edwards* (2008) involves standards regarding when a defendant would be considered competent to act as his own attorney in a trial. The subtle, but important, distinction from the issues discussed in *Godinez* is that whereas *Godinez* addressed the defendant's competency to make the decision to represent himself, *Edwards* focused on the defendant's competency to conduct the defense. Ahmad Edwards was diagnosed with schizophrenia and had been adjudicated as competent to stand trial. He then entered a plea of not guilty and requested to represent himself at trial. The trial judge ruled that as a result of his mental illness, he was not competent to act as his own attorney (proceed *pro se*), and Edwards appealed this finding. He contended (through his appellate attorney) that the judge's ruling violated his constitutional right, under the Sixth Amendment, to represent himself (established in the previous case of *Faretta v. California*, 1975). The Supreme Court denied Edwards' claim and ruled that: "the Constitution permits States to insist upon representation by counsel for those competent enough to stand trial under *Dusky* but who still suffer from severe mental illness to the point where they are not competent to conduct trial proceedings by themselves."(p. 178) In arriving at this conclusion, the Supreme Court declined, however, to establish specific standards for judges to use when determining that a defendant is not competent to serve as his own attorney.

**Amnesia and Competence to Stand Trial**    The issue of amnesia and its relationship to competence to stand trial highlights an important distinction between the forensic psychological evaluation and the ultimate legal determination. *Wilson v. United States* (1968) is a federal case that exemplifies the legal approach to this issue. Robert Wilson, after allegedly committing a robbery, was involved in a car accident, which resulted in a significant head injury and concomitant retrograde amnesia (resulting in total, permanent loss of memory for the time period of the robbery). He subsequently presented with no other deficits, other than his inability to recall, and relate to his attorney, anything related to the alleged offense. He was nonetheless deemed competent to stand trial by the trial court judge, and he appealed based on the argument that his amnesia impaired his ability to aid his attorney in developing his defense. The U.S. Supreme Court ruled that amnesia *per se* is not a bar to competence to stand trial; rather, the trial judge would need to consider, on a case-by-case basis, whether the amnesia affected competency abilities, taking into account the extent to which the amnesia affected the defendant's ability to consult with and assist his lawyer and to testify in his own behalf. In addition, the trial judge would need to consider the extent to which evidence could be reconstructed, the prosecution's assistance in helping to reconstruct such evidence, and the strength of the prosecution's case. It should be noted that these are all legal determinations, not based on psychological assessment of the defendant. Thus, although forensic psychologists have an important role to play in such cases in helping the court to determine whether the defendant has genuine amnesia, the extent of the memory loss, and the likelihood of recovery of memories, the decision about whether the defendant would thus be considered incompetent to stand trial will ultimately be based on legal considerations.

Disposition of Incompetent Defendants    In many jurisdictions, once a defendant is adjudicated as incompetent to stand trial, he or she may be committed to a psychiatric hospital for treatment. This had led to situations in which defendants were psychiatrically hospitalized for lengthy periods of time, far exceeding the possible sentences they could have received if they had been convicted. In 1972, in the case of *Jackson v. Indiana*, the U.S. Supreme Court ruled that such indefinite commitment of incompetent defendants violated both the due process and equal protection clauses of the Fourteenth Amendment to the Constitution. The Court noted that the standards for committing an incompetent defendant were less stringent than those for committing citizens who were not charged with crimes and could result in the indefinite commitment of an individual who would never be able to stand trial. They therefore ruled that a defendant committed solely based on a determination of incompetency to stand trial "cannot be held more than the reasonable period of time necessary to determine whether there is a substantial probability that he will attain that capacity in the foreseeable future". Furthermore, continued commitment would be based on a showing of progress toward attaining competency. The court did not set a specific time-frame, leaving that up to individual states. For forensic psychologists, this means that evaluations for competency to stand trial include an assessment of the likelihood that the defendant could be restored to competency, within time-frames established within the particular jurisdiction.

## B. CRIMINAL RESPONSIBILITY

A basic principle of criminal law is that to be found guilty of an offense, an individual must have committed an *actus reus* (literally, a "bad act") and must have done so with *mens rea* (i.e., a "guilty mind"). Most jurisdictions in the United States (46 states, the federal system, and the military) have provisions for acquittal of defendants who are deemed to be legally insane. However, the standards that are used vary. The most common standard is the *M'Naghten* standard, or a variation of it. This stems from English law dating back to 1843. This standard, often referred to as the "right–wrong test," states:

> "[t]o establish a defense on the ground of insanity, it must be proved that, at the time of the committing of the act, the party accused was laboring under such a defect of reason, from disease of the mind, as not to know the nature and quality of the act he was doing or if he did know it, that he did not know he was doing what was wrong."

The second most common standard is known as the American Law Institute (ALI) standard, which was developed in 1962. This standard states that a defendant would be found not guilty by reason of insanity if, "as a result of mental illness or mental defect he lacked substantial capacity either to appreciate the wrongfulness of his conduct or to conform his conduct to the requirements of the law." The ALI rule includes both a *cognitive prong* (appreciation of wrongfulness) and a *volitional* prong (conform conduct). New Hampshire is the only state currently using what is known as the "product test"—that is, a defendant will be found insane if the offense was a product of a mental illness. Four states (Idaho, Kansas, Montana, and Utah) have abolished the insanity defense. The U.S. Supreme Court has never ruled on whether there is a requirement to allow for a defense of not guilty by reason of insanity. In the case of *Clark v. Arizona* (2006), the Supreme Court stated, "it is clear that no particular formulation has evolved into a baseline for due process" (p. 2722). Thus, no minimum standard has been established.

In addition to variations in the legal standard for insanity, there are also differences in the threshold question about the underlying mental condition (i.e., "mental illness," "mental disease," "mental retardation," "mental defect"). Even when these terms are defined in statute, there is room for interpretation of whether a particular diagnosis meets the criterion. The DMS-IV TR (2000) provides a caveat that " [i]n most situations, the clinical diagnosis of a *DSM-IV* mental disorder is not sufficient to establish the existence for legal purpose of a "mental disorder," "mental disability," "mental disease," or "mental defect" (p. xxxiii). Although studies of insanity acquittees have found that most successful insanity defenses involve a psychotic disorder (e.g., Packer, 1987; Callahan, Steadman, McGreevey, & Clark-Robbins, 1991; Cochrane, Grisso, & Frederick, 2001; Warren, Murrie, Chauhan, & Morris, 2004), other disorders can qualify if they are of sufficient severity to impact the functional criteria (i.e., the cognitive and/ or volitional prong). However, antisocial personality disorder is typically excluded as a basis for an insanity defense. The ALI standard explicitly states that the terms mental disease or defect "do not include an abnormality manifested only by repeated criminal or otherwise antisocial conduct."

Another important exclusion relates to intoxication. Voluntary intoxication resulting from consumption of alcohol or drugs is not considered a basis for an insanity defense (e.g., *Kane v. United States*, 1968). The rationale is that the defendant should not benefit from a condition he or she brought upon him- or herself. However, there are some exceptions for what are considered "fixed" or "settled" conditions. Fixed conditions refer to long-term, permanent sequelae of substance abuse, such as dementia or Korsakoff's psychosis. Most jurisdictions will allow such conditions to qualify for the insanity defense (e.g., *People v. Lim Dum Dong*, 1938; *State v. Hartfield,* 1990). Settled conditions refer to situations in which a psychotic disorder was triggered by substance use but continues well beyond the point of intoxication (e.g., *People v. Kelly*, 1973, in which a young woman committed an assault in a psychotic state, which began months earlier when she ingested large quantities of LSD and mescaline). Most states will allow such conditions to qualify for the insanity defense.

Disposition Issues    One of the controversial aspects of the insanity defense is the mistaken public assumption that the insanity defense is abused, in the sense that it is overused and results in defendants avoiding confinement. However, data from a number of jurisdictions (e.g. Steadman, McGreevy, Morissey, Callahan, Robbins, & Cirincione, 1993; Melton et al., 2007) confirm that the insanity defense is rarely used and, when used, is successful in only about one-fourth of the cases. Furthermore, insanity acquittees may end up being hospitalized for longer than their maximum criminal sentence would have been. The Supreme Court (*Jones v. United States*, 1983) ruled that there is no relationship between the maximum sentence for an offense and the length of confinement in a psychiatric hospital for a defendant acquitted by reason of insanity, because the purpose of the former is punishment and the purpose of the latter is treatment. Thus, Mr. Jones was committed to a psychiatric hospital for many years beyond the maximum 1-year sentence he would have received had he been convicted of larceny (attempting to steal a jacket from a department store). However, in the case of *Foucha v. Louisiana*, 1992, the Supreme Court clarified that continued commitment of insanity acquittees was based not only on evidence that they would pose a risk of harm if released, but that this risk was tied to a mental illness.

Legal Burden and Standard of Proof    Similarly to the standards for competency to stand trial, there are differences across jurisdictions in terms of who has the legal burden and what the standard of proof is. Some jurisdictions place the burden on the state (and vary as to the standard of proof, from preponderance of the evidence to beyond a reasonable doubt). However, other jurisdictions place the burden on the defendant to prove, by a preponderance of the evidence, that he or she was legally insane. The decision to pursue an insanity defense is up to the defendant, as the Supreme Court has ruled (*Frendak v. United States*, 1979) that a judge may not impose an insanity defense on a defendant who competently declines to use that plea.

There are also differences regarding the standards for release of insanity acquittees from psychiatric care. Although some jurisdictions place the burden on the State to prove that the acquittee is still mentally ill and dangerous, the Supreme Court (in the *Jones* case discussed above) held that a state may place the burden on the acquittee to prove, by a preponderance of the evidence, that he is no longer mentally ill and dangerous. Furthermore, a number of states have instituted conditional release programs, which allow for continued supervision and monitoring of acquittees once they are released to the community, with provisions for re-hospitalization if they violate terms of their release.

C. CAPITAL PUNISHMENT

Psychologists may become involved in death penalty cases at several points: pre-trial, pre-sentencing (i.e., post-conviction), and prior to execution. In the case of *Atkins v. Virginia* (2002), the Supreme Court ruled that it was unconstitutional to execute mentally retarded defendants. Thus, in some jurisdictions, psychologists may be retained to evaluate defendants in the pre-trial stage to determine if they meet legal criteria for mental retardation. If so, the defendant will not be eligible for the death penalty.

More commonly, psychologists may become involved in capital sentencing evaluations, after a finding of guilty, to assess the defendant relevant to mitigating or aggravating factors. In 1972, the Supreme Court (*Furman v. Georgia*) found that the death penalty in Georgia and Texas violated both the Eighth Amendment to the Constitution (prohibition against cruel and unusual punishment) and the Fourteenth Amendment (guaranteeing due process), because of evidence that the decisions were made arbitrarily. This resulted in a national moratorium on executions in the United States, until the Supreme Court ruling in 1976 (*Gregg v. Georgia*) that upheld Georgia's new capital sentencing statute, which included a requirement of at least one aggravating factor be found by a standard of beyond a reasonable doubt and allowed the defense to present evidence of mitigating facts and circumstances. In 1978, in the case of *Lockett v. Ohio*, the court went further and held that "any aspect of the defendant's character or record and any circumstances of the offense" could be offered as evidence of mitigation. Thus, such evaluations involve a very thorough and comprehensive evaluation of all aspects of the defendant's history, as well as an assessment of the defendant's mental state at the time of the offense.

Forensic psychologists may also be called upon to assess a convicted defendant's competency to be executed. In the case of *Ford v. Wainwright* (1986), the Supreme Court considered the case of an inmate who had not demonstrated evidence of mental illness at the time of the crime or his trial but who had developed delusional beliefs in prisons, which involved both paranoid thinking and an irrational belief that he could not be executed. The Court ruled that it was unconstitutional (a violation of the cruel and unusual punishment clause of the Eighth Amendment) to execute an "insane" individual. It should be noted that this terminology does not refer to the standard legal definitions of insanity as discussed in the section on Criminal Responsibility. Rather, the Supreme Court used this term to refer to an individual "whose mental illness prevents him from comprehending the reasons for the penalty or its implications" (p. 418). Subsequently, in the case of *Panetti v. Quarterman* (2007), the Court expanded on this concept and ruled that "a prisoner's awareness of the State's rationale for an execution is not the same as a rational understanding of it" (p. 2862). In this case, Mr. Panetti (diagnosed with schizophrenia or schizoaffective disorder) understood that the state's purported reason for wanting to execute him was punishment for having committed murder but stated that this was a sham and that the real reason was to stop him from preaching about spiritual warfare between the forces of darkness and forces of light. The court's ruling established that simply "knowing" that he was being executed for a crime was not sufficient to establish competency to executed, in the face of a delusional and irrational belief system related to the execution. However, the Court declined to provide more specific guidance, thus leaving it up to individual courts to determine whether an inmate's understanding is rational or not.

## III. Civil Wrongs

### A. PERSONAL INJURY (TORTS)

In tort (civil wrong) cases, forensic psychologists are most likely to be involved in cases alleging either intentional or negligent infliction of emotional harm or distress. All tort claims involve four elements:

- A duty owed (by the defendant in the case to the plaintiff): the duty involved is legally defined—it may be a duty to maintain a safe environment (e.g., if the plaintiff slipped on a wet floor and sustained a head injury), a duty to meet a standard of care (as in malpractice cases), a duty for a therapist to protect third parties (as in the *Tarasoff* case), or any other duties stemming from legal obligations governing expected standards of conduct.

- A breach of duty: the determination of whether the defendant breached a duty is based on a "reasonable person" standard (i.e., it is an objective standard of expected conduct, not the plaintiff's subjective perception). In most cases, the determination of whether a duty was breached will be a matter of fact for the jury (or judge) to decide. However, in cases of malpractice, for example, expert opinion will be relevant to a determination of whether the defendant's acts (or omissions) would be considered to meet a reasonable standard of care.

- Damages sustained by the plaintiff: The breach needs to have resulted in an injury or damages that are compensable. Whether the injury is compensable will depend on the jurisdiction; some jurisdictions will not recognize a claim for emotional damages, unless there was also a physical injury or impact (e.g., *Christie Brothers Circus v. Turnage*, 1928; *Gough v. Natural Gas Pipeline, 1993*), whereas others will (e.g., *Molien v. Kaiser Foundation Hospital*,1980). In addition, courts have ruled that a plaintiff who was not injured but was in the "zone of danger" (*Dillon v. Legg*, 1968) can recover damages for emotional harm. In that case, a mother was able to obtain compensation for emotional trauma caused by seeing her daughter run over by a car.

• Proximate cause: The final element in tort law is that the defendant's actions or omissions must be considered the "proximate cause" of the plaintiff's injury. The legal approach to causality is very different from a psychological or scientific understanding. Psychologists often consider multiple contributing factors and predisposing conditions and understand the outcome to be a complex function of these various factors. In the legal system, the issue of liability by necessity requires a perhaps arbitrary determination of whether one event was the direct cause of another. Thus, causality for legal purposes has focused on whether the injury was a reasonably foreseeable consequence (e.g., *Plaisance v. Texaco, Inc.*, 1991) of the breach of duty. Other terminology used to assess proximate cause is whether the injury would have occurred "but for" the defendant's conduct. The issue becomes quite complicated when there is a chain of events (e.g., *Palsgraf v. Long Island Railroad*, 1928).

In this context, a major legal tenet is that the defendant takes the plaintiff "as he found him." This means that if the plaintiff were particularly vulnerable (or predisposed to the injury) and thus suffered an injury from the breach of duty that most people would not have suffered, then the defendant is still liable. This is also sometimes referred to as the "eggshell skull doctrine" (referring to a situation in which a plaintiff has a fragile skull and thus suffers more serious brain injury than the average person). In contrast to the objective standard used to establish breach of duty, the injury is assessed based on the plaintiff's specific circumstances. Thus, for the forensic psychologist, an important part of the evaluation is to address whether the plaintiff's injuries were pre-existing (e.g., that the defendant was already suffering from depression, which was not exacerbated by the event), in which case the defendant's breach is not likely to be found to be the proximate cause. By contrast if the plaintiff was functioning well prior to the event, even though she may have been particularly vulnerable to the stressor, the trier of fact is likely to determine that the defendant's conduct was the proximate cause of the injury.

## B. EMPLOYMENT ISSUES

**Workers' Compensation**   An area closely related to tort law is workers' compensation. All states and the federal system have adopted workers' compensation laws to provide payment to workers who have been injured in the course of their employment. Workers so injured are entitled to payments that cover both loss of earning capacity as well as costs associated with the injury (such as medical costs). An important distinction from tort law is that the worker can be compensated without demonstrating that the employer was negligent. The deciding factor is whether the injury was work-related.

Many of the issues discussed in the section on Personal Injury (related to damages and proximate cause) are relevant to workers' compensation cases as well. (Issues related to duty and breach of duty are not relevant, as there is no need to demonstrate that the employer was in any way negligent.) The case of *Carter v. General Motors* (1961) illustrates some of these principles. The Supreme Court of Michigan ruled that Mr. Carter could collect workers compensation benefits for a psychiatric disorder brought about by the stress of his employment on an assembly line. This affirmed the concept that emotional injury or disability was compensable in the absence of any physical injury or impact. However, continued compensation was to be contingent on a showing that the individual continued to be disabled (in Mr. Carter's case, the evidence was that approximately a year after his initial "breakdown," he was no longer demonstrating symptoms of his disorder).

Harassment and Discrimination    In 1964, Congress passed the Civil Rights Act, which was a major landmark legislation related to racial discrimination. It also included a reference to discrimination based on sex. Title VII of that act specifically stated: "It shall be an unlawful employment practice for an employer ... to fail or refuse to hire or to discharge any individual, or otherwise to discriminate against any individual with respect to his compensation, terms, conditions, or privileges of employment, because of such individual's race, color, religion, sex, or national origin" (section 703[a]). Subsequent Supreme Court cases have established that sexual harassment creating a hostile or abusive work environment constitutes discrimination based on sex (*Meritor Savings Bank v. Vinson*, 1986), and once it is determined from an objective perspective that there was a hostile and abusive work environment, compensation could be awarded *even* in the absence of specific harm (such as failure to be promoted, or loss of income) or emotional injury to the plaintiff ( *Harris v. Forklift Systems*, 1993). In the case of *Ellison v. Brady* (1991), a Federal Appeals Court ruled that a determination of whether a hostile and abusive environment had been established should be determined based on the perspective of a "reasonable woman." This term acknowledged that women may perceive the work environment differently from men but that the criterion would not be a subjective interpretation by the plaintiff but, rather, what would likely be perceived as abusive by most women. The concept of discrimination based on sex was expanded by the Supreme Court (*Oncale v. Sundowner Offshore Services*, 1998) to include same-sex discrimination (in that case, the plaintiff was a man who claimed sexual harassment by male colleagues at work).

In addition to the Civil Rights Act, another major legislation related to discrimination was the Americans with Disabilities Act, passed by Congress in 1990. This act provided rights to disabled individuals in gaining access to services and employment. Relative to the employment issues, it included provisions that required employers to make reasonable accommodations to allow disabled individuals to perform job functions (e.g., flexible scheduling, additional time to complete work, etc.). It also permitted employers to condition hiring, or continued employment, on the individual not posing a "direct threat to the health or safety" of other individuals in the workplace. As discussed below, this may involve forensic psychological evaluations of whether a particular individual poses a risk of harm because of mental illness.

## IV. Civil Commitment and Involuntary Treatment

### A. COMMITMENT OF PERSONS WITH MENTAL DISORDERS

Although American citizens cannot be preventively detained (i.e., incarcerated solely based on a concern about future risk), there are provisions for involuntary commitment of individuals with mental disorders. In the case of *O'Connor v. Donaldson* (1975), the Supreme Court ruled that states could not involuntarily hospitalize an individual based solely on the presence of mental illness. They wrote: "[a] finding of 'mental illness' alone cannot justify a State's locking a person up against his will and keeping him indefinitely in simple custodial confinement…there is still no constitutional basis for confining such persons involuntarily if they are dangerous to no one and can live safely in freedom" (p. 2493). This landmark case established that civil commitment of mentally ill individuals required a finding that their disorder resulted in risk of harm to themselves or others. Forensic psychologists who conduct evaluations for this purpose need to be familiar with the literature on violence risk assessment, as well as suicide risk and also understand how some of the instruments used may vary depending on the population (e.g., acute vs. long-term, forensic vs. civil, sex offenders, juveniles), as discussed below and in Chapter 3.

In addition to involuntary commitment, mentally ill individuals may be subject to involuntary administration of psychotropic medications. In recognition of the significant intrusion on individual liberties, as well as potentially irreversible side effects of such medications (e.g., tardive dyskinesia), the legal system has developed procedures and safeguards before a patient can be medicated against his or her will. The first issue to be determined is whether the individual is capable of making an informed, competent decision regarding whether to accept the medication (Grisso & Appelbaum, 1998). Once it has been established that the individual cannot make a rational, informed decision about accepting the medication, there are two alternative criteria used. In most jurisdictions, the standard is whether taking the medication would be in the best interest of the individual (e.g., *Rivers v. Katz*, 1986). An alternative standard is "substituted judgment"; in other words, what the patient would decide if he or she were competent to make the decision (e.g., *Rogers v. Okin*, 1986). This latter determination may take into account the individual's religious beliefs, as well as previously stated preferences.

The courts have also dealt with issues of commitment and involuntary administration for individuals who are incarcerated. In the case of *Vitek v. Jones* (1980), the Supreme Court held that prisoners had due process rights that prevented the state from transferring them to a psychiatric facility without appropriate procedures. These procedures include: a hearing in front of an independent decision maker (although the Court did not require this person to be a judge); right to bring witnesses and cross-examine the state's witnesses; and qualified and independent assistance (although not necessarily an attorney). Regarding involuntary psychotropic medication for prisoners, the Supreme Court (*Washington V. Harper*, 1990) upheld a Washington state procedure that allowed such forced treatment based on a hearing in front of a panel, which included a psychiatrist, to determine that the inmate suffered from a mental disorder and posed a risk of harm to self, others, or property. The criteria for prisoners do not have to include a finding of *incompetency to make treatment decisions*, based on the Court's ruling that the state has a compelling interest in providing for safety and security in the prison system.

A more complicated issue arose in the case of *Sell v. United States* (2003), in which the government wanted to administer psychotropic medications to a pre-trial inmate who was adjudicated *incompetent to stand trial* and hospitalized. In that case, the government had not demonstrated that failure to medicate would pose a risk of harm (as in the *Harper* case) but argued that there was a compelling state interest in rendering Sell competent to stand trial so that the legal matter could be resolved. The Supreme Court acknowledged the state's interest in restoring a defendant to competency but again struck a balance between the government's interests and the defendant's liberty interest by requiring the trial court to make four findings before allowing forced medication:

1. The court must find an important governmental interest (such as not freeing a defendant charged with a serious crime) but must consider whether there are other means of ensuring that interest (e.g., in some cases, the individual will remain confined for a lengthy period of time).

2. The court must find that forced medication is substantially likely to render the defendant competent to stand trial (which was in issue in Sell's case, as he was diagnosed with delusional disorder and there was conflicting testimony as to whether this disorder would respond to medication). Furthermore, the court must find that the medication will not interfere significantly with the defendant's ability to assist counsel (referring to possible side effects of the medication).

3. The court must find that less intrusive treatments (such as various forms of psychotherapy) would not be likely to restore the defendant's competency.

4. The court must find that administration of the medication is medically appropriate.

### B. SEX OFFENDER COMMITMENT

A special type of civil commitment process is reserved for sex offenders. A number of states have enacted statutes (often referred to as sexually violent predator [SVP] evaluations) that provide for these individuals to be civilly committed as sexual offenders at the completion of their criminal sentences rather than be released into the community. These individuals do not meet the usual standards for civil commitment, as they are not considered mentally ill (e.g., psychotic disorders) as that term is used for that purpose. Rather, statutory language typically requires a "mental disorder" or "mental abnormality" that may also include a personality disorder. The constitutionality of these statutes was challenged on several grounds:

1. These individuals were not mentally ill, and thus not subject to civil commitment.

2. These individuals were subject to *double jeopardy* (i.e., the individual is punished twice for the same crime; first by being given a prison sentence

and then by being indefinitely committed following completion of the sentence).

3. The sex offender commitment represents an *ex post facto* law (i.e., a law that criminalizes behavior *after* the act had been committed), which is expressly forbidden by the Constitution.

The U.S. Supreme Court dealt with these issues in the case of *Kansas v. Hendricks* (1997). Mr. Hendricks had been committed under a Kansas law that required evidence that the individual "suffers from a mental abnormality or personality disorder which makes the person likely to engage in the predatory acts of sexual violence" (Kansas Statutes Annotated, 1994). The Court ruled that sex offender commitment is a *civil* matter—not a *criminal* one. Thus, the double jeopardy and *ex post facto* clauses of the Constitution do not apply. Furthermore, the Court ruled that there was no requirement for a particular definition of mental disorder or mental illness and that the broader term of a *mental abnormality* or *personality disorder* was a sufficient basis to use for commitment, as it required an element, aside from the previously adjudicated criminal act, to demonstrate impairment in volitional control. Subsequently, in the case of *Kansas v. Crane* (2002), the Supreme Court clarified that the state must show that the mental disorder resulted in a lack of control of sexual behavior but that the loss of control need not be absolute.

## Child Custody and Child Protection

The laws relating to awarding of custody of children following a divorce have evolved significantly since the nineteenth century. Children at that time were considered property (or *chattel*), and as such they were considered to be "owned" by the father. However, in the late nineteenth and early twentieth centuries, the "tender years" doctrine emerged, in which mothers were considered inherently more qualified to raise children, and therefore children were typically placed in the mother's custody following a divorce. However, in the latter part of the twentieth century, a more nuanced approach developed in family law, which no longer assumed that mothers were more fit guardians. Rather, decisions about custody would be made on a case-by-case basis, informed by the "best interests" of the child. This standard was elucidated, for example, in the case of *Painter v. Bannister* (1966), in which the Iowa Supreme Court awarded custody to the maternal grandparents, rather than the biological father. In terms of what constitutes the "best interests" standard, a majority of states have enacted statutes that identify factors to be considered (e.g., the Michigan Child Custody Act of 1970, amended in 1993). The factors include those that are clearly subject to psychological evaluation (e.g., the mental health of the parties involved, the capacity of each parent to provide affection and guidance, the emotional ties existing between the parents and the child) as well as some that may not (e.g., moral fitness of the parents).

Despite this focus on the best interests of the child in custody matters, the Supreme Court has ruled that states cannot use such a standard to compel visitation arrangements with third parties without a finding that the child would otherwise be harmed. This ruling came in the case of *Troxel v. Granville* (2000), which involved a Washington state statute allowing courts to order visitation rights in the best interests of the child. In that case, the paternal grandparents had been awarded a visitation schedule against the wishes of the mother. The Supreme Court ruled that because the mother was not considered unfit, the Fourteenth Amendment's due process clause provided her with a fundamental right to make decisions concerning the care and custody of her children.

Issues of child custody also emerge when there are allegations of child abuse and neglect. Child protection statutes have provisions for allowing the removal of children from an abusive environment. In addition, parental rights may be permanently terminated. In the case of *Santosky v. Kramer* (1982), a New York statute allowed for termination of parents' rights upon a showing, by a *preponderance of the evidence*, that the child was "permanently neglected." The U.S. Supreme Court ruled that the statute violated the parents' due process rights, as it set too low a standard of proof. Instead, the Court determined that states had to use at least a standard of clear and convincing evidence before permanently denying parental rights.

## Juvenile Delinquency Laws

The criminal justice system has long recognized that children are not simply younger versions of adults but have characteristics that warrant different treatment when they commit illegal acts. This is buttressed by the significant literature on development psychology (*see* Chapter 3, p. 67). In the late nineteenth century this concept led to development of juvenile courts, whose core mission is rehabilitation, rather than punishment. The basis for this emphasis is the notion of *parens patriae* (the state's responsibility to function as a guardian of children, looking out for their benefit). As the twentieth century proceeded, it became apparent that the juvenile justice system was not providing the rehabilitation to youth that it had promised but was merely incarcerating them. This led to cases in the 1960s that required the juvenile court to provide youth with many of the same due process rights afforded to criminal defendants. The most important of those cases was *In re Gault*, (1967). Gault was a 15-year-old boy charged with making an obscene telephone call. He was taken into custody and the next day at a hearing was deemed to be a delinquent minor and committed to the Arizona State Industrial School (where he could remain until his 18th birthday). His parents were not present at the hearing, neither he nor they were informed of his right to an attorney, and the alleged victim did not testify. Rather, a police officer testified that Gault had admitted to making lewd comments. The Supreme Court ruled that Gault's due process rights had been violated. They noted that given the significant deprivations of liberty that could result from juvenile court proceedings, the accused had a right to:

1. written notice to the child and his parents of the specific charges, provided sufficiently in advance of the hearing to permit preparation;
2. notification to the child and his parents of the right to be represented by counsel;
3. application of the constitutional privilege against self-incrimination; and
4. the determinations of delinquency had to be based on sworn testimony, with opportunity for cross-examination.

The Court thus ruled that a balance must be struck in juvenile court between its rehabilitative aims and the need to provide constitutional protections. Juveniles were not afforded all the rights of adult defendants, as the ruling did not include a right to a trial by jury. The Supreme Court specifically addressed the issue of trial by jury in *McKeiver v. Pennsylvania*, (1971), noting that a jury trial would make the proceedings so adversarial as to undermine the rehabilitative principles of juvenile court. However, in the case of *In re Winship* (1970), the Supreme Court determined that a finding of delinquency had to be made by the standard used for criminal adjudications of adults—that is, beyond a reasonable doubt.

Another aspect of juvenile justice that has been the focus of appellate cases relates to transfer of jurisdiction of adolescents to adult courts. Although the specific guidelines (such as minimum age, the offenses covered, and the procedures) vary across states, all have developed some mechanism to try juveniles charged with certain serious crimes as adults. Similarly to its ruling in *Gault*, the Supreme Court recognized the need for constitutional safeguards in these transfer (or *waiver*) hearings in the case of *Kent v. United States* (1966). Kent was a 16-year-old boy charged with rape. The juvenile court ordered him to be transferred to district court without the benefit of a hearing and without a clear articulation of the basis for the transfer. The Supreme Court ruled that juveniles subject to such waivers of jurisdiction had due process rights to a full hearing. They wrote that the *parens patriae* philosophy of the juvenile court "is not an invitation to procedural arbitrariness."

The distinction between adults and juveniles is also relevant to determinations about the appropriate severity of punishment. The main issue has been whether individuals who commit offenses as juveniles can be subject to the death penalty. In the case of *Roper v. Simmons* (2005), the Supreme Court ruled that it was a violation of the Eighth Amendment (cruel and unusual punishment) to execute a defendant who had committed an offense prior to age 18 years. In arriving at this conclusion, the Court overruled its previous decision in the case of *Stanford v. Kentucky* (1989), in which it had ruled that defendants who were at least 16 years old at the time of the offense could be executed. The reconsideration of the earlier ruling was based on reasoning similar to that used in the *Atkins* case (related to mentally retarded defendants, p. 39), noting changes in national standards, as well as the recognition that adolescents' immaturity, susceptibility to peer pressure, and continuing struggles to form an identity differentiated them from adults. In *Graham v. Florida* (2010), the Supreme Court expanded this reasoning to rule that it was unconstitutional to impose a life without parole sentence on a juvenile in a non-homicide case. (The court did not address whether such a sentence would be constitutional in cases of homicide).

Several important forensic issues have arisen in juvenile delinquency cases because of the presumed developmental differences between youth and adults in their cognitive and decision-making capacities. One of these is the capacity to waive Miranda rights during police interrogations, as well as risks of coerced confessions. In the case of *Fare v. Michael C.* (1979), the U.S. Supreme Court affirmed that questions of youths' capacities to have waived Miranda rights knowingly, intelligently, and voluntarily were to be judged on the basis of the "totality of the circumstances." This means that there is no bright line in terms of age or other factors when deciding whether a youth had the capacity to waive rights to silence and counsel; rather, all relevant factors should be weighed. These factors include "evaluation of the juvenile's age, experience, education, background, and intelligence and whether he has the capacity to understand the warnings given him, the nature of his Fifth Amendment rights, and the consequences of waiving those rights" (p. 725).

Another developmental capacity question has arisen more recently, pertaining to youths' competence to stand trial in juvenile court. This question was rarely raised before the 1990s, but an increase in youth violence during that decade changed the range and severity of penalties for delinquencies (Grisso, 1997). This, together with new scientific research evidence regarding youths' immature decisional capacities (Scott & Steinberg, 2008), increased the law's scrutiny of youths' capacities to make important decisions (e.g., plea agreements). As a consequence, examiners have recently been asked, with increasing frequency, to perform competence-to-stand-trial evaluations of youth (Grisso & Quinlan, 2005).

# THREE

## Scientific Foundations of Forensic Psychology

As discussed in the previous chapter, knowledge of legal concepts is integral to the development of methodologies and approaches to forensic evaluations. Based on such an understanding, forensic psychologists can then apply psychological expertise to the issue at hand. Much of this expertise is "foundational" for psychology—that is, the forensic psychologist applies knowledge that is basic to the profession. For example, for evaluations of competency to stand trial and criminal responsibility, the forensic psychologist must be competent in the diagnosis of severe psychiatric disorders and understand how the symptoms of these disorders could impact the functional capacities outlined in the law. Forensic psychologists involved in personal injury torts need to be familiar with the symptoms and course of disorders such as depression and post-traumatic stress disorder. Those conducting child custody evaluations must be knowledgeable about parental characteristics that have beneficial and negative effects on children, effects of parental mental disorder on children's development, and the effects of divorce on children. Thus, for much of forensic work, the underlying psychological expertise is not unique to the legal setting but, rather, involves understanding how to apply that knowledge to answer the relevant questions. In addition, there are several topics within psychology in which research has been focused directly on areas that are either uniquely, or predominantly, related to legal issues.

This chapter offers summaries of the conceptual and scientific bases for some important areas of research that inform forensic practice. Before proceeding, however, it is worthwhile to consider some core principles for applying scientific inquiry and methods in forensic evaluations.

The legal system's need for forensic psychological evaluations preceded the development of the scientific field of forensic psychology. For example, the concept of legal insanity can be traced back as far as the Greeks and the Hebrew Mishna, and in eighteenth century England (*Rex v. Arnold,* 1724), the concept of the "wild beast" test was employed (i.e., a defendant was found insane if he was as deprived of reason as a wild beast)—clearly a standard not amenable to empirically derived measurement. As recently as the 1970s, prior to the development of a theoretical or empirical basis for violence risk evaluations, mental health professionals were asked to provide assessments for the courts regarding an individuals' "dangerousness," which resulted in poor reliability and validity (*see* below, p. 53).

A major hallmark of the current field of forensic psychology is the development of a scientific underpinning for the methodologies employed. For example, Grisso (1986, 2003) described a conceptual model that can be applied to the assessment of all legal competencies.

Grisso's model began with a focus on the law's view of the relevant competencies and identifies six characteristics of legal competency constructs: functional, contextual, causal, interactive, judgmental, and dispositional. This model requires an understanding of the legal concepts and how they have been interpreted, which allows operationalization of variables, followed by development of methods to reliably and validly assess the relevant factors. It provides a basis for development of assessment methodologies and instruments (as will be discussed in Chapter 4), which are legally relevant as well as empirically based. Thus, a core principle underlying the development of forensic psychological methodologies is the careful integration of theoretical, conceptual, and empirical approaches to provide forensic psychologists with appropriate tools to address legal issues.

Scientific reasoning is also applied in the interpretation of data, particularly in the context of assessing the connection between clinical data and the functional abilities relevant to the legal constructs. Heilbrun (2001) has described the process of forensic evaluation as analogous to hypothesis testing in a scientific experiment. Although the analogy is limited by the lack of a controlled setting, as well as each evaluation involving an *n* of 1, the type of reasoning applied to the data is guided by scientific principles. Thus, the forensic psychologist develops falsifiable hypotheses, which are then judged based on whether the examinee displays characteristics associated or inconsistent with the hypothesized clinical condition. The psychologist also considers alternative hypotheses, and articulates the rationale for how the data best fit the competing hypotheses. Thus, the opinion offered is not limited to a description of how the data support that opinion but also an analysis of the reasons for rejecting alternative explanations.

In this chapter, therefore, we demonstrate the conceptual and scientific knowledge base for some of the most salient issues relevant for forensic psychology practitioners. The areas covered include: violence risk assessment, including operationalization of the concept of psychopathy; eyewitness identification; elicitation of confessions; child sexual abuse interviews; recovered memory; and development issues related to adolescent criminal behaviors.

## I. Violence Risk Assessment

The issue of violence risk assessment is relatively new in the field of psychology. Until the mid-1970s, this was not an area that was much focused on in clinical training or in the research literature in psychology. The predominant response within psychology and psychiatry to the *Tarasoff v. Board of Regents in California* (1976) case, which held a psychologist liable for failing to protect from harm a victim of the psychologist's client, was that mental health professionals could not predict violence. There was a similar response to the legal system's requests for assessments of future risk related to sentencing, particularly death penalty cases (*Barefoot v. Estelle*,1983). Despite these reservations, the Court continued to require violence risk assessments, including as a basis for involuntarily hospitalizing mentally ill patients (e.g., *O'Connor v. Donaldson* [1975]).

Summarizing the early research in this area, Monahan (1981) concluded that clinicians' predictions of violence behavior were accurate only one-third of the time. The methodology used to predict violence at that time was unstructured clinical judgment—that is, clinicians would use whatever variables they thought might be relevant, and this could vary across assessors. To highlight this point, Pfohl (1979) observed case conferences in a state hospital and described the processes and variables that were used, which were variable across treatment teams. Among the factors cited were: the patient's dreams and fantasies, results of psychological testing, presence of repressed anger, and the subjective feelings of the clinicians. Steadman (1973) found that the ultimate decision about discharge could be predicted solely on the basis of the seriousness of the charges that patients had faced, although psychiatrists offered various rationales and justifications for their decisions. Thus, the state of the field in the 1970s and early 1980s was that there was little empirical evidence to guide clinicians in violence risk assessment, and thus no standardized approaches were employed.

Over the past three decades, a significant literature has emerged to guide clinicians in determining the probability that an individual will engage in violent behavior. The early literature was plagued by lack of standardization of both the definition of violence and how to measure it. Furthermore, there was a lack of data about the base rates of violence within the populations of interest. During the 1980s and 1990s, more refined studies were performed, and this "second-generation" literature (e.g., Otto, 1992) demonstrated that predictive accuracy was better than originally thought, particularly if predictions were short term and when there was more careful attention paid to the dependent variable (i.e., how violent behavior was defined). For example, in a study in an emergency room setting, Lidz, Mulvey, and Gardner (1993) demonstrated that predictive accuracy was significantly better than chance when violence was measured not only by self-report but also by identifying a collateral source who could provide independent information. In their study, 53% of those predicted to be violent engaged in violence during the follow-up period compared to 36% of those predicted not to be violent.

## A. BASE RATES AND ROLE OF MENTAL ILLNESS

Another limiting factor that impacts validity of violence risk prediction relates to the base rate of the phenomenon. Lower base rates limit the positive predictive power (i.e., the percentage of individuals predicted to be violent who commit a violent act) of even very accurate instruments. As much of violence risk assessment by forensic psychologists focuses on mentally disordered individuals, relevant data about the base rates in this population are essential.

A large-scale study, funded by the MacArthur foundation, followed approximately 1,000 patients discharged from acute psychiatric hospitals across three different sites (Monahan et al., 2001), using as an outcome measure a combination of self-report, official records, and a collateral informant. They found a 27.5% rate of violent recidivism over a 1-year period, using a clearly delineated definition of serious violence (*see* Table 3.1).

Another important finding that emerges from the literature rconcerns the issue of the relationship between mental illness and violence. Data obtained from an epidemiological catchment survey found that by self-report, individuals in the community who reported symptoms of a mental illness were significantly more likely to have engaged in at least one violent act over the past year (Swanson et al., 1990). However, individuals who acknowledged substance abuse were found to have the highest rate of violence. A study by Link et al. (1990) found that it was not the presence of

TABLE 3.1 **MacArthur Study (Monahan et al., 2001)**

**Definition of serious violence**
1. Violence in which a weapon was used
2. Any violence which resulted in injury
3. Threats with a weapon in hand
4. Sexual assault

mental illness *per se*, but rather acute psychotic symptoms, that were associated with an increased rate of violence in the community among those with a major mental illness.

The MacArthur study (Monahan et al., 2001) found that discharged patients with a major mental illness were more likely to engage in violence compared to a community sample *only* if they also had a substance abuse problem. Elbogen and Johnson (2009) corroborated this finding using data from a national epidemiological survey. They found higher rates of violence among mentally ill individuals but only significantly so for those with histories of substance abuse or dependence. Studies have also demonstrated the importance of contextual variables, such as neighborhood disadvantage (e.g., Silver et al., 2000), on rates of violence in the community.

B. PSYCHOPATHY

A significant advance in the field of risk assessment has been the operationalization of the term *psychopathy*. This disorder, which is a more in-depth description of a core antisocial personality disorder, was first described by Cleckley (1941). Hare has operationalized this concept, developing the Psychopathy Checklist-Revised (1991) to measure the essential interpersonal (e.g., superficial, arrogant, deceptive, manipulative, and conning), affective (e.g., lack of empathy and remorse, shallow affect), and behavioral (e.g., impulsive, irresponsible, sensation seeking, and engaging in criminal activities) components. Hart et al. (1995) developed a "screening" version (PCL-SV), which was designed specifically for psychiatric populations. Although the PCL tools were not developed as risk-assessment tools *per se* but, rather, as measures of psychopathy, they have been found to be positively correlated with violence recidivism (e.g., Hart & Hare, 1997). In a number of studies across different populations, the obtained score on the PCL instruments has been found to be the most highly correlated factor with future violence. This is the case even when individuals do not score in the psychopathic range using the established cut scores; rather, when looked at dimensionally, higher scores on the instruments are correlated with increased risks of recidivism. For example, in the Violence Risk Appraisal Guide (Harris, Rice, & Quinsey, 1993; Webster, Harris, Rice, Cormier, & Quinsey, 1994), which was developed in a maximum security forensic population, the PCL-R score was correlated 0.34 with future violence (the entire instrument had an $r$ of 0.45). On the Classification of Violence Risk (COVR; Monahan et al., 2000), an instrument developed out of the MacArthur study on a population of acute, civil psychiatric patients, the PCL-SV was also the best predictor. This was the case despite the low rate of psychopathy as measured in this population and using a cut score on the PCL-SV that was well below the range considered to be indicative of psychopathy. It is worth noting that in the MacArthur study, the behavioral factor as measured by the PCL-SV was more predictive of violent recidivism than were the interpersonal and affective factors (e.g., Skeem & Mulvey, 2001).

## C. ACTUARIAL APPROACHES VERSUS STRUCTURED PROFESSIONAL JUDGMENT

The accumulated data from the burgeoning field of violence risk research have resulted in two different approaches to violence risk assessment: the actuarial and the structured professional judgment approach. The actuarial approach involves identifying factors correlated with violent recidivism and assigning weights to each factor, resulting in a formula that categorizes the individual into a risk category. The most widely referenced actuarial instrument for assessing risk of violent recidivism is the Violence Risk Appraisal Guide (VRAG; Harris et al., 1993; Webster et al., 1994). Canadian researchers in Penatanguishene developed the VRAG based on analyses of recidivism data over 10 years in a population of male, maximum security psychiatric and sex offender patients. The original sample was broken down into stanines, and the violent recidivism rate increased linearly across these stanines. Other actuarial instruments have also been developed specifically to predict sex offender recidivism (e.g., Static-99; Hanson & Thornton, 2000), as well as recidivism for a general offender population (e.g., Level of Service/Case Management Inventory; Andrews, Bonta, & Wormith, 2004). Actuarial risk instruments may incorporate variables that are coded based on clinical judgment, but the weighting of the variables is determined by a formula.

By contrast, structured professional judgment (SPJ) instruments do not assign weights to the individual variables. Rather, it is up to the clinician administering and interpreting the instrument to determine how much weight to give various factors and then determine whether the individual is considered low-, moderate-, or high-risk. The most widely used SPJ instrument is the HCR-20, 2nd edition (Webster et al., 1997). The HCR-20 incorporates 20 risk factors based on evidence from the literature of the relationship between these factors and violent recidivism. They are broken down into 10 historical factors (many of which are similar to the variables employed in the VRAG), 5 clinical factors, and 5 risk management factors. The historical factors tend to be static variables, whereas the other factors are dynamic. The clinical factors reflect current clinical status, and the risk management factors reflect anticipated behaviors and contexts. Each variable is given a score of 0 (for not present), 1 (for possibly present, or less severe), and 2 (for definitely present, or more severe). Although many of the research studies establishing the validity of the HCR-20 involved summing the numerical scores, (for a review, *see* Guy, 2008), Douglas, Ogloff, and Hart (2003) found that clinicians' overall ratings of risk (high, moderate, or low) were equal to, and in some cases superior to, the numerical scores in predicting violent recidivism, supporting the validity of using professional judgment to weigh variables. The SPJ approach has also been used to specifically assess risk for domestic violence (Spousal Abuse Risk Assessment Guide; Kropp, Hart, Webster, & Eaves, 1999), for violence in adolescents (Structured Assessment of Violence Risk in Youth; Borum, Bartel, & Forth, 2006), and sexual re-offending (Sexual Violence Risk [SVR]-20, Boer, Hart, Kropp, & Webster, 1997).

The use of actuarial versus SPJ approaches to risk assessment has been a source of significant controversy in the literature. Proponents of the actuarial approach argue that they are more accurate in the aggregate (e.g., Quinsey, Harris, Rice, & Cormier, 2006). Criticisms of this approach, however, have focused both on concerns that placing an individual into a numerically specific risk category overstates the probability of risk for that person (e.g., Hart, Michie, & Cooke, 2007; but *see* Mossman & Sellke, 2007, for a rebuttal) and that there are specific limitations of the available instruments. The criticism of most of the existing actuarial instruments (such as the VRAG) is that they rely exclusively on static factors and do not incorporate dynamic factors, such as changes in mental state, behavioral changes, response to treatment, and changes in context(e.g., Litwack, 2001). However, there is no inherent reason why actuarial instruments cannot be developed to incorporate dynamic variables as well (Douglas & Skeem, 2005).

## D. IMPLICATIONS FOR PRACTICE

The early literature in this field focused on "prediction of violence." However, as the field advanced, a more sophisticated approach evolved that focused on "violence risk assessment and management." This was not simply a rephrasing of the task but, rather, a reformulation based on the growing literature, as well as a reconceptualization of the purposes of risk assessment. "Dangerousness" suggests a categorical approach, whereas "violence risk" more accurately captures a dimensional perspective, in which individuals can be placed on a continuum of degree of risk. Furthermore, "risk assessment" allows for more specific identification of the severity of risk as well as identification of possible targets. "Prediction" implies a decision made at one point in time, whereas "assessment and management" shifts thinking to an ongoing process of both re-evaluating risk at different points in time as well as developing management strategies to reduce the risk.

Clinicians who engage in assessments of violence risk need to be aware of the base rates of violence within the populations they are assessing, the benefits and deficiencies of the instruments that are available, as well as the applicability of those instruments to their particular population. For example, the VRAG was initially validated on all male forensic patients in Canada; it did not include women, acute patients, or the racial and ethnic populations typically seen in U.S. forensic and correctional facilities. By contrast, the COVR was initially validated on a more racially diverse population in the United States, included both men and women, but was restricted to acute civilly committed populations. Forensic psychologists have to remain current with the literature in this area, as these instruments may become cross-validated with other populations. Furthermore, forensic psychologists need to be aware of the benefits and disadvantages of using actuarial or structured professional judgment instruments in choosing how to respond to a specific psycholegal issue and also how to apply an anamnestic approach, which focuses on factors that have been associated with previous violence for the individual being evaluated (e.g., Dvoskin & Heilbrun, 2001; Heilbrun, 2009).

## II. Eyewitness Identification

Attempts to apply psychological knowledge about memory to the legal system began as far back as 1908, with the publication of Hugo Munsterberg's book, *On the Witness Stand*. Although legal scholars did not welcome this early attempt, more recent developments in cognitive psychology have had an impact on the legal understanding of the processes influencing validity of eyewitness testimony. In addition to applying existing knowledge about memory processes to the legal system (e.g., retention intervals, effect of stress on memory, cross-racial identification), there is a body of literature that focuses specifically on cognitive processes that are specific to the legal context.

Research on memory decay dates back to the work of Ebbinghaus in the nineteenth century. Ebbinghaus (1885; translated into English in 1913) demonstrated that memory decays rapidly at first and then more gradually. The application to the law is that this highlights the need for police to obtain information from witnesses as soon as possible after the incident. The longer the delay in obtaining the initial testimony, the greater the likelihood that the recall will not be as accurate. Another robust funding is that high degrees of stress interfere with memory. However, the relationship between stress and accuracy of recall is not linear but, rather, follows the Yerkes-Dodson law (Yerkes & Dodson, 1908) that cognitive performance is optimal at moderate degrees of stress. The relevance to the law is that many crimes—particularly violent offenses—represent high-stress situations and may interfere with accurate recall. In addition, a body of research (e.g., Anthony, Cooper, & Mullen, 1992) has demonstrated that people are more accurate when identifying individuals of their same race than they are when identifying individuals of another race.

More recent research, which is specifically relevant to the legal system, involves studies of "weapon focus" (e.g., Steblay, 1992). These studies have demonstrated that a witness' accuracy of recognition of the face of the perpetrator is lower when a weapon (such as a gun) is involved. The rationale for this phenomenon is that as the witness focuses on the gun, he or she focuses less on the face of the perpetrator and thus the accuracy of the recognition is decreased.

## A. CONCORDANCE AND DISCORDANCE BETWEEN LEGAL ASSUMPTIONS AND PSYCHOLOGICAL DATA

The issue of reliability of eyewitness identification has been dealt with by the Supreme Court, most notably in the cases of *Neil v. Biggers* (1972) and *Manson v. Braithwite* (1977). The court identified five factors to weigh in assessing the validity of eyewitness testimony:

1. the opportunity of the eyewitness to view the offender at the time of the crime;
2. the witness's degree of attention;
3. the accuracy of the witness's prior description of the offender;
4. the level of certainty displayed by the witness at the identification procedure;
5. the length of time between the crime and the identification procedure.

Criteria 1, 2, and 5 are consistent with the scientific literature (e.g., as discussed above, the longer the delay between the incident and the identification, the less accurate the identification). However, criteria 3 and 4, although seemingly "common sense," are contradicted by the scientific literature. For example, studies have not corroborated that accuracy of description is correlated with accuracy of identification (e.g., Piggot & Brigham, 1985; Wells, 1985). However, of more significant concern is the criterion related to the level of confidence displayed by the eyewitness. Meta-analytic analyses have found a modest to moderate correlation between level of certainty and accuracy (e.g., Bothwell, Deffenbacher, & Brigham, 1987; Sporer, Penrod, Read, & Cutler ,1995). This nevertheless means that a significant number of confident witnesses will be mistaken. Furthermore, faulty or biased lineups and photospreads may increase the witness's sense of certainty in his or her identification (e.g., Wells et al., 1998), and this confidence may be irreversible. Jurors are likely to be misled by this level of confidence, as they cannot distinguish between accurate and inaccurate identifications when the witnesses express a high degree of certainty (e.g., Wells, Lindsay, & Ferguson,1979).

## B. GUIDELINES FOR LINEUPS AND PHOTOSPREADS

In response to evidence that the most common cause of wrongful convictions (as determined by DNA evidence) was mistaken eyewitness identification, the American Law-Psychology Society appointed a task force to review the relevant literature and make recommendations for improving the process. A group of well-respected researchers (Wells et al., 1998) published their conclusions, which were based on experimental data supporting "relative judgment theory" as well as on procedures that affect suggestibility. Relative judgment theory states that individuals make a relative, rather than absolute, judgment when making an identification. Thus, they will choose the individual in the lineup who looks most similar to the actual target, even if this is not the actual target (and will do so without being aware of this process). This has been corroborated by experimental studies in which the actual culprit was not in the lineup or photospread. Under those circumstances, there was a higher rate of false identification than there was when the actual subject was present (i.e., rather than state that they did not see the culprit, a significant number of subjects chose the person most similar). In other studies, a statement to the subjects prior to the lineup that the culprit may or may not be in the lineup resulted in fewer misidentifications. There are also data suggesting that sequential lineups (i.e., showing one person at a time, rather than simultaneously having the subject look at the whole lineup) resulted in fewer misidentifications. This finding is also consistent with relative judgment theory, because the subject has to give a yes/no answer and does not know how many more people he or she will see.

The concerns about suggestibility are based on an extensive body of research literature that has demonstrated that once an individual's memory has been altered (including implanted memories for historical events or for eyewitness identification (e.g., Loftus, 1979), the individual may become convinced of the accuracy of his or her memory, and thus the degree of certainty is enhanced. The witness may be subject to suggestiveness by the nature of the lineup or photospread array (e.g., if the suspect stands out in some way, even subtle from the other distractors) or from "demand characteristics" of the situation. This latter term is one that is often used in assessing the validity of experimental procedures. In an experimental setting, it is important for the experimenter, for example, to be unaware of whether the subject is part of the experimental group or the control group, so as not to subtly influence the results. Similarly, a police officer who is aware of which of the people in the lineup or photospread is the suspect may tip off the witness by the use of body language, asking certain questions, or other nonverbal clues (again, not necessarily deliberately).

Based on their review, Wells et al. made four recommendations to improve lineup and photospread procedures:

1. The person who conducts the lineup or photospread should not be aware of which member of the lineup or photospread is the suspect.

2. Eyewitnesses should be told explicitly that the person in question might not be in the lineup or photospread and, therefore, should not feel that they must make an identification. They should also be told that the person administering the lineup does not know which person is the suspect in the case.

3. The suspect should not stand out in the lineup or photospread as being different from the distractors based on the eyewitness's previous description of the culprit or based on other factors that would draw extra attention to the suspect.

4. A clear statement should be taken from the eyewitness at the time of the identification and prior to any feedback as to his or her confidence that the identified person is the actual culprit.

## C. IMPLICATIONS FOR PRACTICE

These recommendations have been adapted by many police departments as well as the U.S. Department of Justice (Technical Working Group for

Eyewitness Evidence, 1999). This represents a successful attempt to apply scientific psychological knowledge to the legal system in a pre-emptive manner (i.e., if the recommendations are followed, then the likelihood of misidentification is reduced). It also provides a basis for psychologists to provide expert testimony as to whether the procedures employed in any individual case met the standards. Such testimony is more likely to be provided by academic and research psychologists, although forensic psychologists who serve as trial consultants may be able to provide guidance to attorneys.

## III. Confessions

One of the most compelling pieces of evidence in a criminal trial is a confession provided by the defendant. However, data from studies of falsely convicted defendants who were subsequently exonerated by DNA evidence suggest that 15% to 20% of those cases involved false confessions (Garrett, 2008; Scheck, Neufeld, & Dwyer, 2000). There is now a significant body of psychological research (summarized in Kassin et al., 2010) studying conditions that can lead to false confessions. These include characteristics of the suspect (such as age and developmental disability) as well as situational factors (characteristics of the interrogation).

Two broad issues are included in the question of confessions as evidence. First, a confession may not be admitted as evidence unless it was obtained after the suspect made a "voluntary, knowing, and intelligent" waiver of rights to silence and legal counsel. Second, even if waiver of rights was valid, courts and juries may consider whether the statement that was made was false.

### A. ADOLESCENTS

The research literature has consistently found that younger adolescents, and those with lower IQ scores, have more difficulties than adults in understanding at least one of the elements of the *Miranda* warning. Although, on average, adolescents who are age 15 years or older with IQ scores in the at least near-average range performed as well as adults, those younger than age 14 years, as well as older adolescents with IQ scores below 85, demonstrate the most significant impairment (e.g., Goldstein et al., 2003; Grisso, 1980, 1981; Redlich, Silverman, & Steiner, 2003; Viljoen, Klaver, & Roesch, 2005). In addition, although a number of jurisdictions require the presence of a parent when an adolescent under age 16 years is interviewed by police, studies have found that this does not typically result in the youth invoking his or her *Miranda* rights (e.g., Grisso & Ring, 1979; Grisso, 1981).

Other studies support the presumption that youth are at greater risk than adults of offering a false confession in their acquiescence to police officers' requests (Feld, 2006; Singh & Gudjonsson, 1992).

## B. DEVELOPMENTAL DISABILITY

Developmentally disabled defendants (e.g., those diagnosed with mental retardation) represent another group that has been found to have difficulties understanding their *Miranda* rights. A consistent finding is that individuals with IQ scores below 70 have difficulty understanding, paraphrasing, and appreciating the *Miranda* warning (e.g., Fulero & Everington, 2004; O'Connell, Garmoe, & Goldstein, 2005). Even more relevant to the issue of false confessions, Everington and Fulero (1999) administered the Gudjonsson Suggestibility Scale (Gudjonsson, 1984), a measure specifically designed to assess suggestibility to interrogation, and found that individuals with mental retardation demonstrated increased likelihood of agreeing with leading questions and were also more likely to change their answers in response to even mild negative feedback.

## C. SITUATIONAL FACTORS

Kassin et al. (2010) also identified situational factors (i.e., aspects of interrogation techniques) that can lead to a risk of false confession. Although there are no available data on the frequency of false confessions caused by these situational factors, data obtained from reviewing actual cases of false confessions, as well as extrapolation from laboratory experiments, suggest that these techniques may increase the risk of a false confession. The most commonly identified factors were: physical custody and isolation, presentation of false evidence, and minimization/implied promises.

Drizin and Leo (2004) reviewed 125 cases of false confessions and reported that the average length of interrogation in these cases was 16 hours. This is consistently longer than the lengths typically reported (e.g., Kassin et al., 2007). Other factors that can enhance the stressful impact of lengthy interrogations are isolation (i.e., the suspect is isolated from family, friends, or other sources of support) and sleep deprivation.

Two other techniques that have been identified in actual false confession cases are presentation of false evidence and minimization. The former involved telling the suspect that there is strong evidence to support his guilt (e.g., DNA, fingerprints, witnesses) when this evidence does not exist. The latter involves the police either minimizing or seeming to excuse the suspect's behavior (e.g., suggesting that he was just going along with someone else or was provoked into acting) or implying that a confession will lead to a lesser sentence. Although there are no data on how often these techniques result in a false (as opposed to true) confession, there are laboratory studies that confirm these phenomena. Russano, Meissner, Kassin, and Narchet (2005) paired subjects with a confederate in a paradigm in which they were instructed to solve problems alone. In some instances, the confederate asked for help from the subject. The subjects were then told that there was evidence of cheating and were interrogated. When the experimenters either minimized ("I'm sure you didn't realize what a big deal it was") or promised leniency (no penalty), the rate of confessions for those who had "cheated" was 81% (true confession), and the rate of confessions among those who had not was 18% (false confessions). When no such techniques were used, the rates were 46% true confessions and 6% false confessions.

## D. TAXONOMY OF FALSE CONFESSIONS

Kassin and Wrightsman (1985) proposed a taxonomy of false confessions, which accounts for both personality and situation variables.

1. Voluntary false confessions. These are the confessions that are most difficult to understand *a priori*, because they do not involve any pressure from police. Rather, individuals will come forward and confess to a crime that they did not commit. In some cases, this may be a deliberate attempt to protect the real perpetrator. However, this phenomenon also occurs when there is no rational motive. This can occur in high-profile cases. For example, in 2006, John Mark Karr came forward to confess to the long-unsolved murder of a young girl, JonBenet Ramsay. It was soon determined that he could not have committed the crime. In such cases, there may be a desire for publicity, an attempt to reduce guilt from previous (real or imagined) crimes, or a psychotic disorder in which the individual genuinely believes that he or she is guilty.

2. Coerced-compliant false confessions. These confessions are the easiest to comprehend. They involve an individual who is convinced of his innocence, nevertheless confessing under the stress of the interrogation, to end the aversive circumstances. Thus, individuals who are interrogated in isolation for many hours may confess to end the interrogation, to obtain a promised benefit (such as being released earlier), or to avoid a worse punishment (such as being told that they face the death penalty unless they confess).

3. Coerced-internalized false confessions. These confessions are also given in response to coercive tactics. However, the individual has come to

believe that he really committed the crime. Gudjonsson and MacKeith (1982) described such individuals as being passive, self-doubting, and distrustful of their own memory. These individuals may accept their guilt without a full memory of the incident or may confabulate to fill in the blanks.

**Implications for Practice**  As with the recommendations for eyewitness identification procedures, the research on false confessions may be used to impact police procedures. In addition, the research can inform *post hoc* evaluations to determine whether factors were present that may have impacted on both the individual's competency to understand the *Miranda* warning and the likelihood of a false confession. Psychologists involved in this area need to consider both dispositional variables related to the suspect as well as situational variables of the interrogation techniques.

## IV. Child Sexual Abuse

Evaluations of child sexual abuse in the legal system occur across a variety of contexts, including criminal cases, child custody disputes, and termination of parental rights cases. Much of the complexity involves assessing the veracity of allegations made by young children, whose verbal skills may be limited and whose ability to distinguish reality from fantasy may be less than that of an adult. Furthermore, allegations may be made in the context of heated custody disputes, raising the possibility of false allegations. There has been a significant body of research on techniques for interviewing children when allegations of sexual abuse arise.

A number of legal cases have addressed issues related to reliability of children's reports of sexual abuse. A prominent example involved Kelly Michaels, a young woman who was accused of sexually molesting a large number of children in a daycare center in New Jersey and who was initially sentenced to 47 years in prison. Her case was overturned, based on evidence of suggestive questioning (*State v. Michaels*, 1993). As part of the appeal process, an amicus brief was presented to the court by the Committee of Concerned Social Scientists (Bruck & Ceci, 1995). The amicus brief discussed in detail numerous research studies that addressed:

1. the effects of interviewer bias on children's reports;
2. the effects of repeated questions;
3. the effects of repeating misinformation across interviews;
4. the emotional tone of the interview;

5. the effects of peer pressure on children's reports;

6. the effects of being interviewed by adults with high status;

7. the effects of stereotype inducement (i.e., conveying that an individual is "bad" influences children's false reports);

8. the use of anatomically detailed dolls;

9. source attribution errors (that is, children may come to believe that they experienced something that was just described to them by others).

The research cited was quite extensive, based on numerous studies of questioning of children. One of the most robust findings was that younger children—particularly those younger than age 5—were especially suscep-tible to suggestibility (e.g., Goodman, Quas et al. 1997). The data regard-ing anatomically detailed dolls are particularly interesting. The rationale for their use is that they allow children to explain what happened to them, without requiring elaborate verbal reports. Saywitz, Goodman, Nicholas, & Moan (1991) studied girls ages 5 and 7 years who had undergone a medi-cal examination, some of whom were given a genital examination. When asked, in an open-ended fashion, "What did the doctor do?", only 22% of the girls who had been examined genitally disclosed this information. However, when the interviewer showed an anatomic doll, pointing to the vagina, and asked, "Did the doctor touch you there?" 69% of the girls disclosed, and only 3% of those who were not subject to a genital examination falsely admitted to being genitally touched. However, a study by Bruck et al. (1995) using 3-year-olds found that the use of the dolls dramatically increased false claims of genital insertion (60%), as well as sexualized play with the dolls, in both a group of girls who had a genital examination and a control group. Thus, particularly with younger children, the use of such dolls can lead to false reports and cannot be relied upon to provide valid information.

Kuenhle (2003) has summarized the current state of knowledge regard-ing the elements of a proper interview of a child when allegations of sexual abuse have occurred. These include:

1. development of rapport with the child;

2. assessment of the child's ability to answer questions and provide details (developmental level);

3. identification of ground rules for the interview (particularly that the child not feel pressured to acquiesce);

4. practice interview on issues unrelated to the sexual abuse;

5. addressing the sexual abuse topic beginning with open-ended questions.

## V. Recovered Memories

One of the most controversial issues related to memory involves the concept of recovered or repressed memory. A number of researchers and clinicians have proposed a model in which highly traumatic memories (such as repetitive sexual abuse as a child) may be repressed and then re-emerge years later (e.g., van der Kolk, 1994; Freyd, 1996; Brown, Scheflin, & Hammond, 1998). Others have questioned the validity of this phenomenon, claiming that memories of traumatic events are not subject to different processes than memories of nontraumatic events (e.g., Ofshe & Watters, 1994; Loftus & Ketcham,1994).

Williams (1994) interviewed 129 women who had documented histories of sexual abuse as children. She found that 38% did not recall the abuse that had been reported 17 years earlier. Although these data demonstrated that some children who have been abused may not retain a memory of the abuse, it did not address the issue of whether the memories could be recovered. More relevant, in terms of legal implications, is that there are no data to document the accuracy of recovered memories. Both the American Psychological Association (APA Working Group on Investigation of Memories of Childhood Abuse, 1998) and the American Psychiatric Association (2000) issued position papers on this issue. Although the position papers acknowledged the controversy and did not offer any conclusions about the genuineness of the phenomenon of recovered memories, they both included caveats regarding the use of such memories to establish "truth." The APA acknowledged "gaps in our knowledge about the processes that lead to accurate and inaccurate recollections of childhood abuse". Similarly, the American Psychiatric Association stated, "Psychiatrists should refrain from making public statements about the historical accuracy of uncorroborated individual patient reports of new memories based on observations made in psychotherapy." This controversy highlights one of the most important distinctions between clinical and forensic practice. In therapeutic settings, it may not be important to ascertain the actual veracity of a memory. However, when applied in a legal setting, with higher standards of proof and very significant consequences, it is essential to admit only evidence that can be corroborated.

## VI. Developmental Capacities and Juvenile Justice

Changes in juvenile laws in the 1990s created a more punitive juvenile justice system, as well as greater use of the mechanism of transfer to criminal court where youth could be tried as adults. Such responses to juveniles' crimes suggested that they should be held fully culpable for their offenses (as though they were adults). Forensic examiners, therefore, have been asked with increasing frequency to address whether youths are competent to stand trial, have the capacity to make plea agreements, or have the capacity to decide about and control their behaviors that often lead to their arrest.

For these purposes, forensic examiners now have a wealth of scientific information with which to generally describe adolescents' decisional capacities in comparison to those of adults. Developmental brain research has provided substantial evidence of continued growth of areas of the brain during adolescence pertaining to emotional regulation and executive functions (Scott & Steinberg, 2008). Other studies have shown how youths' less-mature capacities influence their everyday decision making (Steinberg et al., 2009) as well as their capacities to participate in their trials (e.g., Grisso et al., 2003).

It is important to recognize that these scientific findings related to cognitive development have not led to measures or tools that forensic clinicians can use to assess their youth's "culpability." The scientific information that is available serves as background for explaining youths' decision-making capacities in general and for offering base rates and norms for certain cognitive functions. These can be helpful to the forensic clinician in evaluating a youth, but they do not necessarily "establish" the validity of forensic examiners' opinions in individual cases.

# PART II

# Functional Competencies

# FOUR

# Assessment Strategies

Forensic mental health assessment (FMHA) borrows a great deal from clinical psychological assessment with regard to strategies and assessment methods. Yet FMHA also employs assessment strategies, practices, and tools that would rarely, if ever, be encountered in the practice of general clinical psychology or any of the other psychological specialties. This chapter focuses on those aspects of forensic assessment that are different from assessments in other specialties. We first discuss three general concepts that influence all parts of the forensic assessment process. Then we will review how those are applied to three parts of the assessment process: *(1)* method selection, *(2)* the data collection process, and *(3)* communication of results.

To avoid repetitious citation throughout this chapter, we acknowledge that almost all of the following discussion of guidelines for forensic assessment strategies derive from three basic sources: Melton, Petrila, Poythress, and Slobogin's *Psychological Evaluations for the Courts* (2007), Heilbrun's *Principles of Forensic Mental Health Assessment* (2001); and Heilbrun, Grisso, and Goldstein's *Foundations of Forensic Mental Health Assessment* (2009). Each of these references offers discussions, with more detailed citations, for most of the guidelines that are offered here, and the three sources are in agreement about the best practices that this chapter describes. Additional citations are provided only for points that depart from the above generalization.

## I. General Concepts that Shape the Forensic Assessment Process

Forensic psychological assessments are guided at each step of the process by a consideration for the law, legal system, and legal process for which the assessment is intended. Whereas a clinical evaluation is designed to collect data to inform *clinical decisions in a clinical setting,* forensic evaluations are carefully crafted to collect data to inform *judicial decisions in a court of law.* Almost no clinical evaluation would satisfy the latter purpose, and almost no forensic evaluation would satisfy the former purpose. There are several general concepts, arising out of the legal purpose for forensic evaluations, that guide the forensic assessment process.

## A. INTERPRETING THE ASSESSMENT QUESTION

The first step in every psychological assessment is to assure that one has clearly identified the referral question. Everything flows from this. Selections of methods, procedures during data collection, and interpretation of results all depend on a clear identification of the question one is asked to address.

For forensic assessments, the assessment question always derives from *the law's definition of a particular human condition.* By *human condition,* we mean such legal concepts as "competent to stand trial," "not criminally responsible," "unfit parent," and "unamenable to treatment in the juvenile justice system." These are not clinical conditions. They have no meaning in the traditional clinical psychological treatment of patients. They are not the equivalent of any mental disorder; for example, one can be hospitalized for an acute psychotic episode, yet at the same time one might or might not be "competent," "responsible," "fit," or "amenable" (referring to the above legal human conditions). Therefore, a request for an evaluation to address a legal concept such as "competence to stand trial" must be translated if it is to be addressed by psychology. One must determine what psychological characteristics of an examinee will be relevant for addressing the legal question. Often the relevant factors will have less to do with clinical diagnostic conditions than with questions of specific functional abilities (e.g., to make decisions).

How is this translation performed? Obviously it does not have to be performed anew each time one does a forensic evaluation. For most legal conditions for which forensic evaluations are requested, there is a substantial body of conceptual and empirical literature in forensic psychology that has already done the interpretation. That literature has identified the biological, psychological, and social factors that will be relevant for informing the court about that particular legal human condition.

This is helpful for routine forensic evaluations, but sometimes more is required. For example, occasionally forensic examiners are presented with unusual requests regarding questions for which there is no body of literature to do the legal translation for them (e.g., competence to execute a will). At other times, the law's notion of what is relevant for a particular legal human condition might be contradicted by empirical information in psychology. For example, courts have often presumed that suspects with more previous arrests and exposures to *Miranda* warnings have greater "capacity to waive rights knowingly, intelligently, and voluntarily" (the legal condition in question). Yet many research studies have found that there is no relation between number of arrests or times having heard *Miranda* warnings and actual *Miranda* comprehension. Forensic examiners try to translate the law in ways that are consistent with legal precedent, but sometimes they must do more. They must also know enough about both the law and relevant law-psychology research to recognize when to contradict the law's presumptions or how to assist the law in adjusting its perspective so that it weighs empirically meaningful factors when reaching its legal decision.

The field of forensic psychology has also developed conceptual models that help forensic examiners to translate legal definitions of human conditions into characteristics that can be evaluated. Examples include Grisso's (2003) model for legal competencies (offering five components for analysis of all legal competencies) and the three-part model of Salekin (2001) for conceptualizing juveniles' characteristics relevant for transfer to adult court. In summary, forensic assessment is guided by the specific legal question facing the legal decision maker. For every type of forensic assessment question, there is a body of law controlling the legal decision to be made. The examiner performing the assessment knows the relevant law within the jurisdiction in which the assessment is being performed as well as the legal question. The examiner translates the law into psychological concepts that will determine the types of data that will be relevant for that legal question and then develops an assessment procedure designed specifically to obtain those data.

## B. LEGAL REQUIREMENTS FOR QUALITY

A second concept that influences forensic assessment strategies is the law's need for documentation and accuracy. Psychologists in all assessment situations, of course, strive for accuracy and recognize the importance of documenting their work. But assessments for legal processes must meet somewhat different standards than are found in general clinical practice.

The law's interest in fairness when deciding people's fates places a heavy burden on those who provide evidence for judicial consideration. Therefore, the law has devised various ways to "test" the relevance and reliability of evidence by expert witnesses. For example, before an expert's testimony can be provided, often the court considers whether the basis for the opinion the expert will give (e.g., the methods used to collect data, or the theory that the examiner will use to interpret the data) has been generally accepted in the examiner's field, has been reviewed and critiqued by other professionals, and has demonstrated reliability and validity (e.g., *Daubert v. Merrell Dow Pharmaceuticals*, 1995). The burden is highest in cases in which the expert evidence may influence judicial or jury decisions of great import, such as the potential long-term incarceration or execution of a defendant or the permanent removal of children from their parents.

Recognizing a high standard for integrity of one's methods influences forensic assessment strategy throughout the evaluation process. Selection of methods, the data collection process, and communicating results all must be done with an awareness that one will eventually be called on, quite publicly and often in considerable detail, to account for the integrity and quality of one's methods.

Similarly, high standards for documentation influence forensic assessment strategy. The law requires accurate and complete recording of all evidence in legal proceedings, so that persons who are before courts may challenge evidence and appeal the court's decisions. Forensic assessments, therefore, must involve meticulous notation of all procedures as they occur, as well as eventual summary documentation. This includes recording one's errors, as well as being able to offer not only the reasoning for one's opinion but also the reasoning for rejecting all other possible opinions.

Anticipating these demands for reliability of one's methods and careful documentation and explanation of one's work becomes a central part of the strategy for forensic assessments. Thoughtful consideration is demanded at every step in the assessment process, recognizing that eventually one will be held publicly accountable for every choice one is making at each step.

## C. ROLE OF EXAMINER IN LEGAL CONTEXTS

Forensic assessment strategy is strongly influenced by the examiner's role as an expert in the legal process. Forensic psychologists are contracted as experts in legal cases in several ways. Sometimes their evaluations are requested by the court, so that the examiner has no direct relationship to either party in the case. Often, however, forensic examiners are contracted by one of the parties in the case, in anticipation that the assessment will provide information that might support the client's arguments.

These relationships have implications for how a forensic examiner develops an assessment strategy. It is a common error to presume that forensic examiners construct their assessment procedure to find information that will support the party that has hired them. That is, of course, part of the role. But if that is all that forensic examiners do, then they will fail to serve their clients or the legal system effectively. They must also find all of the information that might *not* support the party's arguments. If they only seek information supporting the client, then they leave both themselves and their clients vulnerable to the appearance of bias, thus damaging their credibility and the interests of their client. More importantly, they provide incomplete evidence to the court, thus risking error and injustice.

In fact, some commentators have chosen to conceptualize the forensic examiner's primary allegiance as being to the legal process and its decision makers, even when one has been contracted by a party in the case. This, however, can be misleading. In most areas of law, when one is contracted by a defendant or respondent in a legal proceeding, one's evidence typically is protected by client privilege and cannot be revealed to the court except by prior agreement by that party. In this sense, one's allegiance is to the client. If one has a primary allegiance to the court, it pertains to one's efforts to get the best data possible to test all reasonable hypotheses and thus to contribute in a helpful way to the court's fact-finding task, not merely to offer evidence supporting the client's position.

These obligations can best be summarized as producing an allegiance to *objectivity*. Legal cases are driven by the parties' desires to construct the strongest arguments for their own position. Yet within this context, the forensic examiner conducts the assessment as a search for data and interpretations that are guided by no presumptions about the right outcome. As described later, this has a substantial impact on how one constructs a forensic assessment. It influences the methods and tools one selects, the process of the assessment, and the way one communicates one's results.

## D. THE RELEVANCE OF FORENSIC EXAMINEE POPULATIONS

Assessment strategy in forensic evaluations is influenced by special characteristics and circumstances of "forensic populations"—that is, individuals who come before the courts as defendants, appellants, claimants, or respondents. Those populations, of course, are diverse and are not a "type," even within a narrow area of forensic practice. But as a group they are different in composition and circumstance from clinical populations in general.

For example, criminal and delinquency populations for whom forensic evaluations are requested typically are disproportionate compared to the general population in terms of racial/ethnic composition. They are also different from general populations regarding the proportion with lower socioeconomic backgrounds, cognitive deficits, trauma histories, and certain types of psychopathology. Different types of disproportionality are found in different areas of forensic assessment—for example, among elderly persons for whom the need for guardianship is in question or among parents facing legal decisions about termination of parental rights.

This influences the design of forensic assessments in several ways—especially when selecting assessment tools. Many well-known and validated clinical instruments have not been validated with these special populations. This is especially true for minority clients, for whom a large number of clinical psychological tests do not have evidence regarding possible differences in validity based on differences in race or ethnicity. This becomes quite important when, as in certain criminal forensic settings, the substantial majority of individuals one evaluates are often members of racial/ethnic minorities that constituted only a small fraction of the subjects in the test's norm samples.

Forensic assessment strategy is also influenced by special concerns about response bias by examinees. The context in which many forensic assessments are performed creates an incentive for examinees to report or behave in ways that exaggerate or mask their deficits. This places a significant burden on the examiner to be able to inform the court regarding the degree of confidence one can place on data provided by the examinee. As described later, forensic examiners must design their assessments in ways that will identify "malingering" or "dissimulation" by examinees or at least will indicate whether special caution is necessary in interpreting the results because of potential response bias.

Let us now examine some more specific ways in which these four concepts influence the forensic examiners' choices when developing a forensic assessment. Our focus in the next three sections is primarily on points of strategy that are different from those found in general clinical evaluation or are simply more frequently encountered in performing forensic assessments.

## II. Selection of Methods

Strategy for a forensic assessment requires an initial selection of methods and tools with which data will be collected. These will vary widely from one forensic question to another, but there are certain ways in which the concepts described earlier influence this selection process across forensic areas. The following description of considerations in selection of methods derives substantially from Heilbrun's (2001) analysis of foundational principles of forensic mental health assessment.

## A. MULTIPLE SOURCES

Forensic assessments typically employ interviews with the examinee, the use of one or more standardized tools to obtain information about the examinee, records from other sources, and inquiry involving what are often called *collateral informants*—that is, others who have had direct contact with the examinee. The practice of obtaining information from this variety of sources is fairly standard across areas of forensic assessment.

There are several reasons that such a wide variety of sources is considered best practice in forensic assessment. All methods have inherent error, and the use of multiple methods to cross-check information reduces the potential for one's conclusions to be based on error associated with any single information source. In addition, forensic examiners often are as interested in inconsistencies between sources as they are in consistencies. Two inconsistent accounts do not necessarily mean that one is wrong and the other right. Both may be valid information but from a different perspective, as when two observers notice different things because they are attending to different aspects of an event. At other times, observations of a person in different social settings may offer seemingly discrepant conclusions about the person's behavioral tendencies; yet both may be true, suggesting that one cannot generalize about the person's tendencies across different social circumstances.

Forensic examiners often must rely less in forensic contexts than in general clinical work on an examinee's self-report of important information. They will more often require corroboration from other sources of data before trusting the examinee's self-report. Examinees, of course, often have information about themselves that cannot be obtained by any other means (e.g., personal feelings and thoughts, or observations of events that involved no other observers). But examinees in legal circumstances often are motivated by the potential outcomes of their cases, causing them to provide biased reports of their mental conditions, motivations, or events in their past. For many types of forensic assessments, one simply cannot base opinion on critical pieces of information for which the examinee's self-report is the only source. The reliability or meaning of the examinee's information must be weighed in light of information obtained from other sources as well. Thus, in a criminal responsibility evaluation, the examinee's report that she was influenced at the time of the offense by "messages I was getting from God" might receive little weight in the examiner's final opinion if it was not consistent with other sources (e.g., others' observations of the examinee at the time of the offense, or a history of similar pathology across time).

For these reasons, one encounters a substantial reliance on forensic assessments of information obtained from past records and from interviews with collateral informants. The process of obtaining data from these sources is discussed later in Strategy in Data Collection Process.

## B. ASSURING RELEVANCE

The selection of assessment methods for forensic evaluations is influenced by the requirement that the information obtained must be relevant for the legal case. The requirement for relevance guides the clinician to select methods that will produce a kind of data that has a clear connection to the forensic question and to avoid methods that will provide data that are not relevant for the forensic question. This has several implications for method selection. Let us consider a case in which the question of competence to stand trial has been raised while applying Grisso's (2003) model for analyzing the demands of a forensic assessment for a legal competency.

The relevance requirement would guide the examiner to select tools that directly assess the *functional abilities* about which the court is concerned regarding a person's capacities to participate in a trial. Given that such a tool was available, the relevance requirement would also guide the examiner to avoid using tools that assess functional abilities in less-relevant contexts—for example, tools that assess functional capacity to manage one's safety and property. If there are significant deficits in the person's functional competency abilities, then the examiner is guided to select other methods to address the *causal* element of legal competencies. That might involve tools that will assess serious mental illness or intellectual deficits as potential causes of the functional deficits. Selection of other methods might be guided by the *interactive* element of legal competencies, and still others by the remedial element.

In other words, tools and methods—including interview questions—must be guided by a translation of the legal question, and everything in the evaluation must have a relevant purpose. Moreover, one should avoid questions, tools, and methods that are not relevant for the forensic question. For example, a forensic examiner in a competence-to-stand-trial case might suspect that the person's serious functional deficits for participating in their trial might also have caused them to make an invalid waiver of their rights when they were questioned by the police at the time of their arrest. Yet the examiner would not ask questions or use specialized tools to explore that possibility, because it is not legally relevant—that is, the question was not raised by any party, so the examiner's self-proclaimed interest in the matter would be injecting legally irrelevant information into the legal process.

## C. ASSURING RELIABILITY

The law's definition of the term *reliability* refers generally to what psychologists call the reliability and validity of their methods. As noted earlier in this chapter, the legal uses of forensic assessment data and examiner's opinions places an especially heavy burden on the examiner to select the most reliable data collection methods available for the specific forensic task one is undertaking. There is no place in forensic assessment for psychological tests and methods that have not been validated for the purpose, and with the population, that is relevant for the forensic case. Rorschach results that are only "clinically interpreted," a measure of psychopathy used with an adolescent when the tool has been validated only with adults, a test that is scored by an algorithm that cannot be explained to the court because it has not been made public even to examiners—these are all circumstances that are less than "best practices" in forensic assessment. This is because all such methods are highly vulnerable to being discredited on cross-examination, based on legal tests (e.g., *Daubert v. Merrell Dow Pharmaceuticals*, 1995) regarding the necessary reliability of methods on which expert testimony is admissible. To use them is to jeopardize the interests of one's client and to offer information to the court that may be misleading because it derives from a method of questionable value.

There are several basic elements in the process of scrutinizing the reliability of one's methods when developing forensic assessment strategy. The most basic element is *standardization*. In general, forensic assessment strategy favors the use of methods that obtain data in the same manner across examinees and across examiners. Even if their ultimate validity is not known, a set of standardized interview questions that inquire into a forensically relevant mental condition minimizes error associated with examiners' potential selective bias across cases. Selection and use of standardized methods, therefore, is a part of best practices in forensic assessment.

*Empirical reliability*, in the traditional psychometric sense, is a second basic element. In general, methods that anchor examiners' ratings or scores in clear definitions will demonstrate greater interexaminer agreement and therefore will be favored in forensic assessment strategies. Such matters take on special significance in forensic cases (compared to general clinical cases), where differences in opinions between two experts testifying for different parties need to be traced to their source. Were the two experts obtaining different data? Or were they obtaining the same data and scoring it differently?

Regarding *validity*, forensic assessment strategy favors the method or tool that has been shown empirically to measure what it says it measures, whether this is a legally relevant functional ability (e.g., understanding of the trial process), a propensity or probability for a particular behavior (e.g., future violence), or an examinee's response style (e.g., likelihood of malingering). Moreover, one must attend to whether the evidence for what can be inferred from the instrument's scores pertains to the specific population to which the examinee belongs. Has there been empirical support for the test's meaning for people of this examinee's gender, age, and racial or cultural background?

Of course, these elements of standardization, reliability, and validity apply in general clinical applications of psychological assessment methods as well. But their implications are somewhat different in forensic circumstances. In general clinical work, it is usually appropriate to select and use the "best" method available, whereas in forensic work, the best available method might not be good enough. For example, various clinical diagnostic tools are used in general clinical practice, although we do not know their degree of accuracy or error when applied to various minority racial/cultural groups. But in some forensic cases, the examiner may have to choose not to use that method—even if there is none better—if that question of reliability when applied to this specific examinee is likely to be raised during testimony, potentially resulting in exclusion of the examiner's opinion entirely.

### D. INSTRUMENT SELECTION FOR SPECIFIC FORENSIC QUESTIONS

Each area of forensic assessment (e.g., competence to stand trial, child custody evaluations) has its own specific issues to address when developing a forensic assessment strategy. Therefore, specific forensic assessment instruments have been developed for use in various areas of forensic assessment. This section reviews some of these issues of strategy pertaining to specific forensic questions.

Before describing method selection issues in each area, a classification of assessment tools used in forensic assessments may be helpful. Forensic assessments typically employ three broad types of psychological tests and tools (Heilbrun, Rogers, & Otto, 2002). This typology includes some overlap but offers a convenient scheme for thinking about selection of tools for forensic purposes.

The first type includes clinical assessment tools that were not developed for forensic purposes and have no special norms or research validation for forensic populations. Examples would include many general personality tests as well as most neuropsychological tests that identify specific cognitive disabilities. The fact that they do not have norms or special validation for forensic populations does not mean they cannot be used in forensic evaluations. Personality traits, or specific cognitive deficits, often are important data when addressing forensic questions. The examiner must simply limit the manner in which the data are used. For example, except in extreme cases, it would not be appropriate to infer from intelligence test data alone that examinees could not understand matters related to participation in their trials (i.e., were incompetent to stand trial), any more than one would infer from intelligence test data that a person was capable of driving a car.

The second type of tool includes clinical instruments that were developed or adapted for use in forensic evaluations. Some are clinical tools like the *Minnesota Multiphasic Personality Inventory* (Butcher et al., 2001), for which a substantial amount of research is available that adapts its results for forensic populations or connects its results to forensic questions. For example, its validity scales have often been researched in studies of malingering in forensic populations, and its scales have been used to construct special classification systems for adult correctional populations. Other tools in this category, like the *Psychopathy Checklist-Revised* (Hare, 2003), were developed to substantially measure dimensions of personality associated with theories of propensity for illegal behavior.

Heilbrun et al. (2002) identify a third type of tool as having been developed specifically to measure dimensions or characteristics that have direct forensic relevance. Often the scales have been derived conceptually from analyses of legal definitions for human conditions and then have been operationalized by constructing items—and engaging in appropriate validation—that offer a direct representation of elements of the legal definition. Since they began to appear about 25 years ago, these tools have often been called *forensic assessment instruments* (Grisso, 1986, 2003) or *psycholegal assessment instruments* (Elwork, 1984). These terms emphasize the hybrid nature of this class of psychometric tools that represent legal concepts referring to psychological constructs.

The following discussions of various areas of forensic assessment offer some comments about assessment strategies specific to each area, as well as a brief description of various forensic assessment tools appropriate for each area. Neither the areas described nor the listings of forensic assessment tools are comprehensive but are intended only to provide representative examples. More extensive lists and descriptions of the forensic assessment tools are provided in Melton, Petrila, Poythress, and Slobogin's *Psychological*

*Evaluation for Courts* (2007) and Grisso's *Evaluating Competencies: Forensic Assessments and Instruments* (2003).

Competencies in Criminal and Delinquency Cases    The law has defined the capacities of defendants in criminal and juvenile delinquency cases relevant for assuring that individuals' rights as defendants are protected. A basic assumption behind these definitions is that the process of adjudicating a charge of illegal behavior must be fair, such that the powers of the state do not take advantage of a defendant who is not capable of protecting his or her own interests. Two main areas of criminal competency that arise in this regard are a suspect's capacities to waive Miranda rights in the process of making a potentially incriminating statement during police investigations and a defendant's competence to stand trial. Forensic evaluations often are requested for the first issue and are almost always involved when the second issue is raised.

Questions of a defendant's *capacities to have waived Miranda rights* at interrogation raise a number of important requirements for forensic assessment strategy. For example, the question is retrospective; it requires an evaluation of the likely mental state of the defendant at that time in the past when the defendant gave a statement to police officers. Assessment strategy, therefore, will require the collection of information about the person's mental state and capacities at the time of the police inquiry, based substantially on the examinee's self-report, police reports, others' observations of the individual surrounding that time, and historic information about the person's general capacities derived from mental health and educational records. Various clinical tests (e.g., intelligence testing) may be relevant but will not be determinative of functioning at the time of the police questioning. In this context, forensic assessment tools have been developed to assess specifically a defendant's abilities to understand and appreciate the significant of *Miranda* rights (e.g., Grisso, 1998; Rogers et al., 2009). They do not provide a measure of the person's abilities at the time of the police inquiry, but they provide a measure of current ability with which to make qualified inferences.

*Competence to stand trial* represents probably the most frequently requested forensic evaluation in criminal and juvenile courts. Strategies for performing competence-to-stand-trial evaluations have been extensively developed and described (Grisso, 2003, 2005; Kruh & Grisso, 2009; Melton et al., 2007; Zapf & Roesch, 2009). They often include assessment methods designed to identify defendants' cognitive capacities and clinical conditions that might impair their capacities to participate meaningfully in their trials. But the fundamental question is the defendant's ability to perform various functions that are defined in legal definitions of defendant competence, pertaining to understanding of trials and their purpose, the capacity to work with counsel, and the ability to make decisions about the exercise and waiver of rights. These abilities often cannot be accurately inferred from data obtained with general clinical assessment tools.

Therefore, a number of instruments have been developed to provide direct examination of these basic functional abilities (e.g., the *Competence Assessment for Standing Trial for Defendants with Mental Retardation*: Everington & Luckasson, 1992; *MacArthur Competence Assessment Tool-Criminal Adjudication*: Poythress et al., 1999; *Fitness Interview Test-Revised*: Roesch et al., 1998; *Evaluation of Competence to Stand Trial-Revised*: Rogers et al., 2003). The instruments are not interchangeable. Some are more comprehensive, whereas others "sample" the relevant abilities. Some observe the examinee's responses to hypothetical situations, whereas others use the defendant's own case as their focus. They vary also in the extent of their validation for various populations, as well as the nature of their norms. Finally, none of them produce an "answer" to the question of a defendant's competence to stand trial. All require a significant amount of training in their interpretation in relation to the ultimate legal question of competence to stand trial.

Criminal Culpability    Forensic examiners are often asked to provide evaluations of defendants in various stages of criminal and delinquency cases during which courts must decide their degree of culpability, especially as it relates to the law's response to their crimes. Examples include evaluations for criminal responsibility and sentencing.

*Criminal responsibility* evaluations focus on a state's definition of not guilty by reason of mental illness. Most states provide for such a finding when a defendant, because of mental illness or mental disability, is considered to have committed the alleged offense without the capacity to know or appreciate the nature of the act or was deficient in the capacity to control their behavior. (*See* Packer, 2009, for the varieties of legal definitions and their meanings). The nature of the question obviously focuses on a retrospective state of mind. As such, the strategy for the evaluation will rely heavily on evidence from the defendant, others' observations at that time, and historical mental health records. Strategies for this evaluation have been standardized in forensic tools (e.g., *Rogers Criminal Responsibility Assessment Scales*, Rogers, 1984). Specialized forensic tools to assess for possible malingering (described in "Response Style") often play an important role in assessment strategy in criminal responsibility evaluations.

Evaluations to assist in *criminal or juvenile sentencing* typically focus on questions of motivation, mental health, or developmental disability that may assist the court's review of mitigating or aggravating circumstances associated with various possible penalties for the offense after it has been adjudicated. Sometimes they also address the likelihood of future harm to others or recidivism (discussed in "Risk of Aggression"). Often, the relevant mitigating or aggravating circumstances focus on characteristics of defendants that can be assessed with clinical tools that have or have not been developed with forensic populations. Instruments have also been developed to assess certain personality characteristics, like psychopathy, that are particularly relevant for legal decisions about sentencing. The most prominent example is the *Psychopathy Checklist-Revised* (Hare, 2003).

Risk of Aggression   The need for evaluations of future risk of aggression, violence, and recidivism arises at many points in criminal, civil, and juvenile justice proceedings. Examples in criminal and juvenile cases include legal decisions about pretrial detainment, transfer of juveniles to criminal court, and adult and juvenile sentencing and parole. Many civil cases require assessments of potential violence as criteria for civil commitment of persons with mental illnesses, as well as release to the community after treatment.

Comprehensive strategies for these evaluations have become highly developed. (For recent and comprehensive reviews, consult Heilbrun, 2009, for adult risk assessments, and Hoge & Andrews, 2010, for juvenile risk assessments.) Some of the more important points of strategy generalizing across forensic areas and examinee ages are: *(1)* the need to employ validated risk factors, *(2)* the need to recognize differences between short- and long-term risk, *(3)* the need to avoid predictions and to employ risk estimates framed within a probability model, and *(4)* the need to recognize that the probability of violence is influenced by both person characteristics and situational factors.

About 30 years of research has led to the development of specialized forensic assessment tools that use validated risk factors to assist forensic clinicians in making estimates of the likelihood of future aggression, violence, or recidivism. Examples with adults include the *Violence Risk Appraisal Guide* (Quinsey et al., 1998), the *Historic-Clinical-Risk Management-20* (Webster et al., 1997), the *Classification of Violence Risk* (Monahan et al., 2003), and the *Psychopathy Checklist-Revised* (Hare, 2003). Examples for adolescents include the *Youth Level of Service/Case Management Inventory* (Hoge & Andrews, 2003) and the *Structured Assessment of Violence Risk in Youth* (Borum, Bartel, & Forth, 2006).

Assessment strategy in this area requires an understanding of the fact that these tools are not interchangeable; they have been developed for use with different populations and in different legal circumstances. Moreover, all have their limitations, and the field of "risk assessment" includes a number of controversies regarding the proper uses of actuarial and SPJ tools (Heilbrun, 2009).

Response Style    As noted earlier, almost every type of forensic evaluation occurs in a context in which examinees have important incentives to manipulate the nature of information they try to convey to the examiner. They may wish to appear disabled to avoid the consequences of criminal charges or to obtain gains related to claims in civil disability cases. They may wish to appear healthy and competent in cases in which they are threatened with loss of jobs in fitness-for-duty cases or with loss of custody rights in child custody and abuse/neglect cases. *Response style* has come to be the field's term that refers to matters of veracity and attempted deception in evaluations.

Questions about the candidness of self-report are important in any clinical evaluation. But the motivational pull for manipulating others' perceptions of oneself is more essentially a part of forensic evaluation contexts than in clinical evaluations in which people are in distress and have a need to provide clinicians accurate information to further the treatment process.

The critical need to assess response styles that might reduce the trust one puts in an examinee's self-report on psychological tests has given rise to specialized strategies for assessing malingering and other forms of dissimulation in forensic evaluations (e.g., Rogers, 2008; Boone, 2007; Larrabee, 2007). These strategies include methods for verifying data across sources, specialized interview strategies, and the use of specialized psychological tests. Forensic examiners have long used the "validity scales" in clinical measures of psychopathology (e.g., the *Minnesota Multiphasic Personality Inventory-2*) to assist in this part of the forensic evaluation task. But recent years have seen the development of specialized and well-validated tools for this purpose—most notably, the *Structured Interview of Reported Symptoms* (Rogers, 1992), the *Validity Indicator Profile* (Frederick, 1997), the *Test of Memory Malingering* (Tombaugh, 1996), and the *Miller Forensic Assessment of Symptoms Test* (Miller, 2001).

**Civil Competencies**   Civil law provides for a number of "competencies" that are intended to protect the welfare of persons with disabilities. For example, persons with serious developmental disabilities, or persons with dementias, may be unable to manage their property or make decisions in their interests. Persons with various disabilities may lack the capacity to make decisions to consent to or refuse medical and psychiatric treatments or to decide about their participation in medical research. Laws pertaining to all citizens are designed to protect individuals' right to decide for themselves about such matters. But laws also provide for those decisions to be made by others (e.g., guardians, courts, or family members) when individuals do not have the capacity to act in their best interests.

In such circumstances, psychologists may be asked to perform evaluations to assess individuals' capacities to inform courts about the extent their incapacities. These evaluations focus, in part, on identifying psychopathology or cognitive deficits, but evidence of such disabilities is not sufficient alone when questions of legal competency are involved. Such assessments also require data to demonstrate the person's actual functional capacities to make decisions in the specific area in question.

Recent texts have described strategies for assessing both clinical and functional capacities related to specific civil competencies (e.g., Grisso & Appelbaum, 1998; Kim, 2010). In addition to traditional clinical methods, a number of specialized psychological tools have been developed to assess functional capacities related to competence to consent to treatment (e.g., *MacArthur Competence Assessment Tool for Treatment*, Grisso & Appelbaum, 1998; *Competence to Consent to Treatment Instrument*, Marson, 1995), competence to consent to clinical research (e.g., *MacArthur Competence Assessment Tool for Clinical Research*, Appelbaum & Grisso, 2001), and competence to manage one's general affairs and property (e.g., *Independent Living Scales*, Loeb, 1996).

**Child Welfare**   Evaluations often are requested in cases of divorcing parents seeking custody arrangements for their children and in cases involving alleged abuse or neglect of children by their parents. The primary role of forensic examiners in these cases is to describe for the court the needs of the children in question as well as the capacities of the parents to meet those needs and to provide for children's safety. Strategy in these evaluations, therefore, typically is not aimed at deciding which parent is "best" or whether a parent has or has not abused/neglected a child. The value of psychological information is to offer a particular type of data (profiles of the children and parents) that the court can take into consideration along with other evidence in the case to reach the ultimate legal decisions.

A number of recent texts (e.g., for child protection, Budd, Clark, & Connell, 2011; for child custody, Fuhrmann & Zibell, 2011) have described the state-of-the-art methods for these evaluations, as well as strategies and options for data collection. Data collection in such cases often is far-reaching, involving substantial reliance on historical records, collateral interviews, and direct observation and interview of parents and children. In addition, most child welfare examiners will use some psychological tests to assess relevant characteristics of the children and their parents.

For evaluating children's needs, strategies for selecting psychological tests usually focus on the wide range of measures available in developmental psychology and developmental clinical psychology. For describing parents' capacities, a number of specialized tools have been developed and validated to describe parenting styles (e.g., *Adult-Adolescent Parenting Inventory*, Bavolek & Keene, 1999; *Parent–Child Relationship Inventory*, Gerard, 1994) or parents' degree of risk for potential child abuse or neglect (e.g., *Child Abuse Potential Inventory*, Milner, 1994; *Parenting Stress Inventory*, Abidin, 1995). None of these tools seek to determine which parent should be given custody of their children or whether they have abused. Their purposes are descriptive and comparative, offering standardized and normed sources of data to supplement the examiner's broader inquiry.

## III. Strategy in the Data Collection Process

Beyond the selection of methods, the actual process of collecting data in forensic assessment cases requires special considerations because of the legal context within and for which the evaluation is being performed.

### A. THE FORENSIC EXAMINER'S ROLE

Forensic examiners' roles in relation to parties in a legal proceeding are quite different from those of examiners in clinical contexts. These roles have a significant impact on the data collection process.

Many clinical psychologists perceive their primary duty to their examinees in a manner similar to their psychiatric colleagues; their primary obligation is to "do no harm" and to proceed in a manner that best protects the examinee's interests. In contrast, as noted earlier, forensic mental health examiners have a primary allegiance to objectivity. Sometimes this means that they will find information that is not at all in the best interest of the examinee. Put another way, forensic psychological examiners have no "patients" to whom they owe a clinical obligation. They serve the legal process—not the clinical interests of the persons whom they evaluate.

Of course, they avoid doing unnecessary harm to examinees. But their obligation to produce accurate information, impartially obtained, sometimes works to the detriment of the persons whom they examine (e.g., when they produce information that does not support the defendant's claim of deficits related to criminal non-responsibility, or when they find serious deficits weighing against a parent's custody of a child).

These conditions of the role of the forensic examiner create a very different relationship between forensic examiner and examinee than between clinical examiner and examinee. Moreover, they create an important obligation for the forensic examiner to manage the relationship in a way that does not deceive the examinee. For example, data collection must begin with a careful explanation to the examinee that the forensic examiner is not their "doctor" and careful disclosure of the legal purposes of the evaluation, how the information will be used, the limits of confidentiality, and the options open to the examinee regarding participation in the assessment. These conditions will vary substantially depending on who has authorized the forensic examiner to perform the evaluation (e.g., the examinee's attorney, the court, the state, or a complainant in a civil suit) and depending on the area of law within which the evaluation is being performed (Melton et al., 2007; Heilbrun, Grisso, & Goldstein, 2009).

## B. GETTING COLLATERAL INFORMATION

It is fairly rare that forensic examiners can proceed to form opinions based solely on interviews with examinees. For reasons explained earlier, most of the important interpretations made by forensic examiners must be formulated with the benefit of other sources of data to protect against examinee bias. In addition, few examinees in forensic cases are able to provide all of the background information that the forensic examiner will need to address the forensic referral question.

All of these circumstances point to the need to talk to persons other than the examinee about the examinee's characteristics. Sources may include family members, acquaintances, witnesses, employers, teachers, or friends. In addition, records often must be obtained from hospitals, schools, and other institutions. The need to obtain this range of "collateral information" raises several issues for the data collection process.

One issue is the matter of the time allowed for a forensic evaluation. Many types of forensic evaluations are controlled by statute or state agency regulations, and often those regulations specify the length of time that is allowed between referral and reporting one's results to the court. This places a demand on the forensic examiner for efficiency in seeking collateral information. Efficiency requires not only a matter of making timely requests for information but also selecting what information is actually necessary and realistic to obtain.

A second issue is the matter of release of information. In ordinary clinical cases, doctor–patient confidentiality and patients' rights requires the patient's consent for doctors to obtain information from other sources. The situation is more complex in many forensic cases. Depending on the forensic examiner's role (e.g., performing the evaluation at the request of the examinee's attorney, or performing an evaluation ordered by the court), the examiner may or may not be required to obtain the examinee's consent to collect information from other sources. Forensic examiners must be thoroughly familiar with those requirements as they pertain to their specific role in a case and as they apply within the specific type of forensic evaluation they are performing.

## C. INTERVIEW STRATEGIES

The context for forensic evaluations raises certain issues in the data collection process involving direct interview of the examinee. These issues are not foreign to general clinical evaluations, but they take on special significance in forensic cases. One of these is the matter of safety of the examiner. Forensic psychologists in criminal cases often interview examinees with significant potential for violent behavior. This risk may be present at the time of the interview, or it may arise sometime in the future if the examinee were to seek out the psychologist to express resentment at testimony that was not in the examinee's favor. Interestingly, psychologists who work routinely in forensic settings are not assaulted with any greater frequency than clinicians in other clinical settings (Leavitt et al., 2006). This might result from their taking greater precautions or from the increased structure and safety-related practices of criminal justice institutions in which their evaluations are performed.

Interviewing forensic examinees sometimes requires interview techniques that are less commonly applied in general clinical settings. For example, forensic examiners sometimes will find it necessary to challenge examinees' reports of events in ways that would be considered insensitive or stress-inducing in ordinary clinical practice. Forensic examiners understand that typically, one obtains better information by maintaining a respectful and sensitive interview style. But the forensic examiner's repertoire must include the ability for more direct challenges when they are necessary—for example, pointing out in a straightforward manner the way that an examinee's defensive statement clearly contradicts some other statement the examinee has made at an earlier time in the interview.

## IV. Interpreting Data and Communicating Results

The legal purposes of forensic evaluations pose a number of demands that arise in the examiner's interpretation of data and the examiner's communication of opinions. Each of these requires skill and an appreciation of strategy associated with the impact of one's opinions on the legal process.

### A. REPORT WRITING

Writing reports to convey one's results and opinions is one of the most important skills of the forensic examiner. Strategy and technique for writing forensic reports has been described in several texts that emphasize the differences between general clinical reports and forensic reports (e.g., Heilbrun, Marczyk, & Matteo, 2002). Virtually all of these differences are related to the legal functions of forensic reports. The fact that they serve as legal documents places special demands on their content, style, and precise documentation. Moreover, they must play a role in a legal decision process, and therefore they must conform to various requirements for legal evidence. Finally, they must be written in a manner that can be understood by non-clinicians, because their "consumers"—often the only people who will read the reports—are lawyers and judges.

Reports for most forensic referral questions follow a predictable sequence of presentation that is unlike most general clinical reports. For example, they must begin by clearly defining the forensic question in a manner consistent with applicable legal definitions and describing the specific manner in which the examinee was informed of the nature, purpose, and limits of confidentiality for the evaluation. Then they proceed to list every source of data employed in the evaluation. In a major section of the report, the examiner must describe all relevant data obtained. The content, and the level of descriptive detail, must be no more than is necessary to reach the examiner's opinion about the forensic referral question but no less than is required to understand the examiner's results. Best practices demand that this section of the report should contain all of the data without interpretations. That is typically followed by a section that includes the examiner's interpretations and no data that were not already described in the report's data section. Opinions must be confined to the forensic question, never offering interpretations or "suggestions" to the court on any other clinical or forensic matter. Principles of forensic report writing will be discussed in more detail in Chapter 5.

## B. TESTIMONY

A unique aspect of forensic evaluation is the examiner's potential role as an expert witness in court. A number of texts have described skills and strategies that forensic examiners must master to satisfy the demands of this role (e.g., Brodsky, 1999; Bank & Packer, 2007).

Clear oral expression of one's results is, of course, a key demand, and one's description of one's results must be fashioned to educate non-clinicians. Moreover, one must do this within the rules of legal process. Thus, one is expected to respond only to questions that are asked, with little room for elaboration according to one's own notion of what might improve the reception of one's opinions. Cross-examination may be challenging, and the forensic expert must be able to resist any tendency toward defensiveness. Understanding the various gambits of cross-examination is essential to reduce the likelihood that one will be drawn into testimony that superficially discredits one's opinions.

Expert testimony is usually stressful in contested cases, and in a sense, the anticipation of being put to this test pervades all aspects of forensic assessment. The selection of assessment methods, attending to the details of data collection strategy, and writing the forensic report—all are improved by an awareness that eventually one might have to account for one's assessment process and interpretations in the public spotlight of the courtroom.

# FIVE

# Forensic Consultation

Forensic consultation involves providing expertise to a third party or agency regarding psycholegal or systems issues. Forensic psychologists may be retained explicitly to function as a consultant to one of the parties in a legal case or to an agency. In such circumstances, the psychologist's role is not to conduct an independent evaluation but, rather, to provide relevant expertise to the retaining party. Drogin and Barrett (2007) note that forensic consultation "is a complex, dynamic, and free-standing discipline with a distinct history, research base, and methodology" (p. 466). One might think that consultation would be a less demanding task than evaluation. In fact, it is not necessarily less complex, and although it has some unique features, it shares many competencies with forensic evaluation and testimony.

For example, there is a sense in which an examiner's written report is a consultation. Even when the psychologist's primary role is that of an evaluator, the results and conclusions are conveyed to parties other than the examinee, most often in the form of a written report. The report is, arguably, the most important and comprehensive vehicle for the forensic evaluator to convey data, interpretations, and conclusions to courts and attorneys. In many situations, the case will be resolved without requiring oral testimony, particularly if the report is thorough and clear. The report thus serves to provide the referral source with sufficient information to allow a determination of how to proceed with the case. In many cases, the report will be reviewed by both parties and/or the judge (e.g., in child custody cases or court-ordered evaluations in criminal cases). Thus, the written report prepared by the forensic psychologist can be considered a form of consultation to the attorneys and the judge. In this chapter, we will begin with a discussion of standards for providing written reports of forensic evaluations. We will then discuss the competencies involved when forensic psychologists function as formal consultants.

## I. Forensic Report Writing

As the report is conceptualized as a form of consultation, it should be written in a manner that is comprehensible to the intended audience (i.e., a non-mental health professional). This requires attention not only to the style and format of the report but also the substance. The report should be comprehensive, including the relevant data as well as documentation of the sources of those data. In addition, the report should contain a clear articulation of the relationship between the data obtained and any conclusions.

Psychologists who are trained in clinical settings learn to write progress notes and reports that are intended to communicate with fellow mental health professionals. In these settings, use of technical jargon allows for more concise communication of the relevant data to fellow mental health professionals. Indeed, psychologists may become so comfortable with these terms, that they do not appreciate that they are really technical terms, rather than a standard part of a lay-audience's vocabulary. However, the audience for forensic reports consists of legal professionals, not clinicians. Petrella and Poythress (1983) described feedback from lawyers and judges about forensic reports they had read. These legal professionals indicated that many terms routinely used by clinicians were unclear to them. These included: "oriented to time, place, and person," "affect," "lability," "loosening of associations," and "delusional ideation" (Melton et al., 2007, p. 586).

Despite this concern, avoidance of all mental health jargon is neither practical nor advisable. These terms do have the advantage of being more concise and thus contribute to readability of reports. Furthermore, they reinforce the idea that the forensic psychologist has specialized expertise. To resolve this dilemma, the best solution is to define all technical terms the first time they are used in a report and then use them subsequently in context. Standardized definitions of psychiatric and psychological terms can be adapted from a number of sources such as the *American Psychological Association's Dictionary of Psychology* (VandenBos, 2006).

The clarity of reports can also be enhanced by breaking the report into sections. The use of discrete sections not only results in a more organized report but allows for a demarcation between data and interpretations. When data and interpretations are merged into one section, it is more difficult for the reader to evaluate independently the forensic psychologist's

TABLE 5.1 **Suggested Template for Forensic Reports**

I. Identifying information
II. Sources of information
III. Notification of limits of confidentiality/privilege
IV. Legal standard
V. Historical information
VI. Mental status/clinical functioning
VII. Results of psychological and/or medical tests ( these may be integrated into the section above)
VIII. Information obtained from examinee(s) directly relevant to forensic issue
IX. Collateral information relevant to the psycholegal issue
X. Clinical opinions relevant to the psycholegal issue

rationale for conclusions reached. Furthermore, evaluators should avoid introducing new data into conclusion sections; if the data are relevant, they should be contained in previous sections. Although there is no uniform format that is universally accepted, the organization outlined in Table 5.1 can serve as a useful template. The most important principles are: the data sections should be organized to clarify the type of information included and should have a coherent organizational framework, and the conclusion sections should provide a clear rationale for the opinions offered (see below, p. 98). Some specific guidelines relevant to each of the sections will be summarized below.

A. IDENTIFYING INFORMATION

The report should begin by including identifying information about the nature of the evaluation and the individual (or individuals—for example, in child custody cases) being evaluated. The referral issue (e.g., competence to stand trial, child custody) and the referral source (i.e., the court or one of the attorneys) should be clearly stated, as well as the date on which the report was completed. In addition, identifying data about the examinee should be briefly noted (e.g., full name, sex, age). This section basically provides the reader with an orientation toward the report.

B. SOURCES OF INFORMATION

For the reader to evaluate the validity of the data included in the report, it is important to document all sources of information, as well as the methodology used, including:

• clinical interviews of the examinee(s), including dates and time spent;
• documents and records reviewed;
• collateral sources contacted;
• tests administered or reviewed.

It is also good practice to reference sources of information that were sought out but could not be obtained (e.g., records that were requested but not received, collateral informants who could not be contacted or who did not return calls). This not only demonstrates that the psychologist did not ignore relevant data but also serves as a basis for providing an amended report if these additional sources subsequently become available.

## C. LIMITS OF CONFIDENTIALITY/PRIVILEGE

The report should document both the psychologist's explanation of the purpose of the interview and the limits of confidentiality, as well as an assessment of the examinee's comprehension. This notification is required by both legal (Chapter 9) and professional ethical (Chapter 7) standards. The report should contain a description of what the psychologist told the examinee about the purpose of the evaluation and the limits of confidentiality and privilege (*see* Chapter8), for a detailed description of the recommended elements of the disclosure). The report should also contain a brief statement as to whether the examinee appeared to understand the explanation. Although in many instances, the information will be admitted into evidence even without a full comprehension by the examinee, there are circumstances in which the judge may limit admissibility. Documentation of this issue will assist the judge in making the relevant legal decisions.

## D. LEGAL STANDARD

The legal standard that governs in the jurisdiction should be cited, including the source of the standard, which may be based on a statute or on case law. Citation serves two purposes. It demonstrates to the reader that the psychologist is employing the proper standard. It also helps frame the conclusions offered later in the report. It is best to simply cite the standard verbatim, with attribution of the source. However, some forensic examiners add a description of how they translated the demands of the legal standard into referral questions that refer to psychological concepts, behaviors, or abilities.

## E. HISTORICAL DATA

The report should contain *relevant* historical data that were obtained from both the examinee as well as collateral sources. In the course of a forensic evaluation, the psychologist is likely to have obtained a great deal of historical information. However, in constructing the report, the psychologist has to decide how much information to provide and in how much detail. A good guiding principle is that information should be included in the report to the extent that it is relevant to the psycholegal issue at hand. Some types of evaluations require comprehensive assessments of personality and functioning (e.g., child custody evaluations, aid in sentencing evaluations), whereas others are much more narrowly focused (e.g., competence to stand trial, guardianships). Similarly, the level of detail included about family members should also be guided by relevancy considerations. A typical example relates to family history of mental illness or substance abuse. Although this may be diagnostically significant, the information can be conveyed without revealing names and extraneous details (e.g., "the defendant has a family history of depression, including one sibling and a grandparent"). However, inclusion of names and identifying information about other individuals is usually contra-indicated (e.g., "He has an older brother, John Smith, who has a long history of heroin abuse and prostitution.").

The format of the organization of the history section should be guided by the goal of making the information comprehensible and coherent to the reader. This can be done either by categorical sections (e.g., early history, schooling, employment, marital, mental health history, etc.) or chronologically. When presenting the data categorically, it is clearer to do so in chronologically ascending order. The degree of emphasis on certain aspects of the history will be driven by the type of evaluation as well as the particulars of the case. For example, a disability evaluation will likely involve emphasis on employment history and functioning, whereas an evaluation for aid in sentencing will focus more on criminal history.

## F. MENTAL STATUS/CLINICAL FUNCTIONING

Across all types of reports, a description of the defendant's clinical functioning and mental status at the time of the evaluation should be provided. This section should include specific data, rather than just conclusory language, to support the mental status assessment. For example, rather than state that the examinee "presented with symptoms of mania," the report should provide descriptors, such as "the examinee spoke in a rapid, pressured manner, and it was difficult to interrupt her."

The forensic psychologist should also attend to the time frame relevant to the psycholegal issue. Some evaluations, such as assessment of criminal responsibility, involve a retrospective analysis of the individual's functioning at some point in the past. Others, such as personal injury cases, may involve a comparison of present and previous functioning. Thus, the mental status section should include not only the current observations and reported symptoms but also a sense of the course of the symptoms. For example, if a defendant was experiencing hallucinations and delusions at the time of the alleged offense but has been treated and is asymptomatic at the time of the evaluation, a description of the defendant's attitude toward these previous symptoms should be noted. Rather than simply stating, "The defendant reports no current paranoid thinking," it would be useful to add, "She acknowledged that, around the time of the alleged offense, she believed that her husband had been poisoning her but now states that she realizes this was not true, and realizes that it was part of her mental illness."

The report should also include information regarding the examinee's medication regimen. The names and dosages of the medications that the examinee is taking at the time of the evaluation should be documented. These data may be relevant to the assessment of both mental status traits, as well as validity of psychological test results. The use of medications may positively or negatively impact these results. For example, an examinee who had recently experienced a manic episode may be euthymic at the time of the interview, with the aid of lithium; alternatively, the individual may appear lethargic and produce delayed responses as a consequence of some prescribed medications.

## G. RESULTS OF PSYCHOLOGICAL TESTS

Forensic reports should include the data from all tests and instruments used by the psychologist or others (including those performed by consultants, such as neurologists or neuropsychologists) The nature of the tests should be explained as well. Thus, if the *Psychopathy Checklist–Revised* (PCL-R) was used, a brief description of the test and its relationship to the issues being addressed should be included. Keeping in mind that the report is a communication to legal—not mental health—professionals, results should be reported in clear, non-technical language. (Consistent with the previous discussion of jargon, some technical terms may be included, as long as they are explained.) When reporting on tests that have specific scores (such as the Wechsler Adult Intelligence Scale [WAIS]-IV), the results should include a confidence interval, so that the reader understands that the result obtained reflects a range, rather than a specific number. Furthermore, the meaning of the score should be explained (e.g., "The examinee's performance on the Validity Indicator Profile [VIP] suggests that he made a good effort throughout the test, and the results of cognitive testing administered are likely an accurate representation of his abilities.").

## H. CASE-SPECIFIC SECTIONS

The sections above are standard across all forensic evaluations. In addition, each type of forensic report will require inclusion of data specific to the psycholegal issue. Competence-to-stand-trial evaluations will include data sections focused on the elements of the construct; criminal responsibility evaluations will include data related to both the defendant's, and others', versions of the alleged offense; child custody evaluations will contain data about the interactions of the parent and child, and so forth. The specific data to be included will be determined by how the legal issue has been defined and operationalized. This part of the report will contain not only data obtained directly from the examinee but also collateral sources of information. It is essential that all data relevant to the conclusions or opinions offered be included; this includes data that may weigh in the opposite direction. As noted in the Specialty Guidelines for Forensic Psychologists (Committee on Ethical Guidelines for Forensic Psychologists, 1991, VII.D), psychologists do not "participate in partisan attempts to avoid, deny, or subvert the presentation of evidence contrary to their own position." This language has been preserved in the latest draft of the revised guidelines (Committee on the Revision of the Specialty Guidelines for Forensic Psychology, 2010).

## I. CLINICAL OPINIONS RELEVANT TO THE PSYCHOLEGAL ISSUE

The final section of the report contains the conclusions arrived at by the forensic psychologist. In this section, the psychologist presents the clinical and forensic formulation of the case, interpreting the data to address the relevant legal matter. As noted earlier, new data should not be introduced here; rather, this section should explain the implications, for the psycholegal issue addressed, of the data presented in previous sections. The purpose of this section is for the forensic psychologist to explain how the data led to the specific conclusions offered. This includes, when relevant, an analysis of contradictory data and alternative explanations that were considered and the rationale for not accepting the alternative conclusion. If the evaluation addresses more than one psycholegal issue (e.g. the insanity defense and diminished capacity), then each issue should be addressed in a separate section.

The crux of the conclusion section is the articulation of the nexus between the data obtained and the opinions offered relative to the psycholegal issue. Skeem and Golding (1998) developed a model for assessing the relationship between symptoms and impairment conveyed in competency reports. This schema can be used for all forensic reports, as it is based on the general principle that the report should clearly convey the logic of the analysis tying the conclusions reached to the data reported. They identified four categories of the relationship between data and conclusions: *none, implied, asserted*, or *articulated*. The *articulated* category is the standard for forensic psychological reports. The following is an adaptation of each of these four categories.

*None:* The evaluator offers a conclusion but does not describe any relationship between the data and the conclusion. Example (criminal responsibility): "The defendant appreciated that his conduct would be considered wrong."

*Implied*: The evaluator provides data that are relevant to the conclusion but then does not link the data to the specific psycholegal standard. Example (child custody): "The mother has a history of substance abuse and acknowledged that she began drinking again recently."

*Asserted*: The evaluator offers a conclusion and references data that are relevant to the conclusion but does not specifically describe the relationship between the data and the conclusion. Example (competency to stand trial): "The defendant's ability to assist his attorney with a reasonable degree of rational understanding is impaired by his delusional beliefs."

*Articulated:* The evaluator clearly specifies the relationship between the data and the specific conclusions offered relevant to the psycholegal issue. Example (civil commitment): "The respondent continues to maintain paranoid beliefs about her sister, claiming that her sister is trying to kill her in order to gain her share of their parents' inheritance. She has previously attempted to stab her sister in the context of this delusional belief, claiming that she had to do so in self-defense. Based on this history, as well as her continued paranoid beliefs about her sister, failure to hospitalize her would likely result in a significant risk of harm to the sister."

The articulation of the opinion should clearly indicate the particular sources of data. Using the last example, the sources of the data regarding the woman's paranoid beliefs should be included. This may be self-reported information, although preferably it also includes other sources as well (such as the sister) or documentation of the paranoid beliefs from previous records or treaters. This is particularly important when there are conflicting or inconsistent sources of information. The forensic psychologist's role is not to make the ultimate determination in the case but to objectively provide data and conclusions, which can then be evaluated by the attorneys and the trier of fact, who can independently decide the validity of the data sources.

## J. NOTE ON ULTIMATE ISSUE OPINIONS

Whether or not forensic psychologists should offer opinions on the ultimate legal issue (as discussed in Chapter 7) is a controversial topic in the field (Rogers & Ewing, 2003; Tillbrook, Mumley, & Grisso, 2003; Borum & Grisso, 1996). However, even if the forensic psychologist supports providing ultimate-issue opinions as a matter of principle or a matter of law (as some jurisdictions require such opinions in certain types of court-ordered evaluations), there are instances in which no such opinion can be offered because there are not adequate data to support the position. In such cases, the forensic psychologist should clearly explain the basis for the inability to offer an opinion. This can occur for a variety of reasons:

• there are conflicting factual data that the psychologist cannot resolve;
• there are inadequate data available (e.g., relevant records have not been received, the examinee is unwilling to discuss certain matters; collateral sources are not available to the psychologist);
• the legal standard has not been resolved (e.g., the standard for deciding whether a defendant is capable of serving as his own attorney has not been determined—*see Indiana v. Edwards*, 2008).

In such situations, the forensic psychologist would explain the factors that limit his or her ability to provide an opinion. Depending on the circumstances, the psychologist may offer multiple formulations to the court or alternative options based on the court's decision either about the legal standard or the factual data. For example, the psychologist could note that if the trier of fact were to accept a certain fact pattern or interpretation of the legal standard, then the clinical data would support one conclusion versus another conclusion based on a different fact pattern or legal standard.

## II. Forensic Consultation to Attorneys

Forensic psychologists may be retained to consult with attorneys on a variety of issues related to the legal case. This may include jury selection, case analysis and formulation, trial strategy, and preparation for direct and cross-examination of mental health experts. In contrast to the initial stance of an evaluator, who begins the process as impartial, a consultant's role is to assist the retaining party. Although the forensic consultant is still bound by professional ethics and guidelines (e.g., not to distort or misrepresent data), there is no obligation to be impartial.

It is noteworthy that the legal profession also recognizes the distinction between the roles of evaluator and consultant. The American Bar Association (ABA) has published *Criminal Justice Mental Health Standards* (1989), which state that evaluators must reach an objective opinion but that consultants should be considered to have "the same obligations and immunities as any member of the prosecution or defense team. Nevertheless, the prosecutor and defense counsel should respect the professional's ethical and professional standards" (§7–1.1.(c)). This principle applies in civil cases as well.

## A. JURY SELECTION

The field of consultation on jury selection is not limited to forensic psychologists. Consultants from other professions may also serve in this capacity (a particularly negative stereotype of such a consultant is the ruthless and unethical attorney in the book *Runaway Jury* (Grisham, 1996, which was later made into a movie). However, when psychologists are involved, they apply *scientific jury selection* (e.g., Kovera, Dickinson, & Cutler, 2003; Lieberman & Sales, 2007; Brodsky, 2009). This term refers to application of empirically validated methodologies derived from experiments with simulated and real juries, as well as surveys (e.g., Schulman, Shaver, Colman, Emrich, & Christie, 1973).

Studies on predictors of jury verdicts have included demographic variables, personality traits, and attitudes. Demographic factors have included race (e.g., Simon, 1967), sex (e.g., Kovera, Gresham, Borgida, Gray, & Regan, 1997), as well as educational and socioeconomic status (e.g., Adler, 1973). Personality trait variables studied include authoritarianism (e.g., Narby, Cutler, & Moran) and internal versus external locus of control (e.g., Phares & Wilson, 1972; Hans, 1992). Attitudinal variables include attitudes toward the death penalty (e.g., Moran & Comfort, 1986), tort reform (e.g., Mroan, Cutler, & De Lisa, 1994), and drug use (Moran, Cutler, & Loftus, 1990). A major application of this research has been to aid in the deselection (e.g., exclusion) of biased jurors (e.g., Brodsky, 2009). Data derived from these studies can help identify individuals who are likely to be inclined, or disinclined, to a particular verdict. However, as noted by Kovera, Dickinson, and Cutler, (2003), it has been difficult to validate whether application of scientific jury selection techniques results in less biased juror decisions. In addition, the strengths of the correlations found have tended to be low to moderate (e.g., Brodsky, 2009). Thus, psychologists who serve as consultants on jury selection need to be familiar with the research particular to the cases on which they are consulting (e.g., civil, death penalty, sex offender, insanity, etc.). They should also be clear about the limited incremental validity these techniques can provide and not make exaggerated claims about efficacy.

## B. CASE-SPECIFIC CONSULTATION

An attorney may retain a forensic psychologist to review documentation, discuss the viability of different strategy options (which may include retaining an evaluating psychologist), and critique reports of opposing experts. In such instances, forensic psychologists do not necessarily form an opinion about the psycholegal issue; rather, they identify additional sources of information to obtain, evaluate the strengths and weaknesses of the existing evidence (which may include reports by other mental health experts), and may suggest direct and cross-examination questions and areas of inquiry.

Review of Records    In reviewing documents (such as school records, employment records, mental health records, police reports), the forensic psychologist will focus on whether the information provided is relevant to, and sufficient for, the psycholegal question raised. For example, in a personal injury case, is there clear enough information about the plaintiff's pre-morbid functioning? In a child custody case, is there sufficient data regarding the child's adjustment? In a criminal case, is there an adequate description of the defendant's behaviors related to the alleged offense? If there are records of previous mental health treatment, do they provide an adequate basis for determining whether the diagnoses offered were based on presence of specific symptoms?

Record reviews may also be requested, for example, by agencies such as insurance companies in disability claims. The forensic psychologist may be asked to review the documentation provided by a mental health treatment professional. The consultant would then focus on the functional issues relevant to determination of disability and whether the documentation adequately addresses those issues. The following are examples of the types of questions that a consultant might address in such a case:

1. Was the diagnosis offered based solely on self-report of the individual?
2. Did the therapist have any data about the claimant's functioning at work prior to the index event?
3. If the therapist opines that her client is unable to return to work, does the therapist understand the client's specific job duties?
4. How do the claimant's symptoms specifically interfere with his ability to perform those job duties?
5. Is the claimant involved in treatment to address the specific symptoms?
6. Is the claimant adherent to treatment, including attending sessions, and taking prescribed medications?
7. What is the therapist's assessment of the claimant's prognosis, particularly in terms of ability to return to work?

The consulting psychologist may also be asked to contact the treatment provider and obtain additional information to help the insurer decide whether there are enough data to make a determination about the claim or whether an independent evaluation is needed. In this context, it is important for the forensic consultant to be aware of the differences between therapists and forensic evaluators in terms of level of scrutiny applied to the data and cognitive set (as discussed in Chapter 8). If the consultant employs a critical tone toward the therapist, conveying that the documentation is inadequate, it is unlikely that the therapist will provide the relevant information in a cooperative manner. Rather, the consultant should ask the questions in a respectful tone, keeping in mind that the level of detail required to address the forensic issue is greater than that necessary for the therapeutic process.

**Review of Forensic Mental Health Reports**   A forensic psychological consultant is often asked to review reports that have been generated by the evaluators in the case to help the attorney determine the best course of action. The consultant needs to be knowledgeable about the legal standard, the manner in which that standard has been operationalized, and the assessment tools appropriate for evaluating the issue and must be able to assess whether the evaluators' conclusions are supported by adequate data. The psychologist would then be in a position to consult with the attorney about how to proceed in the case. Furthermore, if the case were to go to trial, the psychologist would be able to offer advice about direct and cross-examination of the expert witnesses. The following are examples of the issues that the consultant may address:

1. Does it appear that the evaluator has the requisite expertise to perform the evaluation (e.g., based on review of a vita)?

2. Did the evaluator obtain adequate and relevant data to address the issue?

3. Are there other sources of information that would be necessary, or helpful, to obtain to address the psycholegal issue (e.g., records, collateral contacts)?

4. Did the evaluator employ appropriate methodology, including proper use of psychological tests and/or forensic assessment instruments?

5. Are the conclusions offered consistent with the data? Are there alternative explanations that would be consistent with the data?

As noted above, the consultant is not opining on the ultimate issue involved but, rather, is providing the attorney with a critique of the data and opinions offered by the evaluators. The consultant should provide an objective assessment of both the strengths and weaknesses of all reports reviewed (including reports by the attorney's retained evaluator). The consultation should provide the attorney with sufficient information to decide on the next course of action. It is worth keeping in mind that a consultant has provided a valuable service to the attorney, even in those cases where the assessment is that the attorney's case is weak; in such circumstances, the attorney may indeed decide to pursue more fruitful approaches to the case. A sample vignette of a consultation is described below.

## C. SAMPLE CONSULTATION ON COMPETENCY-TO-STAND-TRIAL CASE

Tim Jones is a 25-year-old man, charged with breaking and entering and assault and battery with a dangerous weapon. It is alleged that he broke into a home at night when the owner of the home awoke and discovered him. Mr. Jones reportedly picked up a chair and hit the man over the head with it, and then ran away. His attorney requested a competence-to-stand-trial evaluation because he stated that Mr. Jones did not seem to understand his explanations of plea options and appeared confused. The defendant was evaluated by a court-appointed psychologist, Dr. Smith, who opined that Mr. Jones was not mentally retarded, was exaggerating his lack of understanding, and could assist his attorney if he chose to do so. The defense attorney hired a consultant to review the report and make a recommendation as to how to proceed.

After reviewing the report, the consultant offered the following feedback:

1. Dr. Smith had not reviewed any school records but obtained information from the defendant that he had been in classes for a "learning disability."

2. This expert had administered the WAIS-IV, on which the defendant obtained a full-scale IQ score of 60, but the psychologist concluded that he had not put out maximum effort. The test was scored accurately. However, Dr. Smith had not administered any tests to assess validity of responding or effort.

3. Dr. Smith appropriately used the CAST-MR but concluded that the defendant's poor performance was volitional, as he deliberately provided wrong answers. The basis for this conclusion was not adequately articulated in the report.

4. Although Dr. Smith had assessed most of the abilities usually associated with competence to stand trial, he did not specifically address the

defendant's ability to weigh options and work with his lawyer to agree on a defense strategy (including whether or not to accept a plea bargain).

Based on this analysis, the consultant informed the attorney that Mr. Jones may have been feigning or exaggerating lack of knowledge but that Dr. Smith had not provided adequate evidence of malingering, had not made an effort to obtain school records but had relied on Mr. Jones' description of having been placed in an "LD" class, and had not fully explored the issue of Mr. Jones's ability to assist in his defense by participating in making reasoned choices among alternatives. As a result of this consultation, the attorney chose to obtain an independent evaluation by another psychologist regarding his client's competence to stand trial.

## III. Consultation to Organizations

Forensic psychologists may also be called on to consult to organizations (such as hospitals, clinics, mental health departments, correctional institutions) regarding development of policies and procedures. In such cases, the focus is not on a particular case but, rather, a consultation on incorporating practices that represent the state of the science. The consultation may involve specifically forensic activities, such as providing guidance on recommended assessment practices. For example, a consultant can draw on the literature regarding use of tests and instruments for various forensic evaluations. Table 5.2 below provides examples of such research and the relevant areas of practice.

Forensic psychologists may also be asked to consult to institutions concerning clinical practices that are informed by specialized forensic expertise. For example, hospitals and outpatient providers may benefit from a

TABLE 5.2 **Selected Studies of Psychological Tests Used in Forensic Evaluations**

| AUTHORS | GROUP SURVEYED | EVALUATION TYPE |
|---|---|---|
| Borum & Grisso (1995) | Forensic psychologists and psychiatrists | Competence to stand trial and criminal responsibility |
| Boccaccini & Brodsky (1999) | Concurrent members of Division 12 (Clinical) and Division 41 (Psychology and Law) of APA | Emotional injury |
| Lally (2003) | ABPP diplomates in Forensic Psychology | Competence to stand trial, criminal responsibility, risk for violence, risk for sexual violence, competence to waive *Miranda* rights, malingering |
| Archer et al. (2006) | ABPP diplomates in Forensic Psychology and Division 41 of APA | Forensic evaluations of adults |

consultation regarding best practices for assessing and documenting violence risk. Such assessments may not be "forensic" (in the sense that they are not used for legal purpose) but involve areas in which forensic psychologists are uniquely knowledgeable. Tolman and Mullendore (2003) conducted a survey comparing risk assessment evaluations provided by clinical psychologists versus those provided by ABPP (American Board of Professional Psychology) Forensic Diplomates. They found that the Forensic Diplomates were more knowledgeable about the scientific literature on violence risk assessment and were more likely to utilize modern risk assessment instruments.

A forensic psychologist serving as a consultant to an agency or facility would draw on the scientific literature on violence risk assessment to help improve standards of practice in the clinical setting. As discussed in Chapter 3, choice of instruments may depend on the nature of the population (e.g., correctional, forensic, civil, acute, chronic). The role of the forensic psychologist in such a circumstance is to consult to the organization and make recommendations about tools and procedures that are relevant to the particular task and population.

# SIX

# Supervision, Training, and Management

Principles of supervision in forensic psychology stem from the basic conceptualization of the specialty as building on the foundations of scientific and professional psychology. Forensic psychologists receive foundational training as clinical psychologists and then develop specialized expertise in applying this psychological knowledge to legally relevant questions.

Achieving competence in basic clinical skills, such as interviewing, assessment, testing, and clinical formulation is a necessary, but not sufficient, basis for competent practice as a forensic psychologist. Research into quality of forensic reports (e.g., Nicholson & Norwood, 2000) has produced consistent findings, identifying a number of specific deficiencies. The issue is not lack of standards for the field, as there is a significant literature outlining the standards across the many areas within forensic psychology (see Chapter 1). Rather, the problems stem from lack of adherence to the standards among some practitioners. Commenting on these studies, Packer (2008) concluded that: "[a] very likely explanation for these findings is that many forensic evaluations are performed by psychologists and psychiatrists who have not received adequate training in the area and thus lack knowledge of the concepts, methodology, and standards required" (p. 245).

Some of these issues have been addressed through the development of Education and Training (E&T) Guidelines for Forensic Psychology (www.cospp.org). However, these are focused primarily on formal postdoctoral training programs. The demand for forensic evaluation services greatly outstrips the capacity of academic institutions to provide such formal training (e.g., Packer, 2008). This imbalance between "supply" and "demand" for forensic evaluation services is most evident in public sector settings that focus on criminal adjudications. Forensic psychologists are often involved in administrative and leadership positions in such settings, and face challenges in developing systems to efficiently provide forensic mental health evaluation services. This chapter will begin with an overview of some of the common problems identified with forensic reports, and we will then discuss the principles of training that have been developed to address those issues. We will then focus on issues relevant to forensic psychologists who develop and manage forensic systems.

## I. Research on Quality of Forensic Reports

Nicholson and Norwood (2000) and Wettstein (2005) have reviewed a number of studies regarding quality of forensic mental health reports. Most of the studies were conducted on evaluations in criminal matters (as these are more often done under the auspices of a state authority), although some involved civil or family matters. Zapf et al. (2004) reviewed reports of defendants who were recommended as incompetent to stand trial. They found significant omissions of a number of important competency domains, such as the defendant's appreciation of his or her role in the legal proceedings and the defendant's amenability to treatment for restoration of competency related abilities. In a review of criminal responsibility evaluations, Warren et al. (2004) found that in many cases, evaluators had offered opinions without having obtained essential documents or information, such as defendants' statements about the alleged offense, previous psychiatric records, or witness accounts. Skeem and Golding (1998) reviewed the quality of competence-to-stand-trial reports, utilizing a measure of the extent to which opinions offered were clearly articulated and tied to the data (as described in Chapter 5 ). They found that only about a one-third of forensic reports reviewed included an articulation of the relationship between symptoms and the functional domains relevant to competence to stand trial. Summarizing the research literature in this area, Wettstein (2005) commented that "[o]ne of the most common report weaknesses is the failure to substantiate expert opinions and the related failure to relate psychopathology to expert opinions regarding psycholegal abilities. The relationships among symptom, diagnosis, psychological test-identified deficits, and psycholegal functional impairment is too often neglected" (p. 168).

Grisso (2010) categorized the problems raised by reviewers of reports submitted by candidates for board certification in forensic psychology (American Board of Forensic Psychology—ABFP). He listed the 10 most common errors identified in these reports (see Table 6.1). In addition, he

**TABLE 6.1 Ten Most Frequent Faults in Forensic Report Writing**

1. Opinions without sufficient explanations
2. Forensic purpose unclear
3. Organization problems
4. Irrelevant data or opinions
5. Failure to consider alternative hypotheses
6. Inadequate data
7. Data and interpretation mixed
8. Over-reliance on single source of data
9. Language problems
10. Improper test uses

*Adapted from Grisso (2010).*

identified 30 discrete factors, and presented them as prescriptive recommendations for forensic report writing. Although, as Grisso noted, these factors do not necessarily constitute an exhaustive list, they do provide useful information for supervisors in forensic settings.

Packer (2009) identified common deficiencies in evaluators' reasoning in forensic reports. Although these errors were described in the context of criminal responsibility reports, they reflect broader problems observed across the range of forensic evaluations. The categories of errors include: lack of understanding of the relevant psycholegal construct, reasoning with uncorroborated information, illusory correlations, failure to consider alternative explanations, and overreaching.

1. Lack of understanding of the relevant psycholegal construct occurs particularly when psychologists not formally trained in the forensic arena provide evaluations for the legal system. As discussed in Chapter 2, legal constructs may differ from either "common-sense" or psychological approaches. For example, legal concepts of causality, such as "proximate cause" (p. 41 above), differ from psychology's causal explanations. In addition, definitions and interpretations of legal standards (such as insanity) may differ across jurisdictions.
2. Reasoning with uncorroborated information refers to the error of failing to obtain sufficient data, from multiple sources, to address the legal question. This can occur when an evaluator relies exclusively on the examinee's self-report and fails to seek out collateral contacts or documents that can provide information to corroborate, or raise questions about, the examinee's accounts.
3. Illusory correlation refers to the error of assuming that once a diagnosis has been established, the disorder necessarily impacts the psycholegal abilities (e.g., ability to manages one's affairs, ability to provide

adequate parenting, ability to appreciate the wrongfulness of one's actions). However, a basic tenet of forensic psychological evaluations is that there is no one-to-one correspondence that exists between any clinical condition and a legal standard; rather, there must be an explanation of how the disorder specifically impacts the legally relevant abilities.

4. Failure to consider alternative explanations refers to the error of focusing on one interpretation of data and then searching out data that are consistent with that interpretation. This is known as confirmation bias (e.g., Nickerson, 1998). Although this type of interpretive error is not unique to forensic evaluations, the adversarial nature of the legal system encourages this type of thinking (i.e., the lawyer for each side seeks to present only data consistent with his or her position), and thus the forensic psychologist must be particularly vigilant to avoid this error. As discussed in Chapter 3, scientific reasoning requires consideration of hypotheses and evaluation of data that either are consistent with the hypotheses or disconfirm them.

5. Overreaching refers to the error of arriving at a conclusion although there are insufficient data. This can occur particularly when the data obtained are ambiguous or elements are missing (e.g., there are conflicting accounts of the facts of a case, relevant documents or informants are not available, the examinee has limited memory for the relevant time period, test results are ambiguous) but can also reflect a response to perceived pressure to offer a definitive opinion rather than be seen as "waffling." This error also occurs when psychologists inappropriately equate the results of a Forensic Assessment Instrument (FAI) such as the CAST-MR (Everington & Luckasson, 1992) or the RCRAS (Rogers, 1984) with the ultimate legal issue.

## II. Training

The E&T Guidelines for Forensic Psychology (www.cospp.org) identify forensic psychology as a postdoctoral level specialty. This means that graduate-level training is not sufficient to obtain the relevant competencies. Rather, psychologists can master the basic competencies of general psychological practice at the graduate level but require additional training and experience to become competent forensic practitioners. There are currently at least 22 graduate programs in psychology that offer concentrations or emphases in forensic psychology (http://ap-ls.org/education/

ClinicalDoctoral.php) and over 60 predoctoral internships that offer forensic rotations (http://ap-ls.org/education/Internship.php). However, there are fewer than 20 postdoctoral fellowship or residency programs in forensic psychology (http://ap-ls.org/education/PostDoc.php). Given the limited opportunities available for fellowship training, many forensic psychologists obtain their postdoctoral training and supervision outside of formal fellowship or residency programs. Although the E&T Guidelines are geared toward formal training settings, most of the principles are relevant to settings in which psychologists obtain supervised training and experience in forensic evaluations.

The E&T guidelines specify the exit requirements (i.e., requisite competencies that must be obtained) for postdoctoral residents, which serves as a template for the training directors and supervisors. These exit criteria require that the resident:

1. obtain knowledge of the basic principles of the legal system, including how the legal system works, legal doctrines that are relevant for mental health evaluations, as well as core legal cases relevant to forensic psychology and their implications for practice, covering the breadth of forensic psychology;

2. obtain knowledge of forensic psychological evaluation methods, including specialized assessment instruments used in forensic psychological practice;

3. obtain knowledge of, and practice consistent with, the Specialty Guidelines for Forensic Psychologists and the Ethical Principles and Code of Conduct for Psychologists;

4. obtain knowledge of rules, procedures, and techniques related to expert witness testimony;

5. attain advanced skill in providing forensic psychological services sufficient to practice on an independent basis; these skills must be demonstrated in at least two distinct areas of forensic psychological practice and must include the following:

   a. ability to conduct a forensic interview;

   b. ability to use and interpret structured assessment instruments;

   c. ability to obtain the relevant data, including collateral sources of information;

   d. ability to integrate results and formulate interpretations consistent with data, relevant for the conclusions related to the legal question, and consistent with ethical and practice guidelines;

e. ability to write reports that are clear, comprehensive, articulate, and appropriately focused on the referral issue;

f. ability to provide expert testimony in a clear, articulate manner, consistent with ethical and practice guidelines;

6. demonstrate ability to critically evaluate research and how it applies to forensic practice;

7. meet requirements for eligibility for state or provincial licensure or certification for the independent practice of psychology;

8. meet requirements for eligibility for board certification in forensic psychology by the American Board of Professional Psychology.

## A. DIDACTIC TRAINING

Some of the requirements focus primarily on didactic aspects of training. It is noteworthy that education in forensic psychology must be broad, covering the range of forensic areas, including criminal, civil, adult, and juvenile evaluations. This does not mean that training must prepare the residents to be competent practitioners in all those areas but, rather, that they must be familiar with the literature (both psychological and legal) relevant to forensic practice. Education in the legal aspects of forensic psychology presents a particular challenge. Ideally, legal professionals would be incorporated as part of the teaching faculty. However, this is not always possible. Forensic psychologists can provide these didactic presentations, with an understanding that what is being taught is the relevant application of legal concepts to the psycholegal areas.

## B. Training in Forensic Practice

The fifth criterion focuses on providing trainees with the relevant skills to practice competently. Most trainees will have garnered experience primarily in therapeutic settings. Therefore, postdoctoral training needs to begin with an orientation to the role of a forensic evaluator, including the nature of the relationships to be established with examinees as well as legal professionals and an appreciation of the ethical standards that apply in the legal context. Initial supervision often focuses on helping the trainee to develop a level of comfort with the need to establish a balance between developing sufficient rapport with the examinee in order to obtain useful information and the need to be skeptical and confrontative at times.

Other aspects of supervision unique to the forensic setting flow from the analysis of deficiencies identified in the literature. The supervisor typically works with the trainee to ensure understanding of the referral issue, to aid in developing possible hypotheses, and to identify the methodology and sources of information that will be needed (including the collateral sources of information to be sought out and any structured tools or psychological tests that may be appropriate). Once the data are collected, the supervisor works with the trainee to determine whether the data are sufficient to allow a conclusion to be drawn, to consider alternative hypotheses, and to decide the formulation that is most consistent with the data. Perhaps the most labor-intensive part of forensic supervision involves issues related to report writing.

Forensic report writing differs significantly from the style of writing usually produced in clinical progress notes. These differences are a function of the close scrutiny given to these reports, as well as the nature of the audience (legal professionals rather than mental health professionals). Furthermore, forensic evaluations are focused on specific psycholegal issues, which typically are more narrow in scope than open-ended diagnostic assessment in therapeutic contexts. Thus, the supervisor usually will provide the trainee with a template to organize the material and will focus on ensuring that the report is written in language that is comprehensible to the legal audience, with all technical terms clearly explained and clinical conclusions supported by data.

The aspect of report writing that typically requires the most attention in supervision relates to the opinion sections. As discussed above, this is the area that has most often been found to be deficient in studies of quality of forensic reports. Supervision may entail encouraging the trainee to explore multiple hypotheses, to articulate clearly the bases for any opinions offered, to acknowledge contradictory data, and to explain why alternative explanations were not adopted.

Initial experiences of providing expert testimony are often the most anxiety-provoking for trainees. They are often uncomfortable being seen as "experts" by the courts, as this term has a specialized meaning in the legal system. A new practitioner, and particular trainees who are often not yet licensed, may feel that they do not have sufficient experience to be considered an expert in the field. However, in the legal system, an expert is an individual who has specialized knowledge beyond the ken of the average juror. Supervisors need to remind trainees that their expertise stems from their many years of training at the graduate and internship levels, augmented by their postdoctoral training. Thus, although they may not have conducted numerous forensic evaluations when they begin to testify, they have significant experience and received specialized education in clinical assessment as well as treatment of mental disorders.

## C. RESEARCH

The sixth criterion involves "ability to critically evaluate research and how it applies to forensic practice." Clinical practitioners of forensic psychology must keep abreast of research in the field, including developments in assessment tools (Chapter 4), as well as advances in the knowledge base of psychology relevant to forensic practice (Chapter 3). Although this statement applies to all psychologists across specialties, practice within the context of the legal system requires heightened scrutiny of methods and instruments used. The standards for admissibility of new methodologies, including psychological tests, as evidence in legal cases are higher than the standards for clinical practice (see Chapter 9). Forensic psychologists, for example, must be prepared to explain to the court whether a particular test has been peer-reviewed, has a known error rate, and has been generally accepted in the field (e.g., *Daubert v. Merrell Dow*, 1993). This requires, therefore, both a familiarity with the literature, as well as an ability to evaluate the strengths and weaknesses of the relevant research data. Fellowship programs can vary in how these skills are taught and assessed; some programs may require that the fellow engage in a research project, whereas others may require a literature review or provide seminars in which the trainees are exposed to one or more areas of research related to forensic psychological practice.

# III. Forensic Systems

All 50 states and the Federal Government have developed systems for providing public sector forensic mental health evaluations. These typically involve pre-trial evaluations for issues such as competency to stand trial and criminal responsibility. Forensic psychologists are often involved in leadership positions in such public sector systems and need to be knowledgeable about models of service delivery, as well as issues related to training and quality assurance. The types of forensic evaluations systems have been categorized as fitting into one of five models (Poythress et al., 1991; Grisso et al., 1994, Melton et al., 2007).

## A. MODELS FOR FORENSIC SYSTEMS

**Hospital-Based: Inpatient Model**   This model utilizes inpatient hospitals to provide pre-trial forensic evaluations. This allows for in-depth evaluation over a lengthy period of time, as well as opportunities for treatment during the evaluation process. However, this is a resource-intensive model, as defendants are transported from local jails or courts to an inpatient psychiatric facility, which involves a full array of hospital services, including medical examination, laboratory tests, and nursing care. Furthermore, it involves the most significant infringement on liberty interests, as the evaluation requires involuntary commitment, often for a defendant who otherwise does not meet clinical criteria for hospitalization. Most states have therefore moved away from an exclusive reliance on this model.

Hospital-Based: Outpatient Model   Some states continue to use centralized hospitals for forensic evaluations, but the defendant is not admitted to the facility. Rather, he or she is transported to the hospital, and the evaluation is performed on an outpatient basis. The evaluation is completed in 1 day, and the individual is then returned to jail or court. This model is less resource-intensive than the inpatient model but still requires transportation from local sites to a centralized facility. Furthermore, reports are typically not submitted the same day but are received by the court days or weeks later.

Community-Based: Community Agency Model   This model allows forensic evaluations to be completed locally, either at the courthouse (court clinics), the jail, or at a local agency (such as a community mental health center). The evaluations may either be provided directly by state employees or through contracts with a local agency. These evaluations can be completed more quickly, often on the same day the defendant is arraigned (e.g., Massachusetts; Packer, 1994). This model is also considerably more cost-effective than the previous models, although there may be fixed costs (such as salaries of state employees, or guaranteed contracts with the agencies involved). Adoption of this approach was aided by research that indicated that assessments of competence to stand trial could be adequately conducted in a briefer manner (e.g., Melton et al., 1985).

Community-Based: Private Practitioner Model   This model is similar to the community agency one but relies on private practitioners who contract either directly with the court or with a state agency (such as a Department of Mental Health). The defendants may be evaluated either at a jail or at the evaluator's office. These evaluations typically do not take place on the day of arraignment, as arrangements need to be made to identify a particular evaluator and make the referral. This model provides more flexibility than the community agency system, as evaluators are assigned as the need arises. However, this also provides more limited oversight of the process by the court or state agency.

Mixed Model   Finally, some states have chosen to employ a model that mixes elements of all the preceding models. This may result from geography—for example, when a state has some urban population areas close to central facilities but also more distant communities.

### B. TRAINING AND CERTIFICATION

All of these models require administrators and managers to consider how to ensure that forensic evaluators are qualified to perform evaluations. As with service models, states differ in the extent to which they provide relevant training or require certification. Frost et al. (2006) reviewed models of training and certification used across the country. Although many states set credential requirements for public sector pre-trial forensic evaluations (such as requiring a doctoral degree, or a specific number of years of experience), only 10 states had formal certification for forensic evaluators. A number of states provided some form of mandatory training for evaluators, although these mostly involved attendance at workshops or continuing education. Massachusetts (Fein et al., 1991; Frost et al., 2006) has the most intensive training and certification system, which involves attendance at workshops, supervision of forensic evaluations, a written examination, and review of work samples. Related to certification is developing a system for quality assurance. This may involve peer review or external review of selected reports (e.g., Packer & Leavitt, 1998).

Forensic psychologists in the public sector often become involved in both direct supervision, as well as system development. The literature on quality of forensic evaluations and systems issues provides a knowledge base on which to draw. The most effective model for delivery of forensic mental health services, as well as training and quality assurance for evaluations, will depend on the specific circumstances in each jurisdiction.

# PART III

# Foundational Competencies

# SEVEN

# Ethics

The very nature of forensic work, with its interface with the legal system, creates unique ethical challenges for psychologists practicing in this arena. The legal context in which forensic psychologists practice differs significantly from therapeutic contexts. Greenberg and Shuman (1997) identified 10 significant differences between therapeutic and forensic practice (*see* Table 7.1). In addition, forensic psychologists must deal with pressures from the legal system, which has a very different set of ethical standards. The legal system is an adversarial one, in which each side presents its version of facts and interpretation. Lawyers are not required to provide an even-handed account but, rather, bring forward the arguments that support their side and leave it to the opposing attorney to provide the evidence for the opposing side. Thus, forensic psychologists must be particularly vigilant about maintaining objectivity while providing services within a system based on adversarial advocacy.

In recognition of these issues, the American Psychological Association (APA), in its 1992 version of the *Ethical Principles of Psychologists and Code of Conduct* (APA, 1992) devoted a separate section to "Forensic Activities." In the most recent version (APA, 2002), the issues related to forensic practice were incorporated into the established standards. This change represented a recognition that although there are specific manifestations of ethical issues that arise in forensic practice, they constitute variations on the ethical principles that apply to all psychological practice. The American Psychology-Law Society (AP-LS) and the American Academy of Forensic Psychology (AAFP) developed Specialty Guidelines for Forensic Psychologists, hereafter referred to as SGFP (Committee on Ethical Guidelines for Forensic Psychologists, 1991), to provide more specific guidance on how forensic psychologists can apply the ethical principles of psychology to forensic practice. These

TABLE 7.1 **Differences Between Forensic and Therapeutic Roles**

1. Whose client is patient/litigant
2. The relational privilege that governs disclosure in each relationship
3. The cognitive set and evaluative attitude of each expert
4. The differing areas of competency of each expert
5. The nature of the hypotheses tested by each expert
6. The scrutiny applied to the information utilized in the process and the role of historical truth
7. The amount and control of structure in each relationship
8. The nature and degree of adversarialness in each relationship
9. The goal of the professional in each relationship
10. The impact on each relationship of critical judgment by the expert

*Greenberg and Shuman (1997).*

guidelines are currently under revision (draft version available at http://www.ap-ls.org/aboutpsychlaw/SpecialtyGuidelines.php).

The ethical concerns that are frequently raised in forensic practice include the following areas:

- Definitions of "the client"
- Role boundaries
- Maintaining objectivity
- Minimizing harm to examinees
- Psychological testing in forensic settings
- Boundaries of competence

This chapter begins by discussing the categories of ethical issues raised specifically in forensic practice and providing examples of how these issues are addressed by the APA Code of Conduct and the SGFP. We then present vignettes of ethical conflicts that arise when one is providing forensic psychological services.

## I. Defining the Client

In clinical psychological practice, the client is the individual, family, or group who is being treated or evaluated. However, in forensic practice, the examinee is not the psychologist's client; rather, the client is either the court, attorney, or entity (such as a school system or an insurance company) that has retained the psychologist. This important distinction changes the nature of the psychologist's relationship with the examinee and also creates additional expectations. It is incumbent upon the psychologist not only to recognize who the client is but to be very explicit with all parties involved about the ramifications.

## A. RELATIONSHIP TO EXAMINEES

Most people think of psychologists as treatment providers whose goal is to help them. In the forensic setting, the psychologist is not performing an evaluation to provide assistance or relief to the examinee but, rather, to provide objective data that will be used for a legal purpose. This significantly impacts the nature of the relationship with the examinee. It is incumbent upon the forensic psychologist not only to maintain an objective stance but also to fully inform the examinee of the nature of the relationship, the limits of confidentiality, and the purpose of the evaluation. This notification is designed to avoid misleading the examinee into thinking that the forensic psychologist is working in his or her interest.

The psychologist is not functioning as a treater, or "helper," but as an evaluator retained by a third party. Even when the psychologist has been retained by the examinee's attorney, it is important to make this distinction. Although the attorney is an advocate for the individual, the psychologist's data and opinions may or may not be beneficial to her, and the psychologist is not motivated to help the examinee prevail in the legal proceeding.

In therapeutic settings, there is an expectation that communications between the client and psychologist will be privileged and kept confidential (with rare exceptions). However, in forensic evaluations, the information obtained may be shared with others, including the opposing party and the court. As the examinee may not be aware of this, there is a risk that he or she will be lulled into a false sense of trust that certain information will be maintained in confidence. Thus, the psychologist should clearly explain, at the outset of the evaluation process, that all statements made by the examinee, as well the psychologist's observations and conclusions, may be shared with the referring party and may be revealed in written and oral testimony.

The last important element to consider is the specific purpose for which the forensic evaluation is being undertaken. Forensic psychologists cannot obtain information for one legal purpose and then subsequently use it for another without explicit permission. The case of *Estelle v. Smith (1981)* provides an excellent example. In that case, Mr. Smith, who was charged with murder, was evaluated for competence to stand trial by a psychiatrist. After he was convicted, the jury had to decide whether to impose the death penalty or life in prison. At the sentencing hearing, the psychiatrist who had conducted the competence evaluation testified about Mr. Smith's potential dangerousness (an aggravating factor relative to the death penalty). The U.S. Supreme Court ruled that this testimony was inadmissible because Mr.Smith had not been informed at the time of the interview that the evaluation could also be used at the sentencing phase. Although this was a legal ruling, it underscores the ethical issue: psychologists need to be candid and clear, at the time of the interview, regarding what the information obtained will be used for. This issue has been squarely addressed in the SGFP (IV.E.3): "After a psychologist has advised the subject of a clinical forensic evaluation of the intended uses of the evaluation and its work product, the psychologist may not use the evaluation work product for other purposes without explicit waiver to do so by the client or the client's legal representative" (pp. 559–560).

## B. COMMUNICATING WITH OTHER PARTIES

As obtaining third-party information is an integral component of forensic evaluations, the psychologist should provide a similar explanation to collateral informants who are contacted. In addition, the psychologist needs to be clear about his or her role, as it may impact the appropriateness of contacting certain parties, including the opposing attorney and the court. If the evaluation has been court-ordered, the order will likely specify who will get the report (i.e., the court, one or both attorneys), and the psychologist should not share the information with parties not specifically authorized. In some jurisdictions, the psychologist must submit the report directly to the court and not to either of the attorneys. In addition, if the psychologist is retained by a defense attorney, then that attorney may not want this fact known to the prosecution. This may limit some of the psychologist's options and may necessitate negotiating with the attorney how to obtain relevant information. For example, the psychologist may need direct information from witnesses, and will then have to coordinate with the attorney regarding how to obtain these data in an appropriate manner.

## C. REPORTING UNETHICAL BEHAVIOR BY AN OPPOSING PSYCHOLOGIST

When the psychologist's client is the attorney retaining him, this can sometimes create a dilemma relative to other elements of the Psychology Code of Conduct. For example, the APA code (1.04) states: "[w]hen psychologists believe that there may have been an ethical violation by another psychologist, they attempt to resolve the issue by bringing it to the attention of that individual, if an informal resolution appears appropriate and the intervention does not violate any confidentiality rights that may be involved." For example, in the context of a forensic evaluation, a psychologist hired by a plaintiff in a personal injury case may become aware of potentially unethical behavior by a colleague retained by the defendant . However, the psychologist has an obligation to the plaintiff's attorney, who may not want the opposing psychologist to be informed prior to cross-examination. In such a circumstance, the psychologist has an obligation to his client (the attorney), which would likely override the obligation to bring the matter to the attention of the colleague at that point. Furthermore, forensic psychologists should be careful not to abuse the ethics complaint process as a means to intimidate opposing experts. In such instances, it may be advisable to wait until the legal case has been resolved before addressing the potential ethical concern.

## II. Dealing With Role Boundaries

### A. DUAL-ROLE RELATIONSHIPS

Psychologists are advised to avoid dual-role relationships in forensic contexts whenever possible, as potential conflicts of interest and threats to objectivity can arise in such circumstances. Objectivity is important for the integrity and validity of the forensic evaluation process. Thus, accepting a role as a forensic evaluator for an individual with whom the psychologist has a personal relationship is fraught with difficulties. More typical, however, is a situation in which the psychologist may have multiple professional roles with the examinee. This can occur in contexts in which the psychologist has served in a therapeutic role and is subsequently asked to perform a forensic evaluation. The roles and responsibilities that attach to a therapeutic relationship are inherently different from, and in opposition to, the stance required for a forensic evaluation (e.g., Greenberg & Shuman, 2007; Strasburger, Gutheil, & Brodsky, 1997).

The SGFP and the APA Code of Conduct note the problems with dual-role relationships but recognize that there are circumstances in which such relationships are unavoidable. For example, the SGFP includes the following (IV.D. 2.): "When it is necessary to provide both evaluation and treatment services to a party in a legal proceeding (as may be the case in small forensic hospital settings or small communities), the forensic psychologist takes reasonable steps to minimize the potential negative effects of these circumstances on the rights of the party, confidentiality, and the process of treatment and evaluation" (p. 659). Similar issues arise when a mental health or medical emergency requires the forensic psychologist to provide therapeutic services. This can occur, for example, if an examinee is deemed to be imminently suicidal and in need of hospitalization. The need to take immediate action will trump the forensic evaluation role; the psychologist would then need to consider whether continuation in the forensic role is still feasible.

### B. MAINTAINING INDEPENDENCE FROM THE RETAINING PARTY

Forensic psychologists are often retained by one side in an adversarial process. Lawyers will often refer to the retained psychologist at "their witness" and may consider her as part of their "team." However, based on the need for objectivity, the forensic psychologist is independent of the legal team, even if they are working together. This does not mean that the psychologist should refrain from working closely with the attorney to prepare for testimony, including effective means of presentation. However, the psychologist's role is to provide information to the trier of fact, while the lawyer's job is to "win" the case. This distinction is articulated in the SGFP (VII.D), which states that although forensic psychologists are obligated to present testimony fairly, "[t]his principle does not preclude forceful representation of the data and reasoning upon which a conclusion or professional product is based." Thus, psychologists can strategize about the most effective means of presenting testimony, but should not do so by engaging in " partisan attempts to avoid, deny, or subvert the presentation of evidence contrary to their own position" (p. 664). This is particularly relevant because the judicial system is an adversarial one, with each side presenting its case, without an obligation to present a balanced picture. Psychological ethics, however, do require acknowledgment of all the data, even those contrary to the position being taken.

## C. ULTIMATE ISSUE TESTIMONY

Another aspect of maintaining role boundaries relates to whether forensic psychologists should testify as to the ultimate legal issue (e.g., whether child custody should be awarded to the mother or father, whether a juvenile meets criteria for transfer to adult court, whether a criminal defendant is competent to stand trial, etc.). This is a controversial issue in the field, with articulate arguments having been made for both sides of the issue (e.g., Rogers & Ewing, 2003; Tillbrook, Mumley, & Grisso, 2003). The opponents of providing such opinions argue that the ultimate issue is a legal or moral one, which the trier of fact decides. Although the forensic psychologist provides relevant data, giving an ultimate opinion impinges on the role of the judge or jury. Advocates for providing ultimate issue opinions argue that psychologists do not usurp the role of the trier of fact, as they are providing their opinion, which the jury or judge can choose to accept or reject. They also point to practical problems that arise when experts decline to offer such opinions, including confusion for the jury and making it more difficult to understand how the psychological expertise relates to the legal issue at hand.

The SGFP (VII.F.) does not take a position on provision of ultimate issue testimony but does clarify the role of the forensic psychologist by noting that "professional observations, inferences, and conclusions must be distinguished from legal facts, opinions, and conclusions. Forensic psychologists are prepared to explain the relationship between their expert testimony and the legal issues and facts of an instant case" (p. 665). Importantly, this highlights the distinction between the clinical data and the psycholegal opinion. Thus, regardless of whether the forensic psychologist includes an ultimate opinion, the standard is to clearly articulate the data underlying the opinion and how the data support that opinion. Even when psychologists are willing to offer ultimate opinions, they do so only when the data are adequate to support such an opinion. When the data are missing or ambiguous, forensic psychologists should refrain from offering an ultimate opinion, as doing so would involve going beyond the data and thus exceeding the bounds of the psychologist's expertise.

## III. Maintaining Objectivity

### A. PERSONAL VALUES

A central value of forensic evaluation is the need to provide information to the legal system in an objective manner. The issues of identifying who the client is and clarifying role boundaries relate to this issue as well. However, threats to objectivity can arise from other factors as well, including personal values or beliefs, and the nature of the case. In such circumstances, psychologists are advised to consider whether they are capable of maintaining involvement in the case without threatening a fair and objective evaluation.

Capital cases (i.e., criminal cases in which the defendant is facing the death penalty) provide one example of this issue. Although professional ethical guidelines do not prohibit evaluations in capital cases (e.g., Eisenberg, 2004), individual psychologists may face an ethical dilemma. For example, if the psychologist has a strong conviction against the death penalty, and is morally opposed to its imposition under any circumstances, he or she may not feel comfortable providing objective data that may be used by the jury to impose the death sentence. In other cases, a psychologist may have such strong, negative attitudes toward a defendant charged with a particularly heinous crime (such as rape and murder of a child) that he or she would feel incapable of offering testimony that would be advantageous to the defendant, if evidence to that effect were to arise. In such circumstances, the responsibility is on the individual psychologist to consider whether to avoid accepting certain types of cases.

### B. CONTINGENCY FEES

In some types of cases (such as personal injury lawsuits), an attorney may work on a contingency basis. This means that the plaintiff does not pay the attorney directly, but rather the attorney will be reimbursed from monetary damages awarded if the plaintiff wins the lawsuit. This is standard and within the bounds of ethical practice in the legal profession.

However, the forensic psychologist retained to perform an evaluation in the case cannot enter into a similar arrangement. The APA Code of Conduct (3.06) states: "Psychologists refrain from taking on a professional role when personal, scientific, professional, legal, financial, or other interests or relationships could reasonably be expected to impair their objectivity, competence, or effectiveness in performing their functions as psychologists." The SGFP also specifically addresses this issue (IV.B.): "Forensic psychologists do not provide professional services to parties to a legal proceeding on the basis of 'contingent fees,' when those services involve the offering of expert testimony to a court or administrative body, or when they call upon the psychologist to make affirmations or representations intended to be relied upon by third parties" (p. 659). The principle is that the forensic psychologist would have a conflict of interest in such circumstances because if the psychologist's opinion were not favorable to the plaintiff, then the psychologist would not be reimbursed. The requirement to provide an objective, fair evaluation would be compromised by the psychologist's financial incentive driven by the outcome.

This is an example of the difference between the ethos of the legal system and that of psychology. The attorney's role is clearly defined as an advocate for the client, with an obligation to obtain a favorable outcome for the client. The forensic psychologist, by contrast, although having an obligation to the client (in this case, the attorney) to provide a competent service, is bound to do so in an impartial manner. The psychologist needs to arrive at an opinion that is based on the data, regardless of whether it is beneficial or harmful to the attorney's legal argument.

## IV. Minimizing Harm to Examinees

The first principle of the APA Code of Conduct (2003) is "Beneficence and Nonmaleficence." It states, in part: "Psychologists strive to benefit those with whom they work and take care to do no harm. In their professional actions, psychologists seek to safeguard the welfare and rights of those with whom they interact professionally..." (Principle A). The forensic arena—particularly in criminal cases—offers many instances in which psychologists confront this principle.

### A. INCLUSION OF INFORMATION IN REPORTS AND ORAL COMMUNICATION

Although, as noted above, the examinee is not the forensic psychologist's client, this does not mean that there is no obligation to that individual. Although the psychologist is required to be objective and include information that may be detrimental to the individual, this does not mean that all information obtained should be included in the report.

Often, in the context of a thorough evaluation, information is obtained that may be personally embarrassing to the individual or could create legal problems unrelated to the current evaluation (e.g., report of previously undetected crimes). Inclusion of such information in a report could be damaging to the individual's welfare, while fulfilling no obligation or expectation associated with the psychologist's role. Therefore, inclusion of such information risks causing harm unnecessarily. This concept is embodied in SGFP (Section VI.F.2): "With respect to evidence of any type, forensic psychologists avoid offering information from their investigations or evaluations that does not bear directly upon the legal purpose of their professional services and that is not critical as support for their product, evidence or testimony, except where such disclosure is required by law" (p. 662). In determining whether to include a particular piece of information in a report, the forensic psychologist should consider whether the data are relevant to the specific legal issue being determined. Does the particular datum provide useful information on an aspect of the case that will inform the relevant opinion? The answer to this question can be used to help guide the decision about whether to include the data in the report.

A related issue involves pre-trial evaluations of criminal defendants for competence to stand trial. Often, those defendants will appear for a trial at a later time, once they are found competent. Therefore, there is the risk that statements they make to the examiner about the offense—often self-incriminating—could be used against them at their later trial. Most states (and federal law) prohibit the later use (at the trial on guilt) of such information from competence evaluations (e.g., Federal Rules of Procedure, 12.2 (c)). Yet there are ways in which the inclusion of self-incriminating statements in the competence report can influence later events. For example, release of this information to the prosecution may result in discovery of other evidence that could be inculpating (known as "fruits of the statement"). This would create an ethical problem, because the defendant's participation in a competence evaluation could result in the development of evidence that could be used for conviction. Thus, the SGFP specifically cautions forensic psychologists in these circumstances to "avoid including statements from the defendant relating to the time period of the alleged offense" (IV.G.1, p. 663).

## B. PUBLIC STATEMENTS

Forensic work is often conducted in a public forum. Most proceedings are open to the public, and some cases may garner media attention. In these cases, after the psychologist has testified, she may be faced with media requests for interviews. Such requests should be responded to carefully. Ethical guidelines do not prohibit talking to the media, and there may be important goals served by making such statements (such as education of the public, correction of misconceptions). But in doing so, one must protect information that is private, confidential, or privileged. For example, the psychologist may have obtained information from the examinee or made observations that were not included in the oral testimony, and those statements would still be protected. In the context of a media interview, it may be difficult to strictly adhere to the distinction between information that is already in the public domain and information that is still subject to expectations of confidentiality.

## C. RECORD KEEPING

The legal context may require heightened attention to issues of maintaining records. Because the psychologist's data are likely to be used as a basis for a legal determination, it is important to preserve the data in a form that can be discovered by all authorized parties. This includes notes taken as part of the evaluation, including third-party informants, testing, consultations, and any audio or videotaping that was undertaken. The forensic psychologist should be mindful that any documents created, including notes, might eventually have to made accessible to anyone in a legal proceeding who has a right to examine or cross-examine based on that material.

The nature of the legal process also often entails maintaining records for longer periods of time than would be necessary in clinical practice. There are sometimes long lags between the time an evaluation was conducted and the time that the case comes to trial. Furthermore, even after a legal proceeding has been completed, there may be appeals, which can take many years to resolve. Although there are no specific timelines that govern this matter, forensic psychologists consider the importance and relevance of their records in determining the length of time to preserve them. Destroying or deleting records prematurely may harm the parties involved by precluding their ability to pursue legal remedies.

## D. CAPITAL PUNISHMENT CASES

Evaluations of whether an inmate is competent to be executed is a clear example of forensic psychologists confronting the obligation of not doing harm. The Supreme Court has determined (*Ford v. Wainwright,*1986; *Panetti v.Quarterman, 2007*) that it is unconstitutional (cruel and unusual punishment) to execute mentally ill defendants who are so impaired as to not appreciate why they are being subject to the death penalty. Forensic psychologists thus may be called on to evaluate a death row inmate to determine whether he or she is competent to be executed. Some commentators have questioned whether participation in such an evaluation should be considered unethical, because a finding of competence is equivalent to imposing a death sentence, whereas others have pointed out that a blanket professional refusal to do such evaluations would probably result in the execution of some persons who were not discovered to have been incompetent (e.g., Leong et al., 1993). Given these conflicting views, there is no clear consensus in the field, and individual psychologists need to make personal decisions about their involvement in such cases. The decision may be influenced by how the psychologist defines his or her role in the case; some psychologists may draw a distinction between providing clinical data to the court to allow a legal decision versus providing an opinion that the individual is either competent or not competent to be executed (*see* section above on Ultimate Issue Testimony).

## V. Psychological Testing in Forensic Cases

### A. APPROPRIATE USE OF TESTING

As in all psychological assessments, it is important to use "assessment instruments whose validity and reliability have been established for use with members of the population tested" (APA Code, 9.02(b)). In forensic settings, the stakes for examinees are high, thus creating a heightened sensitivity to the proper use of psychological tests. The legal system has recognized this issue, and courts have established stringent standards for admissibility of techniques and methodologies offered as evidence in trials (e.g., *Frye v. U.S.,1923; Daubert v. Merrell Dow, 1993; Kumho Tire v. Carmichael, 1999*). Thus, some instruments that may have some utility in a clinical context would be deemed not to be sufficiently reliable and valid as to be used in forensic settings (e.g., Archer, Buffington-Vollum, Stredny, & Handel, 2006; Lally, 2003).

### B. RELEASE OF PSYCHOLOGICAL TEST DATA AND RESULTS

The principle of maintaining the integrity of psychological testing can come into conflict with the rights of parties in legal proceedings to examine the bases for all opinions offered. Thus, although ideally psychological test data would be released to a qualified psychologist retained by an attorney, courts may order the test released directly to an attorney. In such circumstances, psychologists must comply with the order but can take precautions to protect test integrity. The APA Ethical Principles of Psychologists and Code of Conduct distinguishes between test data (the individual's responses and the psychologist's documented observations or ratings) and test materials (the manuals, instruments, protocols, and test questions or stimuli). Release of the latter is more likely to compromise test security; therefore, psychologists should make all reasonable efforts to provide the attorney with the test data, without releasing the test materials. If a judge nonetheless orders release of the materials, the psychologist would have no choice but to comply. This is consistent with principle 1.02 of the APA Code, which states: "If psychologists' ethical responsibilities conflict with law, regulations, or other governing legal authority, psychologists make known their commitment to the Ethics Code and take steps to resolve the conflict. If the conflict is unresolvable via such means, psychologists may adhere to the requirements of the law, regulations, or other governing legal authority."

A related issue arises when an attorney requests to be present during testing or asks that a recording (audio and/or video) be made. In some instances, the court will order compliance with such requests. Such arrangements can raise concerns about test integrity. Furthermore, concerns have been raised about the impact of such arrangements on test validity (Committee on Psychological Tests and Assessment, 2007). Forensic psychologists should inform the court of any concerns raised and attempt to work out an arrangement that is mutually satisfactory (e.g., if the testing is videotaped, arranging for the camera not to focus on the test materials).

### C. EXPLANATION OF TEST RESULTS TO EXAMINEE

The APA Code of Conduct specifically endorses the principle that it is desirable to explain the results of all tests given to the individual who was tested. However, an explicit provision is made in the code for exceptions, which include forensic evaluations (9.10). This does not mean that forensic psychologists are exempt from the principle, but it acknowledges that in some forensic evaluations, explanation of the results to the party may be precluded or contra-indicated. For example, the party retaining the psychologist may have specifically stipulated that the results are not to be shared with the party. In other instances, security concerns may dictate that the psychologist not inform the examinee. Thus, forensic psychologists need to be aware of the specific requirements in each case and proceed accordingly. When there are no contra-indications, the best practice is to share the results with the examinee.

## VI. Boundaries of Competence

### A. OBTAINING ADEQUATE KNOWLEDGE AND SKILLS

The APA Code of Conduct provides that psychologists should be careful to offer services only in areas in which they have attained competence. There is also a specific reference (2.01.(f)) to forensic work: "When assuming forensic roles, psychologists are or become reasonably familiar with the judicial or administrative rules governing their roles."

In addition to this requirement to obtain knowledge of the legal rules, psychologists practicing in the legal arena need to familiarize themselves with both the legal and psychological concepts that pertain to their areas of practice (Chapter 2). Research on the quality of forensic reports (as discussed in Chapter 6) demonstrates that often psychologists have engaged in forensic work without adequate training, with negative outcomes (poor quality of reports). Given the high volume of cases and the relative dearth of training programs to date (Packer, 2008), some psychologists may be induced to conduct forensic evaluations without an adequate foundation. In addition, forensically trained psychologists should take care to practice only in those forensic areas in which they have adequate clinical expertise. For example, a forensic psychologist with excellent training working with adults may not necessarily have the requisite knowledge and skills to provide forensic evaluations of juveniles (SGFP, III.A.).

## B. ADEQUATE BASES FOR ASSESSMENT

Even when psychologists are competent to practice within a particular area, they need to attend to ensuring that they have used appropriate methods and have obtained sufficient data to address the psycholegal issue. The APA code specifically states: "Psychologists base the opinions contained in their recommendations, reports, and diagnostic or evaluative statements, including forensic testimony, on information and techniques sufficient to substantiate their findings" (9.01(a). In some circumstances, the nature of the evaluation is such that psychologists are asked for an opinion when an individual examination is not possible (e.g., in a retrospective analysis of a deceased's *testamentary capacity*, or ability to make a competent will). In other cases, access may be difficult to obtain (e.g., refusal of a party to be interviewed). Both the APA Code of Conduct and the SGFP address this issue, recommending that "forensic psychologists make every reasonable effort" to conduct an examination of an individual being assessed (SGFP,VI.H.). When, despite such efforts, the examination cannot be conducted, "psychologists document the efforts they made and the result of those efforts, clarify the probable impact of their limited information on the reliability and validity of their opinions, and appropriately limit the nature and extent of their conclusions or recommendations" (APA Code, 9.01(b)).

## VII. Some Case Vignettes

*Case Example 1: Defendant Does Not Understand the Warning*

A forensic psychologist has been appointed by the court to evaluate a defendant for a criminal responsibility evaluation. At the initiation of the session, the psychologist informs the defendant that the purpose of the interview is to provide a report to the court and to both attorneys (prosecution and defense), which could be used to determine whether he meets criteria for legal insanity. She takes care to explain to him that she is not there to provide treatment but to provide an objective evaluation for the court. Nevertheless, when she asks him for his understanding, he persists in stating that she is there to help him. She thus concludes that he does not comprehend the nature of the evaluation. Can she proceed with the interview?

> As the evaluation has been court-ordered, the psychologist could proceed with the interview, noting in her report that the defendant did not understand the nature of the process (and thus preserving the issue for an ultimate legal determination by the judge). However, the best practice would be for the psychologist to contact the defense attorney, notify him of the issue, and obtain his guidance. If the attorney agrees that the evaluation should proceed, then the psychologist can do so and note this in the report. If the attorney objects, the psychologist could notify the judge and respond as directed (SGFP IV.E. 2.). In this manner, the psychologist is able to comply with the order from the court but to do so in a manner that takes into consideration the defendant's rights.

*Case Example 2: Providing Information to the Prosecuting Attorney in a Criminal Case*

A forensic psychologist has been hired by the prosecuting attorney to evaluate a criminal defendant for the purpose of assessing criminal responsibility. The evaluation is requested after a defense expert has conducted an interview but prior to the defense formally asserting an intention to proceed with an insanity defense. As part of the evaluation, the psychologist obtains the defendant's account of the offense and then shares this information with the prosecutor prior to submitting a report. Did the psychologist act appropriately in sharing these data?

The appropriate response may depend on the jurisdiction in which the psychologist is practicing. However, in some states, statements offered by the defendant are protected until such time as the defense formally asserts the insanity defense in court (which may very well be after the evaluation was conducted). Indeed, the American Bar Association's Criminal Justice Standards (Standard 7–3.4) specifically recommends that forensic evaluators not be permitted to share such information prior to the defense providing notice of proceeding with an insanity defense, which will rely on testimony of a mental health expert. Thus, the psychologist should determine the rules in his jurisdiction and act accordingly (SGFP, VI.G.1.). This type of dilemma was captured in the case of *Commonwealth v. Stroyny* (2002), in which a psychiatrist revealed to the prosecutor, prior to the defendant affirmatively asserting that he would proceed with a defense of not guilty by reason of insanity, specific incriminating statements made by the defendant. The court found that the defendant's rights had thus been violated. Although the court put most of the *legal* onus on the prosecutor, this is an example of the need for forensic evaluators to become informed of the defendant's legal rights and to act accordingly.

### Case Example 3: Custody Evaluator Becomes Treater

A psychologist has been appointed by the court to conduct a child custody evaluation. The psychologist conducts a thorough evaluation of all parties involved and recommends that the parents be appointed joint custody and that the child be referred for individual therapy to aid her in dealing with the stresses brought about by the divorce. The judge accepts the recommendations, and both parents then ask the psychologist if she would agree to provide the therapy, as the child seemed very comfortable with her. Should the psychologist agree to become the child's therapist?

This situation raises questions of multiple roles for the psychologist. Had the psychologist been providing treatment prior to the custody battle, it would have been very problematic if she had then agreed to take on the role of forensic evaluator. In that situation, the psychologist's role as a therapist would have conflicted with the need to be an objective, impartial evaluator.

However, once the legal case has been resolved, her previous objective role does not necessarily prevent her from adopting a therapeutic stance with the child. Nonetheless, she should consider the following in determining whether she can shift roles: *(1)* whether all parties understand that by her accepting the child as a client, she would not be available in the future to become involved in any further legal proceedings involving the family (e.g., if one of the parents wanted to change the custody arrangement); and *(2)* whether the evaluation process resulted in tension with one or both of the parents that could interfere with the child's treatment. After weighing these factors, the psychologist could then determine whether she feels that she could fulfill her responsibilities without compromising her role as the child's therapist.

### Case Example 4: Attorney Wants Changes in the Report

A forensic psychologist has been retained by plaintiff's attorney in a personal injury case. The psychologist submits a draft report to the attorney, who requests that he make some changes to the report, specifically: *(1)* changing the sentence, "she was fired from a job at an insurance company" to "she was laid off from a job," as the attorney has documentation that the job termination was the result of budget cuts and not the plaintiff's job performance; and *(2)* omitting a reference to the plaintiff's arrest on DUI charges that occurred when she was a teenager, because this could be used by the defendant to portray her as a substance abuser prior to the accident that precipitated the lawsuit. Can the psychologist make the changes requested?

When attorneys request changes in reports, the forensic psychologist needs to consider whether complying will result in distortion or misrepresentation of the data (SGFP, VII.D.). In this example, there is a significant difference between the two suggested changes. The first change reflects a possible factual error. If the psychologist can verify that the attorney's account is factual, then making the change would constitute a more accurate presentation of the data and would be advisable. However, the second change reflects an attempt to hide information that is accurate but is disadvantageous to the plaintiff. Complying with this request would place the psychologist in the role of a partisan advocate for the retaining attorney, rather than an independent, impartial expert. SGFP VII.D. explicitly states: "Forensic psychologists do not, by either commission or omission, participate in a misrepresentation of their evidence, nor do they participate in partisan attempts to avoid, deny, or subvert the presentation of evidence contrary to their own position." In this example, the information that the attorney wants to delete could be specifically relevant to the issue at hand and thus its exclusion would result in distortion of the data. If the psychologist determines that the DUI charge was not indicative of a significant pattern of substance abuse, he should address that point directly in the report.

### Case Example 5: Attorney Asks to Defer Payment

A forensic psychologist is contacted by an attorney for the plaintiff in a sexual harassment case. The attorney would like the psychologist to evaluate her client to assess whether she suffers from depression, the degree of her functional impairment, recommendations for treatment, and prognosis. The attorney explains that she will pay the psychologist regardless of the outcome of the case, but would like to defer payment until after the case is completed because of cash-flow issues. Can the psychologist accept this arrangement?

As discussed above [p. 126], forensic psychologists cannot accept contingency fees (i.e., payment based on the outcome of the case), as doing so would compromise the integrity and objectivity of the evaluation process. The situation presented here does not constitute a contingency fee, as the attorney explicitly stated that she would pay the psychologist's fees regardless of who prevails in the legal case. Nonetheless, this does have the potential to pressure the psychologist to arrive at an opinion favorable to the retaining attorney. The psychologist could be subtly influenced by the idea that the attorney is more likely to be able to pay if she prevails in the case and thus obtains a large payment. Thus, the psychologist would be well-advised to be cautious about entering into this arrangement.

## Case Example 6: Shredding Documents

A psychologist has a full-time private forensic practice, conducting hundreds of evaluations a year. His standard practice is to take copious hand-written notes of all of his interviews, compose a written report based on those notes, and then discard his notes once the report is submitted. This helps him reduce filing space, and he contends that all of the relevant information from his notes has been incorporated in the report. Is this practice problematic?

> The SGFP, VI.B. states: "Forensic psychologists have an obligation to document and be prepared to make available, subject to court order or the rules of evidence, all data that form the basis for their evidence or services. The standard to be applied to such documentation or recording anticipates that the detail and quality of such documentation will be subject to reasonable judicial scrutiny; this standard is higher than the normative standard for general clinical practice." Because all parties to the proceedings have an expectation that *all* the data that inform the forensic opinion will be subject to examination, deletion of the raw data can be problematic. Although it is true that forensic psychologists typically condense their notes into a report that conveys what they consider the relevant information, the attorneys involved may have different interpretations of the data or may even question the accuracy of some of it. If these data, such as notes, are no longer available, the parties' rights to fully cross-examine may be violated. Furthermore, evaluators choose specific quotes to include in their reports and those to omit, and the attorneys have a right to question why other quotes were not used. Although this can make cross-examination more difficult, this does not justify withholding the data. Thus, the psychologist's practice, although acceptable in a clinical context, does not adequately meet the higher standard required for forensic practice.

## Case Example 7: Evaluating Only Some Parties in a Custody Evaluation

A forensic psychologist has been appointed by the court to evaluate parents and their 10-year-old daughter in a child custody case. She interviews and tests the daughter and the mother individually and then interviews them jointly. She attempts to schedule an evaluation of the father as well as a conjoint interview with the father and daughter, but the father is not available to be interviewed within the time frame set by the court for the evaluation to be completed. The psychologist contacts the court, asking for additional time to complete the evaluation, but the judge does not grant this request. Based on the information obtained, the psychologist submits a report describing the mother as being emotionally stable, having a good relationship with the daughter, marked by closeness as well as ability to set appropriate boundaries. Furthermore, as the judge has specifically requested an opinion on which parent should be granted custody of the daughter, the psychologist recommends that the mother be granted sole custody. Should the psychologist have declined to submit a report because of her inability to evaluate the father?

Both the APA Code and the SGFP address the issue of providing evaluations without complete data. Although psychologists are advised to make "reasonable" attempts to obtain the necessary data, there are circumstances under which this is simply not possible. In this vignette, the psychologist appears to have attempted to evaluate the father but was not able to do so. Furthermore, she contacted the judge and attempted to extend the deadline to conduct the necessary interviews, but this request was denied by the judge. Thus, the psychologist appropriately submitted a report. However, she exceeded the scope of the data by providing an opinion that sole custody should be awarded to the mother. Her data suggested that the mother was a fit parent and the psychologist could have clearly articulated for the court the basis for the conclusions about the mother's suitability. However, she did not have adequate data to compare the mother's fitness with the father's, which was a crucial element in the legal decision. Thus, the psychologist should have explicitly stated in the report that she could offer an opinion about the mother's fitness but could not provide an opinion about which parent should be granted custody.

This vignette also raises questions about ultimate issue opinions. As discussed above (p. 124), there are differences of opinions about whether forensic psychologists should provide an opinion regarding the ultimate legal issue (in this case, which parent should be awarded custody), even when all the relevant data have been obtained. However, proponents of providing such opinions would agree that it was not justified in this case, because the data obtained were not sufficient to answer the court's question.

# EIGHT

# Interpersonal Dimensions of the Forensic Relationship

Although forensic evaluations require psychologists to employ the basic knowledge and skills they have developed as clinicians, the legal context changes the dynamics of the relationship between the forensic psychologist and the parties being evaluated. As discussed in Chapter 6, training in forensic psychology builds on a foundation of general clinical training. Indeed, many forensic psychologists have practices in which they provide both clinical and forensic services. Thus, when they enter the forensic arena, they are required to adopt an orientation toward the examinee that conflicts with the mindset they have traditionally held. This chapter will begin with a focus on those elements that characterize the nature of the forensic psychologist's relationship to examinees, emphasizing the different orientation required relative to therapeutic work. We then move on to discuss issues of cultural diversity that specifically impact forensic evaluations, followed by a description of the interpersonal dynamics that forensic psychologists have with other parties, including collateral informants, attorneys, and the trier of fact (judge or jury).

## I. Relationship to Examinees

### A. IDENTIFYING THE CLIENT

In therapeutic contexts, it is clear that the client is the individual seeking treatment. However, in forensic evaluations, the individual being evaluated is not the psychologist's client; rather, the client is the referral source, which may be a court (when the evaluation is being requested by the judge), an attorney (one of the sides in an adversarial proceeding), or an insurance company (in cases of disability evaluations). This crucial feature of forensic psychological evaluations impacts the nature of the interpersonal relationship with the examinee, beginning at the very outset of the process. Prior to beginning the evaluation, the forensic psychologist informs the examinee of the following elements:

- the psychologist is not providing treatment;
- the psychologist is not working on behalf of the examinee;
- who has retained the psychologist;
- the purpose of the evaluation;
- the information provided will not be subject to the usual rules of confidentiality that apply in therapeutic settings;
- with whom the information obtained, and conclusions arrived at, will be shared, including possible testimony.

The most salient part of this initial explanation is that the forensic evaluation differs significantly from the usual circumstances under which an individual may interact with a psychologist. Furthermore, even when the psychologist has been retained by the examinee's attorney, this does not mean that the psychologist is working in the individual's interest. The forensic psychologist's orientation is to collect data to answer the referral question; the conclusions arrived at may, or may not, be beneficial to the examinee. This affects not only the examinee's orientation toward the psychologist but also requires the forensic psychologist to be comfortable with a different mindset than is required for other settings. Psychologists who are health-care providers develop an identity as healers, with an aim to benefit the clients with whom they are working. The treatment relationship is a mutual, cooperative one, in which the psychologist and client are working together to achieve a therapeutic aim. However, in a forensic context, the examinee and the psychologist may have different aims (the examinee may be interested in obtaining a desired outcome, whereas the psychologist is focused on providing an objective assessment relevant to the psycholegal issue).

One of the distinctions between therapeutic and forensic contexts highlighted by Greenberg and Shuman (1997) is the difference in "cognitive set and evaluative attitude." They describe therapists as adopting a supportive, accepting, and empathic stance, contrasted with the neutrality, objectiveness, and more detached stance of the forensic evaluator. Although this is a reasonable "broad brushstroke" description of the different attitudes, in practice the differences are more subtle. Indeed, the forensic evaluator's role is not to be supportive of the examinee, but this does not preclude the use of empathy. Indeed, development of rapport is necessary to obtain relevant clinical information. An extremely detached stance is unlikely to result in obtaining relevant data; indeed, it may distort the data by provoking a more distrustful and affectively distant demeanor from the examinee.

The challenge for the forensic psychologist is to find a balance that allows relevant data to be collected, without abusing rapport-building skills to lead the examinee into a misguided sense of comfort. Shuman (1993) has raised concerns about clinicians using empathy as a tool to extract information from an examinee. Deliberate attempts to "lull" an examinee into a misplaced trust in the forensic psychologist, to extract information, are not appropriate. However, empathizing with the individual, in the sense of understanding his or her perspective and emotional experience, is a valuable and reasonable tool. Empathy does not necessarily translate into sharing that perspective or allying with the examinee's interests. For example, a defendant in a criminal case may describe a pattern of bullying and intimidation by a co-worker, whom he subsequently stabbed. The forensic psychologist's ability to obtain a full, rich account of the defendant's subjective experience related to the victim would be useful and necessary to arrive at a formulation relevant to the underlying psycholegal issue (e.g., an insanity defense or a claim of extreme emotional disturbance [EED]). In this example, the forensic psychologist may offer an opinion that the defendant was not mentally ill as required for the insanity defense, but the defendant's perspective, particularly if corroborated by other sources, may be relevant to EED, which is based on the defendant's subjective point of view.

Another important aspect of the interpersonal interaction inherent in the forensic evaluation relates to the level of scrutiny the forensic psychologist applies to communications from the examinee. In treatment settings, the psychologist works with the data provided by the client, using this information to arrive at therapeutic goals. Confirmation of the historical accuracy of the client's perspective is not necessary, nor often sought. For example, referencing the controversy about recovered memories of abuse, the American Psychological Association (APA) recommended: "Therapists should avoid endorsing such retrievals as either clearly truthful or clearly confabulated. Instead, the focus should be on aiding the client in developing his or her own sense of what is real and truthful" (APA Working Group on Investigation of Memories of Childhood Abuse, 1998, p. 936). In contrast, in forensic evaluations, the accuracy of the individual's memories and reports is frequently a crucial element in arriving at a conclusion that is legally relevant. Therefore, the forensic psychologist seeks to obtain corroborating or disconfirming information from multiple sources. Indeed, use of collateral sources of information, rather than reliance only on clinical data obtained from the examinee, is one of the hallmarks of forensic work.

This reliance on third-party sources also impacts the interpersonal stance taken by the forensic psychologist toward the examinee. The psychologist clearly conveys that he or she is not taking the individual's report at face value by indicating the need to obtain corroboration. The evaluator needs to develop the skill of conveying this stance in a respectful manner— that is, not suggesting *a priori* that the examinee is being untruthful, but explaining the need for confirmation as part of the objective evaluation process.

In addition, forensic evaluations may require the psychologist to adopt an adversarial or confrontational stance with the examinee. This occurs when the psychologist has reason to believe that the individual is providing inaccurate or inconsistent information or is malingering (falsely endorsing symptoms) or dissimulating (concealing genuine symptoms). The assessment of malingering also involves a different orientation with the examinee. The very nature of tests designed to assess for malingering, as well as clinical techniques, requires the psychologist to communicate with the examinee in a manner that is not direct and straightforward. Tests of malingering would not be effective if the psychologist fully informed the individual of the purpose of the test. Instructions typically involve telling examinees that they will be asked some questions and that they should indicate whether these are symptoms they have experienced. It is important for the psychologist to inquire about rare or incongruous symptoms in a matter-of-fact tone, so as not to divulge that these are not genuine manifestations. Some tests designed to assess for malingering of cognitive symptoms often rely on the individual mistakenly believing that the test is more difficult than it really is. (For example, the examinee who is inclined to exaggerate memory problems is more likely to do so on a test that he or she believes is difficult, than one which is perceived as simpler.) Thus, the very nature of the forensic psychological enterprise may involve being less than straightforward with the examinee about the nature of some of the techniques employed.

Forensic psychologists need to develop competency in confronting examinees when they suspect that the examinee is not providing accurate information. This may occur in the context of the clinical interview and/or after reviewing validity tests. If the examinee is to be confronted by inconsistencies, this should be handled in a firm, yet respectful manner. The psychologist should consider both the tone of the confrontation (explaining that there is inconsistent information or that the symptoms described are not typical) and the timing. It is best to delay confrontation until later in the interview process, as it can interfere with the rapport needed to obtain other information. In addition, the psychologist should avoid presenting the feedback in a manner that educates the individual about true symptoms. For example, the psychologist may explain that the testing indicates that the pattern of symptoms reported is not typical for individuals with a genuine disorder. However, it would be inappropriate to specifically state, "You reported hearing voices coming only from your left side, while most people who experience hallucinations report hearing the voices coming from both sides."

### B. RECOGNIZING CULTURAL DIVERSITY

**Clinical Cultural Diversity**   Awareness of, and sensitivity to, racial, ethnic, and cultural differences are essential competencies required of all clinicians. There is a wealth of literature on the impact of these factors on diagnosis of treatment of minority groups. For example, studies have found that African-Americans are more likely than Caucasians to be diagnosed with schizophrenia and less likely to be diagnosed with a mood disorder (e.g., Adebimpe, 1994; Baker & Bell, 1999), and that Latinos are disproportionately given a diagnosis of major depression, compared with European-Americans (e.g., Minsky, Vega, Miskimen, Gara, & Escoba, 2003). In addition, experiences identified in the DSM-IV as psychopathological may represent common beliefs in other cultures. As an example, across a number of cultures there is a widespread belief in communications with, and from, deceased ancestors (e.g., Gaines, 1995). Psychologists need to be aware of this cultural phenomenon to distinguish between a culturally normative experience and one indicative of a mental illness.

In addition to the impact of cultural variables on the description and manifestation of symptoms, there are also influences on the interpersonal stance of the individual toward the psychologist. Individuals from other cultures, as well as minority groups within the United States, may have different expectations of how to interact with authority figures, including psychologists, which may be misinterpreted (e.g., Tseng, Matthews, & Elwyn, 2004). Furthermore, difficulties arise when assessing individuals who do not speak English, and require interpreters (e.g., Kaufert & Putsch, 1997). Subtle nuances of language use, as well as the ability to determine the quality of the communication (e.g., degree of thought disorder), may sometimes get "lost in translation." Psychologists need to develop competency in working with interpreters, including changing the pace and tone of the questions when necessary and establishing clear guidelines with the interpreter.

These issues cut across all specialties of psychology. However, some of these have special significance for forensic psychologists because of the high stakes involved in legal cases and because of the nature of the relationship between the psychologist and the examinee. Misinterpretation of a culturally accepted belief as a sign of mental illness is problematic in a therapeutic relationship; however, over time the clinician can re-assess the diagnosis. Forensic evaluations tend to occur over shorter periods of time, and the consequences of a mistaken diagnosis can have far-reaching implications for the examinee. Furthermore, unlike clinical settings, typically the examinee is not seeking out the psychologist but, rather, has been referred by an attorney or a court. In these circumstances, the forensic psychologist is more likely to be perceived as an authority figure or a state agent, which can play into cultural assumptions that distort the examinee's stance. For example, an examinee may avoid eye contact and be reluctant to share information with the evaluator; this may be interpreted as indicative of paranoia or of deliberate lack of cooperation, when it may represent a deferential or distrustful attitude toward authority based on past experiences. This dynamic applies not only with individuals from different countries but also to minorities within the United States, particularly when the forensic psychologist is from the majority culture (see below regarding racial disparities).

Cultural Diversity in Familiarity With Legal Concepts　The organization, structure, and rules of a legal system are not universal but are developed across cultures and countries. Basic elements of the American jurisprudence system may not be familiar to individuals from other cultures. Among these elements are: the right against self-incrimination; the right to an attorney; trial by jury; and laws related to marriage, divorce, child custody. Tseng et al. (2004) discuss in detail how these cultural differences can be relevant for a variety of forensic evaluations. For example, an evaluation of competence to stand trial includes an assessment of the individual's "rational as well as factual understanding of the proceedings against him" (*Dusky v. United States,* 1960). The forensic psychologist has to be able to tease apart the role of cultural differences from the effects of psychopathology in contributing to impairment in the defendant's understanding of the court process. In the area of marital law, in some cultures only fathers may initiate divorce and may be automatically granted custody of the children (e.g., Chaleby, 2001). These expectations could impact the attitude of the parents in a child custody evaluation.

Racial Disparities Within the Legal System   Within the criminal justice system, minorities are disproportionately represented within prison populations. The rate of incarceration is higher for African-Americans and Latinos than for Caucasians (e.g., Bureau of Justice Statistics, 2009) . In a study in Washington state, Grekin, Jemelka, & Trupin (1994) found that relative to Caucasians, mentally disordered minorities were more likely to be imprisoned than hospitalized.

There have been a limited number of studies of the impact of race on forensic mental health evaluations within the criminal justice system, without a clear pattern emerging. For example, in a study of insanity acquittees in Michigan, there was no difference in the percentage of African-American versus Caucasian defendants recommended as insane by forensic evaluators, although African-Americans were less likely to be referred for a sanity evaluation (Packer, 1987). By contrast, in a large study in Virginia, there was a small but statistically significant difference in percentage of defendants recommended as insane (11.4% for Caucasians, 8.5% for minorities) but no difference in percentages referred for evaluation (Warren et al., 2004). Studies of competency-to-stand-trial evaluations have found that African-Americans were more likely to be adjudicated as incompetent to stand trial (in Alabama; Cooper & Zapf, 2003), and more likely to be referred after a screening at a court clinic for further inpatient evaluations (in Massachusetts; Pinals, Packer, Fisher, & Roy-Bujnowski, 2004).

Given the lack of consistency in the results across these various jurisdictions, the explanation for the differential dispositions of defendants across racial groups is not clear. The differences may result from differences in arrest rates, referral rates for forensic evaluations clinical presentations, and/or clinician bias (e.g., Rogers & Shuman, 2000). Regardless of the reasons, forensic psychologists need to be aware of this disparate treatment and be sensitive to any factors that could influence their clinical assessment and dispositional recommendations.

Race of Victim in Capital Sentencing Cases   The case of *McCleskey v. Kemp* (1987) provides an illustrative example of a study of impact of race on jurors. McCleskey was a Black man convicted in Georgia of murdering a White*

---

* Note: the Baldus study referred to the race of defendants and victims as "Black" and "White," so those terms are used in this section

police officer during the course of a robbery. He was convicted by a jury and sentenced to death. He appealed, claiming that in Georgia, the capital sentencing process was administered in a racially discriminatory manner. To support his claim, he cited a study by Baldus, Woodworth, and Pulaski (1990) that involved an analysis of more than 2,000 murder cases in Georgia during the 1970s. They found that the defendants charged with killing White victims were given the death penalty more often than defendants charged with killing Black victims. Strikingly, the most significant racial variable in their data was the race of the victim, rather than the race of the defendant. They found that defendants charged with killing White victims were given the death penalty in 11% of cases, whereas those charged with killing Black victims were given the death penalty in only 1% of the cases. Overall, 4% of Black defendants were given the death penalty versus 7% of White defendants. These data can be understood in the context of most homicides occurring intraracially (i.e., Black victims were most often killed by Black defendants; thus, Black defendants were less likely to be given the death penalty because their victims were predominantly Black).

McCleskey used these data to argue that the death penalty was being administered unfairly. However, the U.S. Supreme Court was reluctant to accept aggregate social science data and did not overturn his death sentence. They ruled that McCleskey had not shown that there was impropriety in his particular case or that the jury's decision to sentence him to death was based on the victim's race. This case highlighted a basic distinction between social science data (based on aggregated data, and statistically significant findings), and the legal system's focus on the individual case. However, these types of data are important for psychologists who serve as consultants to attorneys in capital punishment cases, both in terms of jury selection as well as developing strategic arguments (*see* Chapter 5 on Consultation).

## II. Relations with Other Participants in the Legal Process

### A. RELATIONSHIP WITH COLLATERAL INFORMANTS

As discussed in Chapter 4, a major feature of forensic evaluations is the need to obtain multiple sources of information. In addition to the clinical interview, it is often necessary to contact third parties who can provide information about the examinee's history and functioning. In addition, in criminal cases it may be necessary to obtain more specific details related to the alleged offense from witnesses and/or police officers. Although for many evaluations the psychologist is not required to obtain consent of the examinee to contact third parties, in most cases it is good practice, to maintain good rapport, to inform the examinee that the parties will be contacted.

The nature of the relationship between the forensic psychologist and a third-party source is quite different than the relationship with examinees. The psychologist is in a position of requesting that the individual voluntarily provide information that may be used in answering the legal question. The individual being contacted has no obligation to provide information to the psychologist and in some instances may have no interest in doing so. Furthermore, the collateral may not fully understand the psychologist's role. For example, family members may assume that the psychologist is providing treatment to the examinee; others may ask if they can provide information "off the record." The forensic psychologist, therefore, needs to structure the relationship at the outset, by clarifying his or her role and how the information obtained will be used (including clarifying that any information provided may be included in a written report and/or oral testimony). Furthermore, the psychologist should remain mindful that the purpose of the interaction is to obtain factual information from the informant. This requires careful probing and questioning, particularly when the individual offers opinions or conclusions; the psychologist is interested in obtaining the facts and observations that underlie such opinions. This questioning should be done in a respectful manner but may require detailed inquiries and requests for specific examples.

### B. RELATIONSHIP WITH ATTORNEYS

The nature of the initial relationship with the attorneys in a case will depend substantially on the referral source. Forensic psychologists may be retained directly by an attorney for one of the sides in a case. In some instances, the psychologist may be retained by the court (e.g., in child custody evaluations, or in criminal cases). These two scenarios will have different implications for the manner in which the psychologist relates to the attorneys. When the forensic psychologist is appointed as the court's expert, he or she has an impartial relationship with each attorney. However, after the evaluation is completed, the psychologist may be called as a witness by one of the parties, in which case the nature of the relationship may change (*see* below, section on Testimony).

When retained by an attorney for one side in a legal proceeding, forensic psychologists need to be mindful of structuring the relationship at the time of the initial contact. The attorney will likely attempt to explain to the psychologist the purpose of the evaluation and often will convey his or her approach to the case. This may or may not be a deliberate attempt by the attorney to influence the evaluator, but the psychologist must learn to filter out any "spin." Below are two examples of such an initial interaction.

> *Tort case*: "I am an attorney representing a summer camp that is being sued by the mother of a child who was abused by a former employee, who was fired. The abuse occurred over a 1-month period and was relatively mild. The boy had a history of difficulties prior to coming to camp, had been in therapy, and was prescribed a number of medications. We think it likely that most of his problems relate to early childhood issues and not to the abuse. I am looking for a psychologist to evaluate the boy and review his records."

> *Criminal case*: "I am a prosecuting attorney and am looking for a psychologist to evaluate a defendant charged with attempted murder of a police officer. The defense has obtained an evaluation from a psychologist who claims that the defendant was psychotic at the time, although there was evidence that he was drinking. We have had many cases with this defendant and believe that he is only violent when he drinks, but he continues drinking. I am looking for an evaluation of criminal responsibility, particularly whether it was his intoxication that led to the assault."

In addition to any biasing statements by the attorney, the very nature of the fiscal relationship (i.e., the psychologist is being retained by the attorney) can influence the evaluator's perspective, even if subtly. Zusman and Simon (1983) coined the term *forensic identification* to describe this dynamic. Rogers and Shuman (2000) recommend not discussing initial impressions with the attorney until the evaluation has been completed, to avoid the attorney influencing which data are gathered and/or the opinion formed. In addition, during the initial interaction, the psychologist can reframe the issue in a more neutral manner. Using the examples above, the psychologist can state:

> "I will evaluate the boy to determine his current level of functioning, how he was functioning prior to the abuse, and whether any problems he is having were caused, or exacerbated, by the abuse."

> "I will evaluate the defendant for criminal responsibility and offer an assessment of the contributions of psychosis versus intoxication to the defendant's mental status."

When the evaluation has been completed, the psychologist often contacts the attorney to share his or her findings. At that point, the attorney may or may not want a report produced (i.e., if the psychologist's opinion does not support the attorney's position). If a report is provided, the attorney may want to offer some edits or suggestions. This is another point at which the psychologist needs to be very careful about structuring the relationship with the attorney. The basic principle is that the report must reflect the views of the psychologist, not the attorney. However, some changes may be reasonable if they: *(1)* are minor stylistic or grammatical; *(2)* are based on the attorney's representation that there is an issue of admissibility (i.e., the information is not admissible in court); *(3)* corrects a factual inaccuracy in the original report; or *(4)* the psychologist determines that the change is a reasonable one that does not distort the data or opinion.

Another opportunity for clarifying the nature of the relationship with the attorney occurs in preparation for trial. Some attorneys consider the expert witness to be part of the "team." Most often, if the forensic psychologist is being called to testify, his or her opinion does support the position of the attorney. However, this does not equate to being a member of the "team," or aligning with the attorney's interests. As discussed below (p. 149), the forensic psychologist maintains objectivity on the witness stand. Although the adversarial system allows the attorney to present only data that are supportive of his or her position, the psychologist is ethically bound to report data that might not support the attorney's position (*see* Chapter 7). Thus, the psychologist may need to clarify this distinction with the retaining attorney, explaining the areas in which he or she may not be able to fully support the attorney's position.

This issue also emerges when attorneys request that the evaluator also provide consultation about defense strategy. Ideally, the roles of evaluator and consultant will be kept distinct. The former involves a stance of impartiality, whereas the latter allows the psychologist to work in the interest of the retaining attorney (*see* Chapter 5 Forensic Consultation). The forensic psychologist should explain to the attorney the inconsistency between these two roles and how accepting the dual role would impair his or her objectivity and credibility.

There are other circumstances under which a forensic psychologist may initially be retained in one role (evaluator vs. consultant) and then asked to switch roles. This may occur, for example, when the psychologist informs the attorney that his or her opinion is not consistent with the attorney's position. The attorney may then request that the psychologist consult on other issues, such as cross-examining other witnesses. This change in role is not problematic, as the psychologist will not be testifying, and because the alliance involved with being a consultant did not taint the impartial evaluation.

However, it is much more problematic if the psychologist is initially retained as a consultant (e.g., to review other reports and advise the attorney about the best way to present the case) and is then asked to evaluate the party and testify. In such a case, the initial allegiance to the attorney as a consultant has compromised the psychologist's impartiality; an evaluation conducted at that point would very likely be influenced by the relationship. This can be considered analogous to a situation in which a psychologist who has served as a therapist does not accept a request to function as a forensic evaluator for that client; the dual-role relationship in that circumstance would compromise impartiality and objectivity (e.g., Greenberg & Shuman, 1997; Strasburger, Gutheil, & Brodsky, 1997).

## C. ONE'S RELATION TO THE COURT DURING TESTIMONY

Testifying as an expert witness in court involves a significant role shift for psychologists. In a therapeutic or evaluative setting (including forensic ones), the psychologist is typically in control, can set the ground rules (e.g., instructions for taking a psychological test, format of the therapy session), and structure the nature of the interaction. However, when entering a courtroom, the psychologist enters a different arena in which the rules are set by others, the control is maintained by the attorneys and the judge, and there are limits placed on what the psychologist may say and when.

The relation of the forensic psychologist to the court is influenced by three obligations: obedience to the court's authority, education of the court, and conducting oneself in a manner that assures the court of one's competence (credibility) as a source of information.

Regarding obedience, judicial authority is paramount in any judicial hearing. As explained later, even after the psychologist is on the witness stand, the court may rule that all or part the examiner's testimony will not be heard. The examiner has no "right" to describe her forensic evidence in whatever manner she sees fit. The court operates under a set of rules that is designed to afford due process—not an unbridled search for "the truth" but a revelation of facts and opinions constrained by complex rules of evidence and procedure meant to assure fairness. The examiner must obey the authority of the judge when exercising those rules.

Regarding education of the court, psychologists fulfill their role to the party that is calling them to court and to the court itself when their primary focus is on educating the court regarding their data and opinions. As described later, this requires special attention to constructing their testimony so that nonclinical professionals can clearly understand and use their information.

Regarding credibility, the psychologist's information will not be used or credited in the court's deliberations if it is not believed or trusted. Believability begins with accurate information and a clear logic between data and opinion. But it is influenced also by the psychologist's style and demeanor.

One of the challenges to maintaining credibility is the adversarial systems allowance for aggressive cross-examination techniques designed specifically to discredit one's testimony (e.g., Brodsky, 1991; Brodsky, 1999). Table 8.1 below, adapted from Bank and Packer (2007), categorizes some of the approaches commonly used by attorneys. Psychologists working in clinical settings are less likely to be accustomed to this type of treatment. In a clinical setting, if a client is being challenging or demeaning, this may become grist for the therapeutic mill or may result in the psychologist choosing to end the relationship. However, on the witness stand, the psychologist needs to learn to adapt to these techniques and to nonetheless attempt to convey data and opinions in a clear manner. This involves adopting a certain mindset, which includes: being an educator or consultant; appreciating that attorneys may engage in "showmanship" and not taking the attacks personally; and maintaining composure.

A helpful framework for forensic psychologists functioning as expert witnesses is to recognize that the courtroom is a public forum, consisting of a lay public, rather than fellow mental health professionals. The strength of the data and the validity of the psychologist's analysis are the most important factors in presenting forensic opinions in written reports. However, once called to the witness stand, the psychologist's effectiveness as a witness will also be determined by his or her skills as a persuasive communicator. Bank (2001) describes a Courtroom Communications Model, which applies theory and research on persuasive communication from social psychology to the courtroom setting. This model describes three important elements that contribute to the credibility of an expert witness: expertise, trustworthiness, and presentational style.

TABLE 8.1 **Methods of Discrediting Expert Witnesses**

1. Demonstrating that the witness does not possess the specific expertise needed for the case.
2. Arguing that the methodology used to collect and analyze data is faulty.
3. Claiming that the witness made errors in statements of fact.
4. Noting that the witness made prior statements inconsistent with his or her current courtroom testimony.
5. Portraying the witness as biased (i.e., undermining the trustworthiness dimension of credibility).
6. Attacking the general character of the witness.

*Bank and Packer (2007).*

## III. Elements of Expert Credibility

### A. EXPERTISE

As will be discussed in Chapter 9, the basis for allowing expert testimony is a recognition that the expert has specialized knowledge, beyond the ken of the average juror. Although the legal system is an adversarial one, the expert's role is to provide specialized information and context that is relevant to the legal issue at hand. The first phase of testimony is called *"voir dire"* (literally, "to speak the truth"), in which the witness is questioned about his or her credentials for the judge to determine whether the witness should be qualified as an expert. As the determination is a legal one, it is not the psychologist's role to claim to be an "expert." Rather, the witness lays out his or her credentials, which include foundational training as a psychologist, as well as the relevant (to the case at hand) training and experience he or she has obtained. Presentation of one's credentials in a clear, professional style not only aids the judge in formally recognizing the psychologist as an expert but also contributes to the jurors' perception of the psychologist's expertise. Although the psychologist's responses throughout testimony will be relevant to the jurors' perceptions of his or her expertise, the groundwork for this dimension is laid during the *voir dire*.

*Voir dire* might also raise questions about the foundations for the opinions that the expert will be offering if allowed to testify. Alternatively, this might happen after the expert has been "qualified" by the court, when certain types of data and opinions are being offered in the course of testimony. For example, an opposing attorney might object to the inclusion of data or opinions based on a particular method, raising a challenge to the validity of the method itself.

### B. TRUSTWORTHINESS

Once the psychologist has been recognized as an expert for the purposes of the forensic questions in the present case, the dimension of trustworthiness will have a significant impact on the perception of his or her credibility. The dynamics of the testimonial process involve the retaining attorney engaging in direct examination, in a manner designed to allow the witness to explain his or her methodology, data, and conclusions. This is followed by cross-examination by the opposing attorney, designed to question the validity of the psychologist's data and opinions. The trustworthiness of the witness is enhanced when he or she is not perceived as trying to "help" the cause of the retaining attorney but, rather, is functioning as an educator, explaining to the lay audience the specialized area of expertise.

Furthermore, acknowledging weak points during the direct testimony, rather than waiting for the opposing side to point them out, enhances trustworthiness. The more the expert is seen as independent of the retaining attorney (e.g., by not parroting back answers, but by explaining in depth), the greater the credibility. During cross-examination, the opposing attorney may try to suggest that the witness is biased because he or she was retained and paid by the other side. For example, the expert may be asked how much he or she is being paid for his testimony, suggesting that he or she is a "hired gun." If this point is raised, the witness should clarify that he or she is being paid for his or her time, rather than to produce a particular result (a subtle but important distinction). As with direct testimony, the expert is best-served by maintaining a stance of being an educator, as opposed to an adversary.

Trustworthiness is also influenced by the witness' demeanor. It is comparatively easier to maintain a relaxed, cooperative demeanor when being questioned in a supportive manner under direct examination than it is to do so when being "attacked" under cross-examination. However, dramatic changes in demeanor between direct and cross-examination can undermine the psychologist's trustworthiness by suggesting that he or she is too aligned with one side. In addition, a more confident style during direct, paired with a more hesitant style during cross, can lead jurors to believe that the expert is not being fully candid. Being aware of this natural tendency, expert witnesses can be more mindful during direct examination to adopt a slower, more thoughtful response style to limit the disparity.

Casual observers of a trial may be surprised to see the opposing attorneys, who had been vilifying each other in the courtroom, sharing a laugh or a cordial conversation in the hallway. This dynamic reflects the nature of the adversarial system; in the courtroom, the attorneys may need to play a role to convey their points to the jury (or judge). Psychologists who enter the court as witnesses need to be aware of this process and realize that the same attorney who is lambasting them today may choose to hire them for the next case. The tone and style of cross-examination is usually not a reflection on the witness but, rather, on the strategy that the attorney thinks will be most effective in winning the case. Reminding oneself of this phenomenon can help the witness avoid becoming overly anxious on the stand and maintain a professional demeanor. In addition, attorneys may employ sarcasm, a demeaning attitude, or overt hostility as part of the cross-examination technique. Psychologists need to be aware that responding in kind only undermines their credibility. One of the skills forensic psychologists need to develop is the ability to maintain composure, dignity, and a professional stance, even in the face of behavior by the attorney that does not conform to these standards.

Although Table 8.1 lists a number of the most common cross-examination methods, the specific techniques used by attorneys to discredit witnesses are varied and numerous. Brodsky (1991; 1999) describes a number of these techniques and suggests ways in which to respond to them appropriately. The general message for forensic psychologists who enter the courtroom is to thoroughly prepare, consider the strengths and weaknesses of the conclusions offered, and to anticipate of the substance and style of examination (both direct and cross).

# NINE

# Laws Relevant to the Practice of Forensic Psychology

In Chapter 2 we reviewed the legal basis for the substantive areas of forensic practice. This chapter will focus on the laws related to the practice of psychology, with particular emphasis on those issues that directly impact forensic practitioners. The chapter begins with a broad discussion of laws pertaining to confidentiality and privilege of communications to psychologists as well as their applicability to forensic evaluations. It then focuses on expert witness testimony, including issues of qualifications of experts, criteria for acceptance of expertise by the court, and liability issues related to expert testimony. The chapter concludes with a discussion of interjurisdictional practice, which is particularly relevant to forensic psychologists who may have specialized expertise in a particular area and are retained to work on cases in states in which they are not licensed.

## I. Confidentiality and Privilege

Confidentiality and privileged communications are related, but different, concepts. Confidentiality refers to the expectation that information that a client provides to a psychologist will not be shared with others. Privilege, which actually is "testimonial privilege," refers to the right of an individual to prevent information that was disclosed in a protected relationship (in this instance, to a psychologist) to be offered as testimony in a legal proceeding. There are both statutes and case law that address the circumstances under which confidentiality and/or privilege may be breached. Forensic psychologists need to be knowledgeable about these issues, both in their roles as evaluators as well as when they are asked for consultation by their clinical colleagues.

## A. PRIVILEGE IN FORENSIC EVALUATIONS

The very nature of forensic evaluations (i.e., they are typically conducted explicitly for the purpose of providing relevant information to a court) creates exceptions to the expectation that communications will be privileged. However, even in such circumstances, the forensic psychologist should explicitly inform the examinee of the lack of privilege and the purpose of the interview (e.g., *Estelle v. Smith,*1981). Furthermore, when the psychologist has been retained by the examinee's attorney, the communications may be protected by attorney–client privilege (which may offer more protections than communications to a psychologist). For example, in criminal cases, most jurisdictions recognize that an expert retained by the defense is covered by attorney work product privilege and therefore cannot be compelled to testify without the consent of the defense (*United States v. Alvarez,* 1975). In that case, the Federal Appeals Court ruled that an expert hired by the defense to conduct an insanity evaluation could not be called as a witness by the prosecution. The court wrote: "We reject the contention that the assertion of insanity at the time of the offense waives the attorney–client privilege with respect to psychiatric consultations made in preparation for trial."

However, even this principle is not universally accepted. For example, this ruling was contradicted in another jurisdiction, in which a Federal Appeals Court (*United States ex rel. Edney v. Smith,* 1976) allowed the prosecution to call as an expert witness a psychiatrist who had been hired by the defense to evaluate the defendant for insanity (and whose opinion did not support that claim). The court acknowledged the issue of attorney–client privilege but decided that it could be overcome "by the strong counterbalancing interest of the State in accurate fact-finding by its courts (p. 1054)." As these opposing cases demonstrate, there is a tension between a defendant's right to protect disclosure of incriminating information and the state's right to obtain a fair verdict. How this balance is struck may be determined differently depending on the jurisdiction. A forensic psychologist who is retained by an attorney should clarify at the very outset of the process which set of rules govern in the particular state.

## B. EXCEPTIONS TO CONFIDENTIALITY

Although maintenance of the confidentiality of communications between psychologists and their patients is a core value, there are circumstances in which the legal system allows or even requires that confidentiality to be breached. Two of the most common exceptions to confidentiality involve situations in which the patient may pose a risk of harm to others and laws requiring "mandated reporting." Although this applies to all forms of psychological practice, the issues may be particularly salient in forensic settings because of the nature of the inquiries and communication between the forensic psychologist and the examinee. Across a number of types of forensic evaluations, issues of risk of harm are a focus of inquiry, and thus the forensic psychologist often must inquire about the examinee's thoughts and intentions of harming others. Eliciting this type of information is often a core element, for example, in civil commitment and sex offender evaluations, as well as in some evaluations in criminal cases (e.g., aid in sentencing, criminal responsibility). Furthermore, evaluations relevant to child custody and child welfare frequently involve inquiries regarding both present and previous behaviors toward children. Thus, forensic psychologists need to be aware of the legal rules regarding confidentiality that govern in the jurisdictions in which they practice. The laws are not uniform and vary across states and the federal system based on statutes as well as case law. The discussion below focuses on the most common elements that are typically addressed.

Duty to Protect   Most psychologists are familiar with the case of *Tarasoff v. Board of Regents* (1976), which is often incorrectly referred to as an issue of "duty to warn." Indeed, in 1974, the California Supreme Court had ruled that a psychologist, who had been treating Posenjit Poddar, had breached his duty to warn Ms. Tarasoff that Mr. Poddar had threatened to kill her. However, in 1976, the case was re-heard by the same court, which then clarified that a therapist had a duty to *protect* a potential victim of his client (which is a broader concept than warning, as it involves a broader range of options). As this case was heard in state court, it had precedential value only in California. However, other states, either through case law or statutes, soon incorporated a similar concept. It is worth noting, however, that not all states endorsed this concept and that there are differences across jurisdictions in how the duty is defined and applied. For example, the Pennsylvania courts adopted the more narrow "duty to warn" standard (*Emerich v. Philadelphia Center for Human Development, Inc.*, 1998).

The elements in the duty, when recognized, include the presence of a threat that is credible to an identifiable victim. The psychologist (or other mental health professional) can discharge the duty by warning the intended victim or (in jurisdictions that have adopted the duty to protect standard) by taking other reasonable action to protect the person (e.g., notifying the police or having the person civilly committed). The following cases provide examples of how various courts have ruled on the elements of the duty to protect.

Specific Threat   Although the *Tarasoff* case involved a specific threat to the victim, some courts have expanded the concept to include cases in which there was not a specific threat, but the therapist was held liable for failure to protect an identifiable victim, based on other indications that the client posed a threat. In the case of *McIntosh v. Milano* (1979) in New Jersey, the court ruled that a psychiatrist or therapist "may have a duty to take whatever steps are reasonably necessary to protect an intended or potential victim of his patient when he determines, or should determine... that the patient is or may present a probability of danger to that person (pp. 511–512)." This duty was found despite the absence of any specific threat by the patient toward the victim, whom he killed.

Similarly, in *Jablonski v. United States* (1983), Mr. Jablonski, an outpatient at a V.A. Hospital, killed the woman with whom he had been living. Although he had not made any explicit threats toward the victim, the district court found the hospital liable for not taking steps to protect the woman. A salient issue in this case was the hospital's failure to obtain previous records from other facilities, which would have demonstrated a history of violence on his part toward women with whom he was involved. The appeals court upheld the district court's ruling against the hospital, despite the absence of an overt threat.

Identifiable Victim   Another element in many of these cases is whether there is an identifiable victim. Courts have provided conflicting opinions regarding this issue. For example, in the case of *Lipari v. Sears* (1980), a V.A. hospital was found liable in a case of an outpatient who entered a nightclub and sprayed the room with bullets. The victims were strangers to the patient, and thus not identifiable victims, but the appeals court nevertheless upheld the district court's finding that the hospital's duty extended to the victims. By contrast, in *Thompson v. County of Alameda* (1980), the Supreme Court of California Appeals ruled that the county was not liable for the death of an individual killed by a juvenile offender who had been released from custody the previous day. The ruling was based on the juvenile having made "nonspecific threats of harm directed at nonspecific victims."

It is important to note that on this issue, as with the general issue of "duty to protect," the standards will vary by jurisdiction. In addition to case law, a number of states have enacted statutes that pertain to this matter and that determine practice in their jurisdiction. Forensic psychologists should be familiar with both the general legal concepts and local laws and precedents.

## C. MANDATED REPORTING LAWS

Most states have established laws identifying classes of professionals (including psychologists) who are required to breach confidentiality to report certain types of abuse (most notably child abuse). The specific requirements are enumerated in individual state statutes and may require a psychologist to breach confidentiality if a client discloses that he has abused a child, or another protected group, such as the elderly or disabled. This is considered an exception to confidentiality, as the information is typically reported to a state agency rather than a court. Forensic evaluations have the potential for creating a conflict between opposing legal concepts in this area; the psychologist may be covered by the mandated reporting laws, but in many jurisdictions, lawyers are not. However, consider the situation in which a defendant discloses to a psychologist, retained by the defense attorney, that he has been abusing his stepson. The psychologist would be torn between the statutory obligation to report the abuse and the counterargument that the psychologist is working for the attorney, and thus the communication is covered by the more protective rules of attorney–client confidentiality. This issue has yet to be resolved by higher courts, so psychologists would need to seek specific legal advice (not from the retaining attorney, as that attorney is representing the defendant's interests, not the psychologist's) about how to proceed.

## II. Experts and Evidence

As discussed in Chapter 4, the standard for acceptance of expertise for legal purposes is higher than that used in clinical practice. Courts have ruled on issues of how to determine whether a new technique, procedure, or test should be admissible in evidence; rules of expert testimony; and on standards for determining who is an expert.

### A. RULES OF EVIDENCE

The Federal Rules of Evidence (FRE) include a section on expert testimony. Although these rules govern in federal courts, individual states have similar rules that are relevant in their jurisdictions. FRE 702 established standards for allowing expert witnesses more leeway than lay-witnesses in offering opinions based on specialized knowledge. In the case of *Daubert v. Merrell Dow Pharmaceuticals, Inc.* (1993), the Supreme Court relied on the FRE to

> **Federal Rule of Evidence 702.**
>
> If scientific, technical, or other specialized knowledge will assist the trier of fact to understand the evidence or to determine a fact in issue, a witness qualified as an expert by knowledge, skill, experience, training, or education may testify thereto in the form of an opinion or otherwise, if (1) the testimony is based on sufficient facts or data, (2) the testimony is the product of reliable principles and methods, and (3) the witness has applied the principles and methods reliably to the facts of the case.

establish guidelines for judges to use in determining when new methodologies should be accepted. The *Daubert* court established four guidelines:

1. whether the methodology can be, or has been, tested;
2. whether the proposed method or procedure has been subject to peer review or publication;
3. whether it has a known or potential error rate;
4. whether it is generally accepted in the relevant scientific community.

The *Daubert* decision superseded the previous Supreme Court decision on this issue, which was issued 70 years earlier in the case of *Frye v. United States* (1923). That case raised the question of whether polygraph results could be accepted as valid evidence in legal proceedings. In rejecting polygraphy, the Supreme Court established the standard that the methodology must be "sufficiently established to have gained general acceptance in the particular field in which it belongs." Although the *Daubert* court expanded this standard in the federal jurisdiction, this does not necessarily impact decisions in state courts, some of whom still use the equivalent of the *Frye* standard, whereas others have adopted the broader *Daubert* standard.

The U.S. Supreme Court further refined its ruling in Daubert in two subsequent cases. In the case of *General Electric Co. v. Joiner* (1997), the Court emphasized the discretion that *Daubert* gave to the trial judge to act as "gatekeeper" for accepting expert testimony. They ruled that appeals courts could not overturn the trial judge's decision based on their own judgment of the reliability of the testimony unless they found that the initial ruling constituted a clear abuse of discretion. In the subsequent case of *Kumho Tire Co. v. Carmichael* (1999), the witness was proffered as an expert on tire failure analysis. In its ruling in this case, the Supreme Court expanded the *Daubert* standards to be applied not only to testimony based on "scientific" knowledge but also to testimony that was based on "technical" expertise or other specialized knowledge (p. 142). This case is particularly relevant to forensic psychologists, as arguably not all testimony is based on scientific expertise but may also be founded on professional experience.

## B. ACCEPTANCE OF PSYCHOLOGISTS AS EXPERT WITNESSES

Although psychologists are routinely accepted as expert witnesses in a wide range of legal cases today, this was not always the case. The landmark case of *Jenkins v. United States* (1962) was the first to explicitly recognize that psychologists could be considered experts in the diagnosis of mental illness. In that case, the trial judge's decision not to admit testimony from three psychologists, in a competence-to-stand-trial case, because they did not possess a medical degree was overturned by the appeals court. Rather, the court recognized that psychologists may have relevant training and expertise in diagnosing and treating mental disorders. However, they noted that the possession of a doctoral degree in psychology was not, in itself, sufficient to warrant acceptance as an expert. Referencing the range of training available to psychologists, the court determined that "[t]he critical factor in respect to admissibility is the actual experience of the witness and the probable probative value of his opinion" (p. 646) and recognized that doctoral training in psychology, followed by internship and practical experience, was sufficient to allow a psychologist to testify about clinical diagnoses. It is also worth noting that the appeals court specifically mentioned the attainment of a diplomate from the American Board of Examiners in Professional Psychology (which has since changed its name to American Board of Professional Psychology) as one indicator of expertise.

## C. ADMISSION OF TESTIMONY BASED ON DATA NOT ADMISSIBLE IN EVIDENCE

As discussed in Chapter 4, a major tenet of forensic evaluations is that data must be obtained from multiple sources. This includes not only the examinee but also review of records, as well as interviews of third parties (also referred to as "collateral informants"). Legal issues may be raised when the information from the collateral source has not been admitted into evidence. Such information may be considered "hearsay."

Acknowledging that experts routinely rely on such data to arrive at an opinion, rules of evidence provide for admission of such testimony by the expert if it is "of a type reasonably relied upon by experts in the particular field in forming opinions or inferences upon the subject" (FRE 703; *see* below). Thus, forensic psychologists should be prepared to explain the rationale for relying on such evidence, including that this is standard practice. The case of *People v. Goldstein* (2005) highlights this issue. In that case, a psychiatrist, in arriving at an opinion regarding insanity, relied on statements provided by third-party sources. Although under direct and cross-examination, the psychiatrist appeared to understate that reliance on such third-party evidence was accepted and standard practice (instead referring to a few prominent psychiatrists' endorsement of the approach), the trial court nonetheless ruled that the testimony could be admitted. In this particular case, the appeals court confirmed that third-party information is admissible. However, they then ruled that because the particular statements relied on were so relevant to the ultimate determination in the case, and the individuals who had made those statements were not called to testify, they should not have been admitted into evidence (mirroring the language in the last sentence of FRE 703 that the court should allow such evidence only if the "probative value in assisting the jury to evaluate the expert's opinion substantially outweighs their prejudicial effect"). This type of ruling should not deter forensic psychologists from continuing to seek out collateral information; rather, it is the responsibility of the attorney to determine when it is necessary to call the informants to testify.

## D. ULTIMATE ISSUE TESTIMONY

Chapter 7 discussed the ethical and professional issues relevant to forensic psychologists offering opinions in court on the ultimate legal issue. This issue has also been addressed by the legal system—most notably in rules of evidence (*see* below, FRE 704). The rule allows experts, including psychologists, to provide ultimate issue testimony. The notes accompanying the rule discuss the difficulties inherent in forbidding such testimony—most notably that it could lead to confusing "circumlocutions," which can make the opinions seem less certain. Nevertheless, in 1984, section (b) was added to the rule, excluding specifically ultimate opinions only in respect to mental state at the time of the offense in criminal cases (i.e., insanity defense, diminished capacity defenses). Notably, this specific prohibition was added in the wake of John Hinckley's acquittal by reason of insanity for the attempted murder of President Ronald Reagan.

Despite this specific language in the FRE, many states have not incorporated this change. Indeed, a number of states have language in their statutes that specifically calls for experts to give ultimate issue opinions in insanity cases (e.g., Michigan Compiled Laws, §768.20a(6)(c) specifically calls for examiners to provide opinions "on the issue of the defendant's insanity at the time the alleged offense was committed"). Thus, forensic psychologists need to be aware of the laws governing the particular jurisdictions in which they practice.

## Federal Rule of Evidence 703. Bases of Opinion Testimony by Experts

The facts or data in the particular case upon which an expert bases an opinion or inference may be those perceived by or made known to the expert at or before the hearing. If of a type reasonably relied upon by experts in the particular field in forming opinions or inferences upon the subject, the facts or data need not be admissible in evidence in order for the opinion or inference to be admitted. Facts or data that are otherwise inadmissible shall not be disclosed to the jury by the proponent of the opinion or inference unless the court determines that their probative value in assisting the jury to evaluate the expert's opinion substantially outweighs their prejudicial effect.

## Federal Rule of Evidence 704. Opinion on Ultimate Issue

(a) Except as provided in subdivision (b), testimony in the form of an opinion or inference otherwise admissible is not objectionable because it embraces an ultimate issue to be decided by the trier of fact.

(b) No expert witness testifying with respect to the mental state or condition of a defendant in a criminal case may state an opinion or inference as to whether the defendant did or did not have the mental state or condition constituting an element of the crime charged or of a defense thereto. Such ultimate issues are matters for the trier of fact alone.

### E. LIABILITY ISSUES FOR EXPERT WITNESSES

It is settled law that all witnesses are granted immunity from being sued for defamation. This is designed to prevent witnesses from being intimidated from testifying. However, the issue has been raised as to whether this principle should be expanded to provide immunity to expert witnesses from being sued by the retaining party based on a claim that their work product did not meet the standards of the profession. There is as yet no unanimity of opinion on this matter. For example, in the case of *Bruce v. Byrne-Stevens & Assocs. Eng'rs* (1989), the Supreme Court of Washington ruled that witness immunity extends not only to defamation suits but to liability for any negligence in the testimony or the work underyling the testimony. Their rationale was that fear of liability would deter many professionals from providing relevant expertise to the court and would also encourage experts to provide the strongest possible case for those retaining them, thus undermining their objectivity. However, the Missouri Supreme Court ruled to the contrary, in the case of *Murphy v. A. A. Mathews,* (1992), stating that experts should only be given immunity for defamation but could still be liable for negligent work. They wrote: "We do not find the reasoning of the *Byrne-Stevens* plurality persuasive…we do not believe that immunity was meant to or should apply to bar a suit against a privately retained professional who negligently provides litigation support services (p. 680)."

Both of these cases involved engineering work, but the principles apply to expert psychological testimony as well. For example, the Texas Supreme Court, in *James v. Brown* (1982) addressed the issue in a case in which a woman sued three psychiatrists for their role in having her civilly committed. The Court upheld the dismissal of the claims of libel and false imprisonment but allowed the case to proceed as a malpractice claim. Their reasoning was similar to the *Murphy v. Mathews* decision, indicating that although the psychiatrists had immunity for the statements they had made in court, this did not extend to possible negligence in their underlying work.

An interesting expansion of this issue pertains to complaints to state licensing boards and to the APA ethics committee, based on testimony provided by psychologists. In the case of *Deatherage v. Examining Board of Psychology* (1997), the Washington State Supreme Court (which had issued the *Bruce v. Byrnes* opinion above) ruled that a psychologist could be subject to disciplinary action by the state licensing board based on a finding that the work that formed the basis of his expert testimony in child custody cases did not meet professional ethical standards. The licensing board found that he had failed to qualify statements, had mischaracterized statements, had failed to verify information, and had not properly interpreted test data. The Court's rationale was that although the courts had an interest in providing broad immunity to witnesses to preserve the justice system, this did not extend to other nonjudicial supervisory bodies. Similarly, an appeals court in California (*Budwin v. American Psychological Association*, 1994) upheld a censure of a psychologist by the APA for his conduct in a child custody case. The APA had censured Dr. Budwin for violation of the APA Code of Conduct, finding that he had failed to honor his commitment to produce records and had failed to accurately describe, in both his written report and oral testimony, the limits of his interaction and observations with the parties evaluated. The *Budwin* court recognized the value of what is termed *quasi-judicial immunity* (i.e., protecting those who perform functions for the courts, such as psychologists in child custody cases, from liability for their testimony) but determined that this immunity does not apply to professional discipline by a nonjudicial authority (such as the APA).

## III. Multijurisdictional Practice

Psychologists are required by each State to obtain licensure in order to practice in that jurisdiction. Thus, a licensed psychologist in New York would not be permitted to provide psychotherapy in California. The situation with the practice of forensic psychology is more nuanced. Which activities are considered practice of psychology? Is provision of a forensic evaluation the practice of psychology? What about expert testimony?

As with many other issues, the answers to these questions will vary by jurisdiction. Most states consider forensic evaluations to be the practice of psychology. However, there are differences across jurisdictions in terms of requirements; some states require full licensure, whereas others have provisions for temporary or limited licensure to provide evaluations for legal purposes (Tucillo, DeFilippis, Denney, & Dsurney, 2002; Shuman, Cunningham, Connell, & Reid, 2003; DeMers, Van Horne, & Rodolfa, 2008). However, only a few apply this standard to testimony. This distinction can have practical significance, particularly if the forensic psychologist is providing expert testimony in a case that did not require a face-to-face evaluation of an individual. This could happen, for example, in cases such as testamentary capacity (i.e., a *post mortem* analysis of whether an individual had been competent to execute a will) or when the psychologist is called to provide testimony about research (e.g., eyewitness testimony) or standards in the field (e.g., malpractice claims). Forensic psychologists should be aware of the standards in the particular jurisdiction in which they have been retained.

### FORENSIC PSYCHOLOGY AND LAW

All psychologists must be familiar with the laws that govern their practice. However, the level of knowledge required for forensic practice is significantly higher because the very nature of forensic psychological practice involves interface with the law. Forensic psychologists thus must develop competencies related both to the application of psychological expertise to legal concepts, as well as the legal issues related to the practice of psychology. Thus, as part of their professional identity, forensic psychologists are committed to obtaining continuing education and remaining updated both on advances in psychology as well as legal changes (statutes and case law) that affect psychological practice.

# REFERENCES

Abidin, R (1997). *Parenting Stress Index: Professional Manual.* Odessa, FL: Psychological Assessment Resources.

Adebimpe, V.R. (1994). Race, racism, and epidemiological surveys. *Hospital and Community Psychiatry, 45,* 27–31.

Adler, F. (1973). Socioeconomic factors influencing jury verdicts. *New York University Review of Law and Social Change, 3,* 1–10.

American Bar Association, (1989). *Criminal Justice Mental Health Standards.* Washington, DC: ABA

American Psychiatric Association. (2000). Therapies focused on memories of childhood physical and sexual abuse: Position statement. Retrieved from http://www.psych. org/MainMenu/EducationCareerDevelopment/Library/BernsteinReferenceCenter/ PositionStatements.aspx. Accessed April 30, 2010.

American Psychological Association (1992). Ethical principles and code of conduct. *American Psychologist, 47,* 1597–1611.

American Psychological Association (2002). Ethical principles and code of conduct. *American Psychologist, 57,* 1060–1073.

APA Working Group on Investigation of Memories of Childhood Abuse (1998). *Psychology, Public Policy, and the Law, 4,* 933–940.

American Psychology-Law Society. Graduate programs in psychology and law. Retrieved from http://ap-ls.org/education/ClinicalDoctoral.php. Accessed December 31, 2010.

American Psychology-Law Society. Pre-doctoral internship training programs. Retrieved from http://ap-ls.org/education/Internship.php. Accessed December 31, 2010.

American Psychology-Law Society. Forensic postdoctoral fellowship training programs. Retrieved from http://ap-ls.org/education/PostDoc.php. Accessed December 31, 2010.

Anthony, T., Cooper, C., & Mullen, B. (1992). Cross-racial facial identification: A social-cognitive integration. *Personality and Social Psychology Bulletin, 18,* 296–301.

Appelbaum, P. & Grisso, T (2001). *MacArthur Competence Assessment Tool for Clinical Research (MacCAT-CR).* Sarasota, FL: Professional Resource Press.

Archer, R.P., Buffington-Vollum, J., Stredny R.V., & Handel, R.W. (2006). A survey of psychological test use patterns among forensic psychologists. *Journal of Personality Assessment, 87,* 85–95.

Baker, F.M. & Bell, C.C. (1999). Issues in the psychiatric treatment of African Americans. *Psychiatric Services, 50,* 362–368.

Baldus D.C., Woodworth G., & Pulaski C.A.(1990). *Equal justice and the death penalty: A legal and empirical analysis.* Boston: Northeastern University Press.

Bank, S. (2001). From mental health professional to expert witness: Testifying in court. *New Directions for Mental Health Services, 91,* 57–66.

Bank, S. & Packer, I. (2007). Expert witness testimony: law, ethics, and practice. In A. Goldstein (ed.), *Forensic psychology: Emerging topics and expanding roles.* Hoboken, NJ: John Wiley.

Bartol, C. & Bartol, A. (2004). History of forensic psychology. In A. Hess & I. Weiner (Eds.), *The handbook of forensic psychology* (2nd edition) (pp. 3–23). New York: John Wiley.

Bavolek, S. & Keene, R. (1999). *Adult-Adolescent Parenting Inventory-2 manual.* Park City, Utah: Family Development Resources.

Bersoff, D., Goodman-Delahunty, J., Grisso, T., Hans, V., Poythress, N., & Roesch, R. (1997). Training in law and psychology: Models from the Villanova Conference. *American Psychologist, 52,* 1301–1310.

Boccaccini, M.T. & Brodsky, S.L. (1999). Diagnostic test usage by forensic psychologists in emotional injury cases. *Professional Psychology: Research and Practice, 30,* 253–259.

Boone, K. (Ed.) (2007). *The assessment of feigned cognitive impairment: A neuropsychological perspective.* New York: Guilford.

Borum, R., Bartel, P., & Forth, A. (2003). *Manual for the Structured Assessment for Violence Risk in Youth (SAVRY): Version 1.1.* Tampa, FL: Louis de la Parte Florida Mental Health Institute, University of South Florida.

Borum R. & Grisso T. (1995). Psychological test use in criminal forensic evaluations. *Professional Psychology: Research and Practice, 26,* 465–473.

Borum R. & Grisso T. (1996). Establishing standards for criminal forensic reports: An empirical analysis. *Bulletin of the American Academy of Psychiatry and the Law, 24,* 297–317.

Bothwell, R.K., Deffenbacher, K.A., & Brigham, J.C. (1987). Correlation of eyewitness accuracy and confidence: Optimality hypothesis revisited. *Journal of Applied Psychology, 72,* 691–695.

Brigham, J., & Grisso, T. (2003). Forensic psychology. In D. Freedheim (Ed.), *Handbook of psychology: Volume 1, History of psychology* (pp. 391–411). Hoboken, NJ: John Wiley.

Brodsky, S.L.(1973). *Psychologists in the criminal justice system.* Urbana, IL: University of Illinois Press.

Brodsky, S.L. (1991). *Testifying in court: Guidelines and maxims for the expert witness.* Washington, DC: American Psychological Association.

Brodsky, S.L. (1999). *The Expert eExpert Witness: More maxims and guidelines for testifying in court,* Washington, DC: American Psychological Association.

Brodsky, S.L. (2009). *Principles and practice of trial consultation.* New York: Guilford Press.

Brown, D., Scheflin, A.W., & Hammond, D. (1998). *Memeory, trauma treatment, and the law.* New York: W W Norton & Co.

Bruck, M., Ceci, S.J., Francoeur, E., & Resnick, A. (1995). Anatomically detailed dolls do not facilitate preschoolers' reports of a pediatric examination involving genital touching. *Journal of Experimental Psychology: Applied, 1,* 95–109.

Bruck, M. & Ceci, S.J.(1995).*Amicus* brief for the case of *State of NJ v. Michaels* presented by Committee of Concerned Social Scientists. *Psychology, Public Policy, and Law, 1,* 272–322.

Budd, K., Connell, M., & Clark, J. (2011). *Evaluations for child protection.* New York: Oxford.

Bureau of Justice Statistics (2009). Prisoners in 2008. Retrieved from http://bjs.ojp.usdoj.gov/content/pub/pdf/p08.pdf. Accessed April 30, 2010.

Butcher, J., Graham, J., Ben-Porath, Y., Tellegen, A., Dahlstrom, W., & Kaemmer, B. (2001). *MMPI-2: Manual for administration and scoring* (Rev. ed.). Minneapolis: University of Minnesota Press.

Callahan, L.A., Steadman H.J., McGreevy M.A., & Robbins PC. (1991). The volume and characteristics of insanity defense pleas: An eight-state study. *Bulletin of the American Academy of Psychiatry & the Law, 19,* 331–338.

Chaleby, K.S. (2001). *Forensic psychiatry in Islamic jurisprudence.* Herndon, VA: International Institute of Islamic Thought.

Cleckley, H. (1941). *The mask of sanity*. St. Louis, MO: Mosby

Cochrane, R.E., Grisso, T., & Frederick, R.I. (2001). The relationship between criminal charges, diagnoses, and psycholegal opinions among federal pretrial defendants. *Behavioral Sciences and the Law, 19,* 565–582.

Committee on Ethical Guidelines for Forensic Psychologists (1991). Specialty guidelines for forensic psychologists. *Law and Human Behavior, 15,* 655–665.

Committee on Psychological Tests and Assessment (2007). Statement on third party observers in psychological testing and assessment: A framework for decision making. Retrieved from http://www.apa.org/science/programs/testing/third-party-observers.pdf. Accessed December 31, 2010.

Committee on the Revision of the Specialty Guidelines for Forensic Psychology, 2010). Specialty Guidelines for Forensic Psychology. Retrieved from http://www.ap-ls.org/aboutpsychlaw/080110sgfpdraft.pdf. Accessed December 24, 2010.

Cooper, V.G, & Zapf, P.A. (2003). Predictor variables in competency to stand trial decisions. *Law and Human Behavior, 27,* 423–436.

Council of Specialties in Forensic Psychology. *Forensic Psychology: Formal specialty definition.* Retrieved from http://cospp.org/specialties/forensic-psychology. Accessed December 31, 2010.

DeMers, S.T.,Van Horne, B.A., & Rodolfa, E.R. (2008).Changes in training and practice of psychologists: Current challenges for licensing boards. *Professional Psychology: Research and Practice, 39,* 473–479.

Douglas, K S., Ogloff, J.R.P., & Hart, S.D. (2003). Evaluation of a model of violence risk assessment among forensic psychiatric patients. *Psychiatric Services, 54,* 1372–1379.

Douglas, K., Otto, R., & Borum, R. (2003). Psychological assessment in forensic settings. In J. Graham, J. Naglien, & E. Weiner (Eds.), *Handbook of psychology, volume 10: Assessment Psychology* (pp. 345–363). New York: Wiley.

Drizin, S.A., & Leo, R.A. (2004). The problem of false confessions in the post-DNA world. *North Carolina Law Review, 82,* 891–1007.

Drogin,E.Y. & Barrett, C.L. (2007). Off the witness stand: The forensic psychologist as consultant. In A. Goldstein (Ed.), *Forensic psychology: Emerging topics and expanding roles.* Hoboken, NJ: John Wiley.

Ebbinghaus, Hermann (1885). *Memory: A Contribution to Experimental Psychology.* New York: Columbia University (translated into English by Ruger, H.A., & Bussenius, C.E., 1913).

Eisenberg, J. (2004). *Law, Psychology, and Death Penalty Litigation.* Sarasota, FL: Professional Resource Press.

Epperson, D.L.,Kaul, J.D., & Hasselton, D. (1998). *Final report of the development of the Minnesota Sex Offender Screening Tool-Revised* (MnSOST-R). Presentation at the 17th annual Research and Treatment Conference of the Association for the Treatment of Sexual Abusers, Vancouver, British Columbia.

Everington, C. & Fulero, S. (1999). Competence to confess: Measuring understanding and suggestibility of defendants with mental retardation. *Mental Retardation, 37,* 212–220.

Everington, C., & Luckasson, R. (1992). *Competence Assessment for Standing Trial for Defendants with Mental Retardation (CAST\*MR): Test manual.* Worthington, OH: IDS Publishing Corporation.

*Federal Rules of Evidence* (2007).

*Federal Rules of Procedure, 12.2 (c),* (2009).

Fein, R., Appelbaum, K., Barnum, R., Baxter, P., Grisso, T., & Leavitt, N. (1991). The designated forensic professional program: A state government–university partnership to improve forensic mental health services. *Journal of Mental Health Administration, 18,* 223–230.

Feld, B. (2006b). Police interrogations of juveniles: An empirical study of policy and practice. *Journal of Criminal Law and Criminology, 97,* 219–316.

Freyd, J.J. (1996). *Betrayal trauma: The logic of foregetting childhood abuse.* Cambridge, MA: Harvard University Press.

Fuhrmann, G. & Zibell, R. (2011). *Evaluations for child custody.* New York: Oxford.

Frost, L.E., deCamara, R.L., & Earl, T.R. (2006). Training, certification, and regulation of forensic evaluators. *Journal of Forensic Psychology Practice, 6,* 77–91.

Fulero, S. & Everington, C. (2004). Mental retardation, competency to waive Miranda rights, and false confessions. In G. D. Lassiter (Ed.), *Interrogations, confessions, and entrapment* (pp. 163–179). New York: Kluwer Academic/Plenum.

Gaines, A.D. (1995). Culture-specific delusions: Sense and nonsense in cultural context. *The Psychiatric Clinics of North America, 18,* 281–301.

Garrett, B. (2008). Judging Innocence. *Columbia Law Review, 108,* 55–142.

Gerard, A. (1994). *Parent-Child Relationship Inventory: Manual.* Los Angeles, CA: Western Psychological Services.

Golding, S. & Roesch, R., (1983). *Interdisciplinary Fitness Interview training manual.* Unpublished manuscript.

Goldstein, N., Condie, L., Kalbeitzer, R., Osman, D., & Geier, J. (2003). Juvenile offenders' Miranda rights comprehension and self-reported likelihood of false confessions. *Assessment, 10,* 359–369.

Goodman, G.S., Quas, J.A., Batterman-Faunce, J.M. Riddlesberger, M.M., & Kuhn, G. (1997). Children's reactions to and memory for a stressful eent: Influences of age, anatomical dolls, knowledge, and parental attachment. *Applied Developmental Science, 1,* 54–75.

Greenberg, S.A., & Shuman, D.W. (1997). Irreconcilable conflict between therapeutic and forensic roles. *Professional Psychology: Research and Practice, 28,* 50–57.

Grekin P.M., Jemelka R., & Trupin E.W. (1994). Racial differences in the criminalization of the mentally ill. *Bulletin of the American Academy of Psychiatry and the Law, 22,* 411–420.

Grisso, T. (1980). Juveniles' capacities to waive Miranda rights: An empirical analysis. *California Law Review, 68,* 1134–1166.

Grisso, T. (1981). *Juveniles' waiver of rights: Legal and psychological competence.* New York: Plenum.

Grisso, T. (1986). *Evaluating competencies: Forensic assessments and instruments.* New York: Plenum.

Grisso, T. (1987). The economic and scientific future of forensic psychological assessment. *American Psychologist, 42,* 831–839.

Grisso, T. (1988). *Competency to stand trial evaluations: A manual for practice.* Sarasota, FL: Professional Resource Press.

Grisso, T. (1991). A developmental history of the American Psychology-Law Society. *Law and Human Behavior, 15,* 213–231.

Grisso, T. (1997). Juvenile competency to stand trial: Questions in an era of punitive reform. *Criminal Justice, 12,* 4–11.

Grisso, T. (2003). *Evaluating competencies: Forensic assessments and instruments* (second edition). New York: Kluwer Academic/Plenum Press.

Grisso, T. (2006). Foreword. In S. Sparta & G. Koocher (Eds.), *Forensic mental health assessment of children and adolescents.* New York: Oxford University Press.

Grisso (2010): Guidance for Improving Forensic Reports: A Review of Common Errors. Vol. 2 pp. 102–115. Retrieved from http://www.forensicpsychologyunbound.ws/. Accessed December 31, 2010.

Grisso, T., & Appelbaum, P. (1998*). MacArthur Competence Assessment Tool for Treatment (MacCAT-T).* Sarasota, FL: Professional Resource Press.

Grisso, T., Cocozza, J.J., Steadman, H.J., Fisher, W.H., & Greer, A. (1994). The organization of pretrial forensic evaluation services. *Law and Human Behavior, 18,* 377–393.

Grisso, T. & Quinlan, J. (2005). Juvenile court clinical services: A national description. *Juvenile and Family Court Journal, 56,* 9–20.

Grisso, T., & Ring, J. (1979). Parents' attitudes toward juveniles' rights in interrogation. *Criminal Justice and Behavior, 6,* 221–226.

Grisso, T., Steinberg, L., Woolard, J., Cauffman, E., Scott, E., Graham, S., et al. (2003). Juveniles' competence to stand trial: A comparison of adolescents' and adults' capacities as trial defendants. *Law and Human Behavior, 27,* 333–363.

Gudjonsson, G.H. (1984). A new scale of interrogative suggestibility. *Perisoanlity and Individual Differences, 5,* 303–314.

Gudjonsson, G.H. & MacKeith, J.A.C. (1982). False confessions: Psychological effects of interrogation. In A. Trankell (Ed.), *Reconstructing the past: The role of psychologists in criminal trials* (pp. 253–269). Deventer, The Netherlands: Kluwer.

Guy, L.S. (2008). *Performance indicators of the structured professional judgment approach for assessing risk for violence to others: A meta-analytic survey.* Unpublished dissertation, Simon Fraser University, Burnaby, BC, Canada.

Hans, V.P. (1992). Judgments of justice. *Psychological Science, 3,* 218–220.

Hanson, R.K. & Thornton, D. (2000). Improving risk assessments with sex offenders: A comparison of three actuarial scales. *Law and Human Behavior; 24,* 119–136.

Hare, R. (1993). *The Revised Psychopathy Checklist.* Toronto, CA: Multi-Health Systems.

Harrison P.M. & Beck A.J. (2002). Prisoners in 2001. Washington, DC: US Department of Justice, Office of Justice Programs.

Hart, S.D. & Hare, R.D. ( 1997). Psychopahty: Assessment and association with criminal conduct. In D.M. Stoff, J.Breiling, & J.D. Maser (Eds.), *Handbook of antisocial behavior.* New York: Wiley.

Hart, S.D., Kropp, P.R., & Webster, C.D. (1997). *Manual for the Sexual Violence Risk—20: Professional guidelines for assessing risk of sexual violence.* Vancouver, B.C.: The Mental Health, Law, and Policy Institute.

Hart, S.D., Michie, C., & Cooke D.J. (2007) Precision of actuarial risk assessment instruments: Evaluating the 'margins of error' of group v. individual predictions of violence. *British Journal of Psychiatry, 190,* s60–s65.

Healy, W. (1923). *The individual delinquent.* Boston: Little, Brown.

Heilbrun, K. (2001). *Principles of forensic mental health assessment.* New York: Kluwer Academic/Plenum Publishers.

Heilbrun, K. (2009). *Evaluation for risk of violence in adults.* New York: Oxford.

Heilbrun, K., Grisso, T., & Goldstein, A. (2009). *Foundations of forensic mental health assessment.* New York: Oxford.

Heilbrun, K., Marczyk, G., & DeMatteo, D. (eds.) (2002). *Forensic mental health assessment: A casebook.* New York: Oxford.

Heilbrun, K., Rogers, R., & Otto, R. (2002). Forensic assessment: Current status and future directions. In J. Ogloff (Ed.), *Psychology and law: Reviewing the discipline* (pp. 120–147). New York: Kluwer Academic/Plenum Press.

Hoge, R., & Andrews, D. (2002). *Youth Level of Service/Case Management Inventory: User's manual.* North Tonawanda, NY: Multi-Health Systems.

Hoge, R., & Andrews, D. (2010). *Evaluation for risk of violence in juveniles.* New York: Oxford.

Jones, K. (1999). *Taming the troublesome child: American families, child guidance, and the limits of psychiatric authority.* Cambridge, MA: Harvard University Press.

Kaslow, F. (1989). Early history of the American Board of Forensic Psychology. *Forensic Reports, 2,* 305–311.

Kassin, S.M., Drizin, S.A., Grisso, T., Gudjonsson, G.H., Leo, R.A., & Redlich, A.D. (2010). Police-induced confessions: Risk factors and recommendations. *Law and Human Behavior, 34*, 3–38.

Kassin, S.M., Leo, R.A., Meissner, C.A., Richman, K.D., Colwell, L.H., Leach, A-M., & La Fon, D. (2007). Police interviewing and interrogation: A Self-report survey of police practices and beliefs, *Law and Human Behavior, 31*, 381–400.

Kassin, S.M. & Wrightsman, L.S. (1985). Confession evidence. In S. Kassin & L. Wrightsman (Eds.), *The psychology of evidence and trial procedure* (pp. 67–94).Beverly Hills, CA: Sage.;

Kaufert, J.M. & Putsch, R.W. (1997). Communication through interpreters in healthcare: Ethical dilemmas arising from differences in class, culture, language, and power. *Journal of Clinical Ethics, 8,* 71–87.

Kim, S. (2010). *Evaluation of capacity to consent to treatment and research.* New York: Oxford.

Kovera, M.B., Dickinson, J.J. & Cutler, B.L.(2003). Voir Dire and jury selection. In A.M. Goldstein (Ed.). *Handbook of Psychology: Volume 11 Forensic Psychology.* Hoboken, NJ: John Wiley & Sons.

Kovera, M.B., Gresham, A.W., Borgida, E. Gray, E., & Regan, P.C. (1997). Does expert testimony inform or influence juror decision making? A social cognitive analysis. *Journal of Applied Psychology, 82,* 178–191.

Kropp, P., Hart, S., Webster, C., & Eaves D. (1999). *Spousal Assault Risk Assessment Guide User's Manual.* Toronto, Canada: Multi-Health Systems, and B.C. Institute Against Family Violence.

Kruh, I. & Grisso, T. (2009). *Evaluation of juveniles' competence to stand trial.* New York: Oxford.

Kuenhle, K. (2003). Child sexual abuse evaluations. In A.M. Goldstein (Ed.). *Handbook of Psychology: Volume 11 Forensic Psychology.* Hoboken, NJ: John Wiley & Sons.

Laboratory of Community Psychiatry, Harvard Medical School (1973). *Competency to stand trial and mental illness* (DHEW Publication No. ADM77–103). Rockville, MD: National Institute of Mental Health.

Lally, S.J. (2003). What tests are acceptable for use in forensic evaluations: A study of experts. *Professional Psychology; Research and Practice, 34,* 491–498.

Larrabee, G. (ed.) (2007). *Assessment of malingered neuropsychological deficits.* New York: Oxford.

Leavitt, N., Presskreischer, P., Maykuth, P., & Grisso, T. (2006). Aggression toward forensic evaluators: A statewide survey. *Journal of the American Academy of Psychiatry and the Law, 34*, 231–239.

Leong, G.B., Weinstock, R., Silva, J.A., & Eth, S. (1993). Psychiatry and the death penalty. *Journal of the American Academy of Psychiatry and the Law, 28*, 427–432.

Lidz, C., Meisel, A., Zerubavel, E., Carter, M., Sestak, R., & Roth, L. (1984). *Informed consent: A study of decisionmaking in psychiatry.* New York: Guilford.

Lidz, C., Mulvey,E., & Gardner, W.(1993). The accuracy of predicitions of violence to others. *Journal of the American Medical Association, 269*, 1007–1011.

Lieberman, J.D. & Sales, B.D. (2007). *Scientific jury selection.* Washington, DC: American Psychological Association.

Litwack, T.R. (2001). Actuarial vs. clinical assessments of dangerousness. *Psychology, Public Policy and Law, 7*, 409–443.

Loeb, P. (1996). *Independent Living Scales.* San Antonio: Psychological Corporation.

Loftus, E.F. & Ketcham, K. (1994). *The myth of repressed memory.* New York: St. Martin's Press.

Marson, D., Cody, H., Ingram, K., & Harrell, L. (1995). Neuropsychological predictors of competency in Alzheimer;s disease using a rational reasons legal standard. *Archives of Neurology, 52*, 955–959.

Matarazzo, J. (1987). There is only one psychology, no specialties, but many applications. *American Psychologist, 42,* 893–903.

McGarry, A., Curran, W., & Kenefick, D. (1968). Problems of public consultation in medico-legal matters: A symposim. *American Journal of Psychiatry, 125,* 42–45.

Melton, G., Petrila, J., Poythress, J., & Slobogin, C. (1987). *Psychological evaluations for the courts.* New York: Guilford.

Melton, G., Petrila, J., Poythress, J., & Slobogin, C. (2007). *Psychological evaluations for the courts* (3ʳᵈ edition). New York: Guilford.

Michigan Compiled Laws, §768.20a(6)(c)

Miller, H. (2001). *Miller-Forensic Assessment of Symptoms Test.* Lutz, FL: Psychological Assessment Resources.

Milner, J. (1994). Assessing physical child abuse risk: The Child Abuse Potential Inventory. *Clinical Psychology Review, 14,* 547–583.

Minsky, S., Vega, W., Miskimen,T., Gara, M., & Escobar, J.,(2003). Diagnostic patterns in Latino, African American, and European American psychiatric patients. *Archive of General Psychiatry. 60,* 637–644.

Monahan, J. (Ed.) (1980). *Who is the client? The ethics of psychological intervention in the criminal justice system.* Washington, DC: American Psychological Association.

Monahan, J. (1981). *The clinical prediction of violent behavior.* Washington, DC: Government Printing Office (DHHS Publication Number ADM 81–921).

Monahan, J., Steadman, H.J., Robbins, P.C., Silver, E., Appelbaum, P.S., Grisso, T., Mulvey, E.P., & Roth, L.H. (2000). Developing a clinically useful actuarial tool for assessing violence risk. *The British Journal of Psychiatry, 176,* 312–319.

Monahan, J., Steadman, J., Appelbaum, P., Grisso, T., Mulvey, E., Roth, L., Robbins, P., Banks, S., & Silver, E. (2003). *Classification of Violence Risk (COVR).* Lutz, FL: Psychological Assessment Resources.

Monahan, J., Steadman, H.J., Silver, E., Appelbaum, P.S., Robbins, P.C., Mulvey, E.P., Roth, L.H., Grisso, T., & Banks, S. (2001). *Rethinking risk assessment: The MacArthur study of mental disorder and violence.* Oxford: Oxford University Press.

Monahan, J., & Walker, L. (1985). *Social science in law.* Westbury, NY: The Foundation Press.

Monahan, J., & Walker, L. (2006). *Social science in law* (6ᵗʰ edition). Westbury, NY: The Foundation Press.

Moran, G. & Comfort, J.C. (1986). Neither "tentative" nor "fragmentary": Verdict preference of impaneled felony jurors as a function of attitude toward capital punishment. *Journal of Applied Psychology, 71,* 146–155.

Moran, G., Cutler, B.L., & De Lisa, A. (1994). Attitudes toward tort reform, scientific jury seledction, and juror bias: Verdict inclination in criminal and civil trials. *Law and Psychology Review,* 309–328.

Moran, G., Cutler, B.L., & Loftus, E.F. (1990). Jury selection in major controlled substance trials: The need for extended voir dire. *Forensic Reports, 3,* 331–348.

Narby, D.J., Cutler, B.L., & Moran, G. (1993). A meta-analysis of the association between authoritarianism and jurors' perceptions of defendant culpability. *Journal of Applied Psychology, 78,* 38–42.

National Institute of Justice (1999). *Eyewitness evidence: A guide for law enforcement.* Washington, DC: U.S. Department of Justice

Nicholson, R.A. & Norwood, S. (2000). The quality of forensic psychological assessments, reports, and testimony: Acknowledging the gap between promise and practice. *Law and Human Behavior, 24,* 9–44.

Nickerson, R.S. (1998). Confirmation bias: A ubiquitous phenomenon in many guises. *Review of General Psychology, 2,* 175–220.

O'Connell, M.J., Garmoe, W., & Goldstein, N.E.S. (2005). Miranda comprehension in adults with mental retardation and the effects of feedback style on suggestibility. *Law and Human Behavior, 29*, 359–369.

Ofshe, R., & Watters, E. (1994). *Making monsters: False memories, psychotherapy, and sexual hysteria.* New York: Charles Scribner's Sons/Macmillan Publishing.

Otto, R.K., Heilbrun, K., & Grisso, T. (1990). Training and credentialing in forensic psychology. *Behavioral Sciences and the Law, 8*, 217–231.

Otto, R.K. (1992). Prediction of dangerous behavior: A review and analysis of "second generation" research. *Forensic Reports, 5*, 103–133.

Packer, I.K. (1987). Homicide and the insanity defense: A comparison of sane and insane murderers. *Behavioral Sciences and the Law, 5*, 25–35.

Packer, I.K. (2008). Specialized practice in forensic psychology: Opportunities and obstacles. *Professional Psychology: Research and Practice, 39*, 245–249.

Packer, I.K. (2009). *Evaluation of criminal responsibility.* New York: Oxford.

Packer, I.K., & Leavitt, N. (1998). Designing and implementing a quality assurance process for forensic evaluations. *Presented at American Psychology-Law Society Conference,* Redondo Beach, CA.

Petrella, R.C. & Poythress, N.G. (1983). The quality of forensic evaluations: An interdisciplinary study. *Journal of Consulting and Clinical Psychology, 51*, 76–85.

Pfohl .S. (1979). From whom will we be protected? Comparative approaches to the assessment of dangerousness. *International Journal of Law and Psychiatry, 2*, 55–78.

Phares, E.J. & Wilson, K.G. (1972). Responsibility attribution: Role of outcome severity, situational ambiguity, and internal-external control. *Journal of Personality, 40*, 392–406.

Pigott, M.A., & Brigham, J.C. (1985). Relationship between accuracy of prior description and facial recognition. *Journal of Applied Psychology, 70*, 547–555.

Pinals, D.A., Packer I.K., Fisher W., & Roy-Bujnowski. K. (2004). Relationship between race and ethnicity and forensic clinical triage dispositions. *Psychiatric Services, 55, 87–878.*

Poythress, N.G., Otto, R.K., & Heilbrun, K. (1991). Pretrial evaluations for criminal courts: Contemporary models of service delivery. *Journal of Mental Health Administration, 18*, 198–208.

Poythress, N., Monahan, J., Bonnie, R., Otto, R.K., & Hoge, S.K. (2002). *Adjudicative competence: The MacArthur Studies.* New York: Kluwer/Plenum.

Poythress, N., Nicholson, R., Otto, R., Edens, J., Bonnie, R., Monahan, J., & Hoge, S. (1999). *The MacArthur Competence Assessment Tool—Criminal Adjudication: Professional manual.* Odessa, FL: Psychological Assessment Resources.

Quinsey, V., Harris, G., Rice, M., & Cormier, C. (1998). *Violent offenders: Appraising and managing risk.* Washington, DC: American Psychological Association.

Redlich, A.D., Silverman, M., & Steiner, H. (2003). Pre-adjudicative and adjudicative competence in juveniles and young adults. *Behavioral Sciences and the Law, 21*, 393–410.

Roesch, R. & Golding, S. (1980). *Competency to stand trial.* Urbana-Champaign, IL: University of Illinois Press.

Roesch, R., Zapf, P., Eaves, D., & Webster, C. (1998). *Fitness Interview Test (Revised Edition).* Burnaby, British Columbia, Canada: Mental Health, Law and Policy Institute, Simon Fraser University.

Rogers, R. (1984). *Rogers Criminal Responsibility Assessment Scales.* Odessa, FL: Psychological Assessment Resources.

Rogers, R. (1986). *Conducting insanity evaluations.* New York: Van Nostrand Reinhold.

Rogers, R. (Ed.) (1988). *Clinical assessment of malingering and deception.* New York: Guilford.

Rogers, R. (Ed.) (2008). *Clinical assessment of malingering and deception.* New York: Guilford.

Rogers, R., Bagby, R., & Dickens, S. (1992). *Structured Interview of Reported Symptoms Professional Manual.* Odessa, FL: Psychological Assessment Resources.

Rogers, R., & Ewing C.P. (2003). The prohibition of ultimate opinions: A misguided enterprise. *Journal of Forensic Psychology Practice, 3,* 65–75.

Rogers, R., & Shuman, D.W. (2000). *Conducting insanity evaluations* (2nd ed.). New York: Guilford Press.

Rogers, R., Tillbrook, C., & Sewell, K. (2003). *Evaluation of Competence to Stand Trial-Revised.* Lutz, FL: Psychological Assessment Resources.

Roth, L., Lidz, C, Meisel, A., Soloff, P., Kaufman, F., Spiker, D., & Foster, R. (1982). Competency to decide about treatment or research: An overview of some empirical data. *International Journal of Law and Psychiatry, 5,* 29–50.

Russano, M.B., Meissner, C.A., Narchet, F.M., & Kassin, S.M. (2005). Investigating true and false confessions within a novel experimental paradigm. *Psychological Science, 16,* 481–486.

Saks, M. & Baron, C. (1980). *The use/nonuse/misuse of applied social research in the courts.* Cambridge, MA: Abt Books.

Salekin, R. (2001). Juvenile transfer to adult court: How can developmental and child psychology inform policy decision making? In B. Bottoms, M. Kovera, & B. McAuliff (Eds.), *Children, social science, and U.S. law* (pp. 203–232). New York: Cambridge University Press.

Saywitz, K.G., Goodman, G.S., Nicholas, G., & Moan (1991). Children's memories of physical examination that involve genital touch: Implications for reports of child sexual abuse. *Journal of Consulting and Clinical Psychology, 59,* 682–691.

Scheck, B., Neufeld, P., & Dwyer, J. (2000). *Actual innocence.* Garden City, NY: Doubleday.

Scott, E. & Steinberg, L. (2008). *Rethinking juvenile justice.* Cambridge, MA: Harvard University Press.

Schulman, J., Shaver, P., Colman, R., Emrich, P. and Christie, R. (1973, May). Recipe for a jury. *Psychology Today,* 37–84.

Shapiro, D. (1984). *Psychological evaluations and expert testimony: A practical guide for forensic work.* New York: Van Nostrand-Reinhold.

Shapiro, D. (1991). *Forensic psychological assessment: An integrative approach.* Boston: Allyn & Bacon.

Shuman, D. (1986). *Psychiatric and psychological evidence.* New York: McGraw-Hill.

Shuman, D. (2005). *Psychiatric and psychological evidence.* St. Paul, MN: Thomson-West.

Shuman, D.W., Cunningham, M.D., Connell, M.A., & Reid, W.H. (2003). Interstate forensic psychology consultations: A call for reform and proposal for a model rule. *Professional Psychology: Research and Practice, 34,* 233–239.

Simon, R.J. (1967). *The jury and the defense of insanity.* Boston: Little, Brown.

Singh, K. & Gudjonsson, G. (1992). Interrogative suggestibility among adolescent boys and its relationship to intelligence, memory, and cognitive set. *Journal of Adolescence, 15,* 155–161.

Skeem, J. & Golding, S.(1998). Community examiners' evaluations of competence to stand trial: Common problems and suggestions for improvement. *Professional Psychology: Research and Practice, 29,* 357–367.

Skeem, J.L. & Mulvey, E.P. (2001). Psychopathy and community violence among civil psychiatric patients: Results from the MacArthur Violence Risk Assessment Study. *Journal of Consulting and Clinical Psychology, 69,* 358–374.

Sporer, S., Penrod, S., Read, D., & Cutler, B.L. (1995). Gaining confidence in confidence: A new meta-analysis on the confidence-accuracy relationship in eyewitness identification. Unpublished paper, Aberdeen University.

Steadman, H.J. (1973). Some evidence on the inadequacy of the concept and determination of dangerousness in law and psychiatry. *Journal of Psychiatry & Law, 1,* 409–426.

Steblay, N.M. (1992). A meta-analytic review of the weapons focus effect. *Law and Human Behavior, 16,* 413–424.

Steinberg, L., Cauffman, E., Woolard, J., Graham, S., & Banich, M. (2009). Are adolescents less mature than adults? Minors' access to abortion, the juvenile death penalty, and the alleged APA "flip-flop". *American Psychologist, 64,* 583–594.

Strasburger L.H., Gutheil T.G., & Brodsky A. (1997). On wearing two hats: Role conflict. *American Journal of Psychiatry, 154,* 448–456.

Technical Working Group for Eyewitness Evidence (1999). *Eyewitness evidence: A guide for law enforcement.* Washington, DC: US Department of Justice, Office of Justice Programs.

Tepper., A., & Elwork, A. (1984). Competence to consent to treatment as a psycholegal construct. *Law and Human Behavior, 8,* 205–223.

Tillbrook, C., Mumley, D., & Grisso, T. (2003). Avoiding expert opinions on the ultimate legal question: The case for integrity. *Journal of Forensic Psychology Practice, 3,* 77–87.

Tolman, A.O. & Mullendore, K.B. (2003). Risk evaluations for the courts: Is service quality a function of specialization? *Professional Psychology: Research and Practice, 34,* 225–232.

Tombaugh, T. (1996). *Test of Memory Malingering.* San Antonio: Pearson Education.

Tseng, W.S., Matthews, D., & Elwyn, T.S. (2004). *Cultural competence in forensic mental health.* New York: Brunner-Routledge.

Tucillo, J.A., DeFilippis, N.A., Denney, R.L., & Dsurney, J. (2002). Licensure requirements for interjurisdictional forensic evaluations. *Professional Psychology: Research and Practice, 33,* 377–383.

VandenBos, G.R. (2006). *American Psychological Association's Dictionary of Psychology.* Washington DC: American Psychological Association.

van der Kolk, B.A. (1994). The body keeps the score: memory and the evolving psychobiology of posttraumatic stress. *Harvard Review of Psychiatry, 1,* 253–265.

Viljoen, J., Klaver, J., & Roesch, R. (2005). Legal decisions of preadolescent and adolescent defendants: Predictors of confessions, pleas, communication with attorneys, and appeals. *Law and Human Behavior, 29,* 253–278.

Warren, J.I., Murrie, D.C., Chauhan, P., & Morris, J. (2004). Opinion formation in evaluating sanity at the time of the offense: An examination of 5175 pre-trial evaluations. *Behavioral Sciences and the Law, 22,* 171–186.

Webster, C., Douglas, K., Eaves, D., & Hart, S. (1997). *The HCR-20: Assessing the Risk for Violence (Version 2).* Vancouver: Mental health, Law and Policy Institute, Simon Frazier University.

Webster, C., Douglas, K., Eaves, D., & Hart, S. (1997). *HCR-20 Assessing Risk for Violence: Version II.* Burnaby, British Columbia: Mental Health, Law & Policy Institute, Simon Frazier University.

Weiner, I. & Hess, A. (Eds.) (1987). *The handbook of forensic psychology.* New York: John Wiley.

Weiner, I. & Hess, A. (Eds.) (2005). *The handbook of forensic psychology* (3rd edition). New York: John Wiley.

Wells, G.L. (1985). Verbal descriptions of faces from memory: Are they diagnostic of identification accuracy? *Journal of Applied Psychology, 70,* 619–626.

Wells, G.L., Lindsay, R.C.L., & Ferguson, T.J. (1979). Accuracy, confidence, and juror perceptions in eyewitness identification. *Journal of Applied Psychology, 64,* 440–448.

Wells, G.L., Small, M., Penrod, S., Malpass, R.S., Fulero, S.M., & Brimacombe C.A.E. (1998). Eyewitness identification procedures: Recommendations for lineups and photospreads. *Law and Human Behavior, 22,* 603–647.

Wettstein, R.M. (2005). Quality and quality improvement in forensic mental health evaluations. *Journal of the American Academy of Psychiatry and the Law, 33,* 158–175.

Wildman, R., Batchelor, E., Thompson, L., Nelson, F., Moore, J., Patterson, M., & deLaosa, M. (1980). *The Georgia Court Competence Test: An attempt to develop a rapid, quantitative measure for fitness for trial.* Unpublished manuscript, Forensic Services Division, Central State Hospital, Milledgeville, GA.

Williams, L.M. (1994). Recall of childhood trauma: A prospective study of women's memories of child sexual abuse. *Journal of Consulting and Clinical Psychology, 62,* 1167–1176.

Wrightsman, L. (1987). *Psychology and the legal system.* Pacific Grove, CA: Brooks/Cole.

Wrightsman, L., Nietzel, M., Fortune, W., & Greene, E. (2001). *Psychology and the legal system* (3$^{rd}$ edition). Pacific Grove, CA: Brooks/Cole.

Zapf, P., & Roesch, R. (2009). *Evaluation of competence to stand trial.* New York: Oxford.

Zapf, P.A., Hubbard, K.L., Cooper, V.G., Wheeles, M.C., & Ronan, K.A. (2004). Have the courts abdicated their responsibility for determination of competency to stand trial to clinicians? *Journal of Forensic Psychology Practice, 4,* 27–44.

Ziskin, J. (1970). *Coping with psychiatric and psychological testimony.* Beverly Hills, CA: Law and Psychology Press.

Zusman, J. & Simon, J. (1983). Differences in repeated psychiatric examinations of litigants to a lawsuit. *American Journal of Psychiatry, 140,* 1300–1304.

# LEGAL CASES CITED

*Addington v. Texas*, 441 U.S. 418 (1979).

*Ake v. Oklahoma*, 470 U.S. 68 (1985).

*Atkins v. Virginia*, 536 U.S. 304 (2002).

*Barefoot v. Estelle*, 463 U.S. 880 (1983).

*Bruce v. Byrne-Stevens & Assocs. Eng'rs*, 776 P.2d 666 (1989).

*Budwin v. American Psychological Association*, 29 Cal. Rptr. 2d 453 (1994).

*Carter v. General Motors*, 106 NW 2d 105 (1961).

*Christie Brothers Circus v. Turnage*, 144 S.E. 680 (1928).

*Clark v. Arizona*, 126 S. Ct. 2709 (2006).

*Commonwealth v. Stroyny*, 700 N.E. 2d 1201 (2002).

*Cooper v. Oklahoma*, 517 U.S. 348 (1996).

*Daubert v. Merrell Dow*, 509 U.S. 579 (1993).

*Deatherage v. Examining Board of Psychology*, 948 P.2d 828 (1997).

*Dillon v. Legg*, 441 P.2d 912 (1968).

*Dusky v. United States*, 362 U.S. 402 (1960).

*Ellison v. Brady*, 924 F.2d 872 (1991).

*Emerich v. Philadelphia Center for Human Development, Inc.*, 720 A.2d 1032 (1998).

*Estelle v. Smith*, 451 U.S. 454 (1981).

*Fare v. Michael C.*, 442 U.S. 707 (1979).

*Faretta v. California*, 422 U. S. 806 (1975).

*Ford v. Wainwright*, 477 U.S. 399 (1986).

*Foucha v. Louisiana*, 504 U.S. 71 (1992).

*Frendak v. United States*, 408 A.2d 364 (1975).

*Frye v. United States*, 395 F. 1013 (D.C. Circ. 1923).

*Furman v. Georgia*, 408 U.S. 238 (1972).

*Godinez v. Moran*, 509 U.S. 389 (1993).

*Gough v. Natural Gas Pipeline*, 996 F.2d 763 (1993).

*Graham v. Florida*, 130 S. Ct. 2011 (2010).

*Gregg v. Georgia*, 428 U.S. 153 (1976).

*Harris v. Forklift Systems*, 510 U.S. 17 (1993).

*In re Gault*, 387 U.S. 1 (1967).

*In re Winship*, 397 U.S. 358 (1970).

*Indiana v. Edwards*, 554 U.S. 164 (2008).

*Jackson v. Indiana*, 406 U.S. 715 (1972).

*James v. Brown*, 637 S.W.2d 914 (1982).

*Jenkins v. United States*, 307 F.2d 637 (1962).

*Jones v. United States*, 463 U.S. 354 (1983).

*Kansas v. Crane*, 534 U.S. 407 (2002).

*Kansas v. Hendricks*, 521 U.S. 346 (1997).

*Kansas Statutes Annotated* § 59–29a02(a)., (1994).

*Kent v. United States*, 383 U.S. 541 (1966).

*Kumho Tire v Carmichael*, 526 U.S. 137 (1999).

*Lockett v. Ohio*, 438 U.S. 586 (1978).

*Manson v. Brathwaite*, 432 U.S. 98 (1977).

*McCleskey v. Kemp*, 481 U.S. 279 (1987).

*McIntosh v. Milano*, 403 A.2d 500 (1979).

*McKeiver v. Pennsylvania*, 403 U.S. 528 (1971).

*Medina v. California*, 505 U.S. 437 (1992).

*Meritor Savings Bank v. Vinson*, 477 U.S. 57 (1986).

*Michigan Child Custody Act*, MCL §722.23 (1993 amended).

*Molien v. Kaiser Foundation Hospital*, 27 Cal 3d 916 (1980).

*Murphy v. A. A. Mathews*, 841 S.W.2d 671 (1992).

*Neil v. Biggers*, 409 U.S. 188 (1972).

*O'Connor v. Donaldson*, 95 S. Ct. 2486 (1975).

*Oncale v. Sundowner Offshore Services*, 523 U.S. 75 (1998).

*Palsgraf v. Long Island R.R.*, 162 N.E. 99 (1928).

*Painter v. Bannister*, 140 NW 2d 152 (1966).

*Panetti v. Quarterman*, 127 S. Ct. 2842 (2007).

*People v. Hawthorne*, 291 N.W. 205 (Mich., 1940).

*People v. Goldstein*, 843 N.E.2d 727 (2005).

*People v. Kelly*, 516 P.2d 875 (1973).

*People v. Lim Dum Dong*, 78 P.2d 1026 (1938).

*Plaisance v. Texaco, Inc.*, 937 F.2d 1004 (1991).

*Rex v. Arnold*, 16 How. St. Tr. 695 (1724).

*Riggins v Nevada*, 504 U.S. 127 (1992).

*Rivers v. Katz*, 495 NE 2d 337 (1986).

*Rogers v. Okin*, 638 F. Supp. 934 (1986).

*Roper v. Simmons*, 543 U.S. 551 (2005).

*Santosky v. Kramer*, 455 U.S. 745 (1982).

*Sell v. United States*, 539 U.S. 166 (2003).

*Stanford v. Kentucky*, 492 U. S. 361 (1989).

*State v. Hartfield*, 388 S.E.2d 802 (1990).

*State v. Michaels*, 625 A.2d 489 (1993).

*Tarasoff v. Board of Regents*, 551 P.2d 334 (1976).

*Troxel v. Granville*, 530 U.S. 57 (2000).

*United States ex rel. Edney v. Smith*, 425 F. Supp. 1038 (1976).

*United States v. Alvarez*, 519 F.2d 1036 (1975).

*Vitek v. Jones*, 445 U.S. 480 (1980).

*Washington v. Harper*, 494 U.S. 210 (1990).

*Wilson v. United States*, 391 F.2d 460 (1968).

**Adjudicative competence**—a more recent term used for competence to stand trial. A legal construct describing the criminal defendant's ability to understand and participate in legal proceedings at all stages, not just at trial.

**Confidentiality**—the expectation that information that a client provides to a psychologist will not be shared with others; *see* privilege.

**Confirmation bias**—an interpretive error in forensic evaluation in which the evaluator focuses on one interpretation of data and then seeks out data that are consistent with that interpretation.

**Double jeopardy**—being tried twice for the same offense; prohibited by the Fifth Amendment to the U.S. Constitution.

**Eggshell skull doctrine**—a legal doctrine used in tort law that holds an individual liable for all consequences resulting from his or her activities leading to an injury to another person, even if the victim suffers an unusually high level of damages (e.g., due to a pre-existing vulnerability or medical condition).

**Ex post facto clause**—used to refer to a criminal law that applies retroactively, thereby criminalizing conduct that was legal when originally performed; prohibited by the U.S. Constitution.

**Federal Rules of Evidence (FRE)**—enacted in 1975, the FRE govern the introduction of evidence in proceedings, both civil and criminal, in federal courts.

**Privilege**—also known as testimonial privilege; the right of an individual to prevent information that was disclosed in a protected relationship to be offered as testimony in a legal proceeding; *see* confidentiality.

**Proximate cause**—an event sufficiently related to a legally recognizable injury to be held the cause of that injury; the legally recognized primary cause of an injury.

**Relative judgment theory**—states that individuals make a relative, rather than absolute, judgment when making an eyewitness identification.

**Tort**—an act that injures someone in some way and for which the injured person may sue the wrongdoer for damages. Legally, torts are called civil wrongs, as opposed to criminal ones.

**Trier of fact**—a person who determines facts in a legal proceeding.

**Voir dire**—the first phase of testimony in which the witness is questioned about his or her credentials for the judge to determine whether the witness should be qualified as an expert.

# INDEX

AAFP. *See* American Academy of
    Forensic Psychology (AAFP)
ABFP. *See* American Board of Forensic
    Psychology (ABFP)
ABPP. *See* American Board of Professional
    Psychology (ABPP)
*Addington v. Texas*, 32
Adjudicative competence. *See* Competence
    to stand trial
Adolescents, 18, 53, 57
    confessions by, 62–63
    in criminal proceedings, 30
    decisional capacity, 68
    risk of aggression evaluation tool, 85
Adults, 18, 31, 62, 65, 79, 81
    capacities as trial defendants, 48–49, 68
    forensic evaluations of, 131
    with mental retardation, Miranda
      comprehension in, 62–63
    prisons, 25
    risk of aggression evaluation tool, 84, 87
*Adult-Adolescent Parenting Inventory*, 87
Aggression risk, evaluation of, 84–85
ALI. *See* American Law Institute (ALI)
*Alvarez, United States v.*, 155
American Academy of Forensic Psychology
    (AAFP), 11–12, 16, 119
American Association of Correctional
    Psychologists, 10
American Board of Forensic Psychology
    (ABFP), 11, 12, 16, 108
American Board of Professional Psychology
    (ABPP), 3, 15, 11–12, 106, 160
    Forensic Diplomates, 106
American Law Institute (ALI)
    standard, 36, 37
American Psychology-Law Society
    (AP-LS), 4, 10, 11, 12, 14, 16, 60
Americans with Disabilities
    Act of 1990, 29, 43
Amnesia and competence to stand trial, 34–35.
    *See also* Competence to stand trial

Antisocial personality disorder, 37
APA. *See* American Psychological
    Association (APA)
AP-LS. *See* American Psychology-Law
    Society (AP-LS)
Assessment, 13–14, 71–91. *See also* Forensic
    mental health assessment (FMHA)
    adequate bases for, 131–32
    data collection strategies, 87–90
    data interpretation and communicating
      results, 90–91
    instrument selection for specific
      forensic questions, 80–87
    multiple sources, 77–78
    reliability of method selection, 79–80
    selection of methods, 76–87
    validity of method selection, 80
*Atkins v. Virginia*, 29, 39, 49
Attorney–client privilege, 155, 158. *See also*
    Privilege

*Barefoot v. Estelle*, 53
*Best Practices in Forensic Mental Health
    Assessment*, 18, 25
Binet, Alfred, 9
Bipolar disorders
    and competence to stand trial, 32
Board Certification in forensic
    psychology, 108, 112, 116
Breach of duty, 40–41, 156
*Bruce v. Byrne-Stevens &
    Assocs. Eng'rs*, 162, 163
*Budwin v. American Psychological
    Association*, 163
Burden of proof, 30–32

Capital punishment, 38–40
    cases, 128
    race of victim in, 144–45
*Carter v. General Motors*, 42
Case-specific sections, forensic reports, 97–98
CAST-MR, 104, 110

Drug courts, 30
Dual-role relationships, 123–24, 149
Due process, 36, 44, 48, 149
*Dusky v. United States*, 32, 34, 143
Duty to protect, 156–57
Duty to warn, 157

Education and Training (E&T) Guidelines for
  Forensic Psychology, 16–17, 107, 110
  exit requirements, 111–12
  for forensic psychology, 16–17
  principles of, 16
EED. *See* Extreme emotional
  disturbance (EED)
Eggshell skull doctrine, 41
Eighth Amendment
  prohibition against cruel and
  unusual punishment, 39
*Ellison v. Brady*, 42
*Emerich v. Philadelphia Center for
  Human Development*, 156
Employment
  harassment and discrimination, 42–43
  workers' compensation, 41–42
*Estelle v. Smith*, 121–22, 155
Ethical principles of forensic practice, 26–27,
  119–37
  boundaries of competence, 130–32
  case study, 132–37
  client, definitions of, 120–23
  maintaining objectivity, 125–26
  minimizing harm to examinees, 126–29
  psychological testing in
    forensic cases, 129–31
  role boundaries, 123–25
*Ethical Principles of Psychologists and
  Code of Conduct*, 119–32
*Evaluating Competencies–Forensic Assessments
  and Instruments*, 14, 25
*Evaluation of Competence to Stand
  Trial-Revised*, 83
Ex post facto clause, 46
Expert opinions, 6, 7, 10, 13, 40, 108
Expert testimony, 113, 126. *See also*
  Testimony
Expert witnesses, 31
  forensic psychologists
    functioning as, 149–50
  liability issues for, 162–63
  methods of discrediting, 150
Extreme emotional disturbance (EED), 140
Eyewitness identification, 58–62
  implications for practice, 61–62
  lineups and photospreads,
    guidelines for, 60–61
  reliability of, 59–60

FAIs. *See* Forensic assessment
  instruments (FAIs)
False confessions. *See also* Confessions
  coerced-compliant, 64
  coerced-internalized, 64–65
  voluntary, 64
*Family Court Review*, 15
*Fare v. Michael*, 49
*Faretta v. California*, 34
Federal Appeals Court, 42, 155
Federal court system, 29–30
Federal Rules of Evidence (FRE)
  702, 158–60
  703, 160–61, 162
  704, 161, 162
Fernald, Grace, 9
*Fitness Interview Test-Revised*, 83
FMHA. *See* Forensic mental health
  assessment (FMHA)
*Ford v. Wainwright*, 39, 128
Forensic assessment instruments (FAIs), 13, 14,
  83, 110
Forensic consultation, 92–106
  to attorneys, 100–105
  defined, 92
  to organizations, 105–6
  report writing. *See* Writing of
    forensic reports
Forensic identification, 147
Forensic mental health assessment
  (FMHA), 14, 71. *See also* Assessment
  conceptual building blocks for, 13
  principles and methods of, 24–25
  systems-based classification of, 19
Forensic psychiatry, 11
Forensic reports
  inclusion of information in, 126–27
  mental health reports, 103–4
  quality of, 108–10
  writing of. *See* Writing of
    forensic reports
*Forensic Reports*, 15
Forensic Specialty Council, 16
Forensic systems
  community agency model, 115
  inpatient model, 114–15
  mixed model, 116
  outpatient model, 115
  private practitioner model, 115–16
*Foucha v. Louisiana*, 38
Fourteenth Amendment, 32, 33, 35
  guaranteeing due process, 39, 47
FRE. *See* Federal Rules of Evidence (FRE)
*Frendak v. United States*, 38
*Frye v. United States*, 9, 29, 159
*Furman v. Georgia*, 39

# ABOUT THE AUTHORS

**Ira K. Packer, PhD, ABPP,** is currently clinical professor of psychiatry at the University of Massachusetts Medical School (UMMS) and serves as director of the UMMS Forensic Psychology Postdoctoral Fellowship Program. He is the author or co-author of a number of articles including issues related to the insanity defense, expert witness testimony, and training and practice in forensic psychology. He is also the author of the book: *Evaluation of Criminal Responsibility* (Oxford University Press, 2009). In his capacity as Chair of the Forensic Specialty Council, he was the lead author of the Education and Training Guidelines for Forensic Psychology, as well as the petition to the American Psychological Association for renewal of recognition of Forensic Psychology as a specialty in professional psychology.

Dr. Packer has been engaged in the practice of forensic psychology for over 30 years and served as Assistant Commissioner for Forensic Services, Massachusetts Department of Mental Health. He is board-certified in forensic psychology by the American Board of Professional Psychology. He has previously served as president of both the American Board of Forensic Psychology and the American Academy of Forensic Psychology. He received the 2007 Distinguished Contributions to Forensic Psychology award from the American Academy of Forensic Psychology.

**Thomas Grisso, PhD, ABPP,** is Professor, Directory of Psychology, and Director of the Law and Psychiatry Program at the University of Massachusetts Medical School (UMMS). His research has examined the application of psychological assessment to questions of legal competencies and the application of clinical and developmental psychology to law, policy, and practice in criminal and juvenile justice. He has received the American Board of Professional Psychology's Award for Distinguished Contributions (2002) and currently is Executive Director of the American Board of Forensic Psychology. He is co-editor of the Oxford University

Press nineteen-volume series on *Best Practices in Forensic Mental Health Assessment*. Dr. Grisso has received the American Psychological Association's award for Distinguished Contributions to Research in Public Policy (1994), an honorary Doctor of Laws degree from the John Jay College of Criminal Justice, City University of New York (1998), the American Psychiatric Association's Isaac Ray Award (2005), and the U.K.'s Royal College of Psychiatrists Honorary Fellow Award (2006).

# ABOUT THE SERIES EDITORS

**Arthur M. Nezu, Ph.D., ABPP** is Professor of Psychology, Medicine, & Public Health at Drexel University and Special Professor of Forensic Mental Health and Psychiatry at the University at Nottingham in the United Kingdom. He is a Fellow of multiple professional associations, including the American Psychological Association, and is board-certified by the American Board of Professional Psychology in Cognitive and Behavioral Psychology, Clinical Psychology, and Clinical Health Psychology. Dr. Nezu is widely published, is incoming Editor of the *Journal of Consulting and Clinical Psychology*, and has maintained a practice for three decades.

**Christine Maguth Nezu, Ph.D., ABPP**, is Professor of Psychology and Medicine at Drexel University, and Special Professor of Forensic Mental Health and Psychiatry at the University at Nottingham in the United Kingdom. With more than 25 years of experience in clinical private practice, consultation/liaison, research, and teaching, Dr. Maguth Nezu is a board-certified by the American Board of Professional Psychology (ABPP) in Cognitive and Behavioral Psychology and Clinical Psychology. She is also a past president of the ABPP. Her research has been supported by federal, private, and state-funded agencies and she has served as a grant reviewer for the National Institutes of Health.